SharePoint 2010
Site Owner's Manual

SharePoint 2010
Site Owner's Manual

FLEXIBLE COLLABORATION WITHOUT PROGRAMMING

Yvonne M. Harryman

MANNING
SHELTER ISLAND

To my husband and son

Manning Publications Co.
20 Baldwin Road
PO Box 261
Shelter Island, NY 11964

Development editor: Cynthia Kane
Technical proofreader: Phil Cohen
Copyeditor: Linda Recktenwald
Proofreader: Melody Dolab
Typesetter: Dottie Marsico
Cover designer: Leslie Haimes

ISBN 9781933988757
Printed in the United States of America
1 2 3 4 5 6 7 8 9 10 – MAL – 17 16 15 14 13 12

Brief contents

Contents

Preface

I've been working in SharePoint consulting for over 10 years, and with time I began to realize the lack of books on the market that showed tech-savvy business users just how easy SharePoint is to use. I would go in and build systems for major corporations and government agencies around the world, and in most cases toward the end of the engagement there would still be some hours remaining because I had completed the job ahead of schedule. I often would use this time to meet with the business owners and educate them on how to use the new system. I would listen to what their pain points were and make suggestions on how they could leverage SharePoint to help manage and automate their business needs. The reaction from this was amazing: clients would tell me that they had paid companies a significant amount of money in the past to implement similar solutions; they had no idea how easy it was to do this leveraging SharePoint functionality. This is what prompted me to write a book and to make it scenario-based.

You'll find many technical books on SharePoint that discuss how to build out the infrastructure or do development with SharePoint, and you may find a few step-by-step books on SharePoint's out-of-the-box functionality. What's unique about this book is that it teaches you this functionality in a scenario format. I chose to use that format to ensure that you exercise your imagination to realize the many options for using SharePoint's built-in functionality.

I've been working in the SharePoint space for a long time, and I feel strongly that other consultants and I should be going into organizations to help install and build out farms to scale and perform for their user base and to help migrate or implement complex systems on their platform. With that said, there are many systems that could be easily built and have big impact without requiring you to run to the techies. I hope this book educates you on how to spot and envision those opportunities so you can get started using SharePoint in a way that will impress your peers.

Acknowledgments

I'd like to thank Manning Publications, especially publisher Marjan Bace and my editor Cynthia Kane, and everyone who helped with the development and production of the book. Special thanks to Phil Cohen for providing his technical insights during the technical proofread of the final manuscript.

For their thoughtful comments on the content, I'd like to thank the readers who participated in the Manning Early Access Program and provided feedback in the Author Online forum, and to the following reviewers who read the manuscript at various stages during its development: Andrew Totmakov, Monty J. Grusendorf, Anil Radhakrishna, Sean Hogg, Nikander Bruggeman, Margriet Bruggeman, Richard Siddaway, Kunal Mittal, John Powell, Christian Siegers, John Timney, Linley Schaller, Sanchet Dighe, Prajwal Khanal, Ed Richard, Berndt Hamboeck, Rama Krishna, Paula Shank, Tony Niemann, and Amos Bannister.

To my parents, thanks for inspiring me to always achieve great things, and to my family, thanks for enduring the late nights of work on the book. I dedicate this book to my husband Luke, and my son Luca, and thank them for keeping me sane and making sure I always have balance in my life as well as freedom to pursue my passions. Tigy, your video game time may suffer now that the book is done!

Without all the people mentioned here, and also those who worked behind the scenes and whose names I don't know, this book would have never made it to publication.

About this book

Part 1 is designed to acquaint you with SharePoint and to teach you about its functionality. Part 2 will then guide you through the different components of SharePoint. You'll learn about the functionality associated with each of these components in a step-by-step fashion, while building out a usable scenario. Each situation is drawn from a real-world scenario that I've encountered, and you may be able to adapt them for your own use.

Who should read this book

This book is intended for tech-savvy business users:

- An end user of SharePoint who doesn't have a computer science degree but wants to optimize the technology they have at hand
- The developer who doesn't understand SharePoint's built-in capabilities
- The SharePoint developer/user who is new to SharePoint 2010

Roadmap

This book consists of 11 chapters divided into two parts as follows:

Part 1 "Getting started with SharePoint" introduces you to SharePoint terminology, capablities, and out-of-the-box features.

Chapter 1 is an introduction to SharePoint—what it is and why you should be using it—and a look at what is new in SharePoint 2010.

Chapter 2 offers a broad overview of SharePoint 2010 and its out-of-the-box capabilities, along with a look at the functionality associated with the different releases of SharePoint.

Chapter 3 covers the core components of SharePoint and shows how to create a site with out-of-the-box templates.

Part 2 "Implementations using real-world scenarios" will show you how you can customize and create your own site templates, based on real-world scenarios.

Chapter 4 guides you in how to set up a document collaboration site and covers site branding, document libraries and collaboration features, as well as custom lists and lookup fields.

Chapter 5 discusses how to leverage enterprise content management features, such as content types, information management policy, and retention schedules.

In chapter 6 you will learn how to publish content to the web, using hosted internet-facing sites, blogs, lists, discussion boards, and surveys.

Chapter 7 focuses on the business intelligence capabilities of SharePoint and describes different scenarios to show you how you can use it knowledge-mine your data to create business reports.

Chapter 8 covers how to create application sites with SharePoint Designer, including how to manage and create lists, apply conditional formatting, and configure out-of-the-box list workflows.

Chapter 9 discusses how to collect and manage data and integrate it with InfoPath, using forms libraries, InfoPath forms, and forms services.

In chapter 10, you will learn how to use Access with SharePoint, including Access features like linked and local tables, queries, reports, forms, and Access Services.

Chapter 11 helps you to pull it all together with search, My Sites, and web parts that enable you to pull data across sites.

The book has two appendixes: appendix A helps you set up your test environment and install and configure SharePoint on your computer; appendix B will walk you through the steps needed to create your first site.

Code conventions and software requirements

This book doesn't require you to be a developer or do any coding. The solutions will be just as powerful as solutions that are developed from code and will be implemented through the SharePoint user interface and Microsoft Office tools. You'll quickly see how easily you can develop your own solutions using a no-code approach.

Ideally, you should have access to a SharePoint environment for experimenting. If you don't, appendix A will walk you through the steps to set up an environment for building the scenarios. It will also include the details of any software requirements. Appendix B helps you create your first site.

Author Online

Purchase of *SharePoint 2010 Site Owner's Manual* includes free access to a private web forum run by Manning Publications where you can make comments about the book, ask technical questions, and receive help from the author and from other users. To access the forum and subscribe to it, point your web browser to www.manning.com/SharePoint2010SiteOwnersManual. This page provides information on how to get on the forum once you're registered, what kind of help is available, and the rules of conduct on the forum.

Manning's commitment to our readers is to provide a venue where a meaningful dialogue between individual readers and between readers and the author can take place. It's not a commitment to any specific amount of participation on the part of the author, whose contribution to the book's forum remains voluntary (and unpaid). We suggest you try asking the author some challenging questions, lest her interest stray!

The Author Online forum and the archives of previous discussions will be accessible from the publisher's website as long as the book is in print.

About the author

Yvonne M. Hamilton (Harryman) is a Solution Architect at Microsoft, specializing in SharePoint technologies. She has implemented and designed SharePoint solutions for clients such as the White House, US Air Force, National Institute of Health, Iron Mountain, the Gap, State of California, Peter Kiewit and Sons, WellPoint, Baxter, Ingersoll-Rand, and many others. Her key focus areas are Cloud solutions, Microsoft Rapid Application Development tools, Object Oriented Programming and Governance. Yvonne and her teammates have received many awards for the projects that they have designed. Her top awards include a letter of recognition from the White House Chief of Staff and the prestigious Circle of Excellence award at Microsoft; as important are some of the top team awards received directly from clients for work done at the National Institute of Health and Ingersoll-Rand.

Yvonne holds two degrees, a Bachelor's and Master's of Science in Computer Information Systems. Her undergrad was completed at the College of Charleston and the Master's was received from Johns Hopkins University. Yvonne is very active in the SharePoint community. You can find many of her past contributions under Yvonne Harryman; prior to the publication of this book she got married in Ireland and is now Yvonne Hamilton. Yvonne frequently travels around the US designing solutions for clients, but her home is in Seattle, WA, where she lives with her husband Luke, son Luca, and two rescue German Shepherd mixes.

Part 1

Getting started with SharePoint

Part 1 will give you an introduction to SharePoint and a rundown of all the SharePoint out-of-the-box functionality. You won't build out scenarios step by step until part 2. If you like to learn hands on, feel free to jump to part 2 once you've read chapter 1. If you opt to do that, I recommend that before you start implementing your own solutions in SharePoint, you go back and read the rest of part 1. There's a plethora of built-in functionality that may get you 80 percent of the way to your final solution. You should be aware of what those options are so you don't recreate anything that may already exist.

1

Leveraging the power of SharePoint

This chapter covers

- *What SharePoint is*
- *Why you should be using SharePoint*
- *What's new in SharePoint 2010*
- *Introduction to SharePoint by creating a Hello World site*

Increasing collaboration capabilities has become one of the top priorities of businesses around the world. Imagine emailing a document to a customer with edits and then finding out that they had also been making changes to the document; now you have to merge pages of changes. What if you're required to work from home because of a snowstorm, and the latest copy of the report you need is accessible only via your desktop at work? Problems with collaboration have caused many lost hours in companies and have therefore become a priority for businesses to resolve.

Using the array of tools that Microsoft now offers, people are finding effective ways to communicate and share their information. One key tool that's being used to do this type of collaboration is SharePoint. SharePoint is an application that you can use to create websites that help people collaborate and communicate information. End users are using its powerful capabilities in web content management to share information with other users around the world via the web, sharing information with users even if they don't have Microsoft Office, using features such as Office Web Access, Access Services, and Visio Services. SharePoint also enables you to collaborate simultaneously on the information without fear of overwriting each other's changes by using versioning and co-authoring features.

SharePoint tools released in 2007 brought a higher standard of effective collaboration to the workforce. The introduction of a new permissions model for document collaboration, enhanced search features, and the Windows Workflow Foundation, along with many other features, enabled a new level of information management solutions. SharePoint tools released in 2010 have taken collaboration to the next level. This release is packed with enhanced features such as the rich Silverlight UI, a new Ribbon interface, and enhanced tools, which enable the power user to build application sites.

Before you continue reading through a series of scenarios discussed in part 2 that walk you through common problems business users are faced with and how SharePoint comes to the rescue, you need to understand what SharePoint is. In this chapter I'll introduce you to SharePoint, tell you about what's new to SharePoint 2010, and finish with a short example to get you started.

1.1 Say hi to SharePoint

In the real world when you first meet someone you learn a bit about them; likewise, here I'll introduce you to SharePoint. This is a great get-to-know-you chapter for those readers who aren't familiar with SharePoint. Here you'll see what SharePoint is and why it's so great. For those of you already familiar with SharePoint, this should be more of a recap of what you already know. In addition to the initial introduction, I'll also touch on the new features for SharePoint 2010. By the end of this chapter, you and SharePoint will be at the beginning of a long-standing, beautiful friendship.

1.1.1 What is SharePoint?

SharePoint in its most basic form is a website that helps people collaborate and communicate information. It has a wide set of features that, when fully leveraged and configured, is capable of being used as a rich, interactive, and powerful platform. This platform is capable of supporting the most advanced business needs or can be used on your own personal site. Business and personal uses can be found everywhere, and the variations are endless, including, but not limited to, the following:

- Company intranets to communicate the latest company news, share division information, and provide insight into policies such as those of HR and Payroll
- Company team sites for easy collaboration and document management
- Company extranets for easy collaboration with other companies/ partnerships with different organizations
- Public-facing sites available via the World Wide Web for product sales or important communications
- Creation of applications to automate business processes or to gather business intelligence

Here are some examples of personal use:

- Blog sites
- Family sites for sharing photos and videos
- Community sites such as user groups
- Wedding sites

You can create all of these sites without having to understand a single line of code, and all levels of users and developers can learn to use them. Also, if you're using SharePoint Foundation, the license is *free*, which is good to know if you're considering it for personal use. The majority of this book is focused on building out scenarios, like the ones listed here, and guiding you on how to configure these sites step by step, using the out-of-the-box functionality. Don't worry or get overwhelmed; you can do this, even if you aren't a techie. SharePoint is so user-friendly that after completing this book, you'll feel like you have a computer science degree.

1.1.2 Why SharePoint

Many facets differentiate SharePoint from other web content management systems. Let's discuss a few of those aspects:

- *Second to none across the information system work streams* — Microsoft is the only company that gets ranked as leader for all of the following Magic Quadrants by Gartner: enterprise content management, information access technology, BI platforms, horizontal portals, social software, web conferencing, and unified communications. According to the September 2009 Gartner Magic Quadrant reports, no other vendor was listed as leader in all of those areas. They continued to lead in enterprise content management in November 2010.

- *Consolidated collaborative solutions* — SharePoint offers consolidated collaborative solutions; you can meet all of your business intelligence, social computing, internet site, enterprise search, and enterprise content management needs with one tool. The competition will require you to deploy and know multiple tools instead of just one to meet all of those needs.

- *Powers the best intranets* — In the annual 10 best intranets by Nielson Norman Group for 2010, SharePoint remains at the top, with 5 of the 10 selections running on SharePoint.

- *Empowers the tech-savvy business user* — The no-code approach and ease of deployment make it an attractive choice for nontechnical users to quickly adapt to the technology.

- *Office interoperability* — SharePoint offers a rich set of integration features with other Microsoft technologies, including all of the Office products.

- *Cloud-ready* — Lastly, it's cloud-ready. If you don't have the infrastructure to host SharePoint or the on-site skill set required, then go to SharePoint online or use other providers to have them quickly set up SharePoint for you.

Now that you have a good understanding of the differentiators, let's jump into the new features associated with SharePoint 2010.

1.1.3 What's new in SharePoint 2010

In this section I'm going to give you a glimpse into some of the exciting new features associated with SharePoint 2010. In chapters 2 and 3 you'll get a more comprehensive view into what features and functionality are associated with the different versions of SharePoint, but here I want to whet your appetite:

- *Ajax*—Ajax-based usability allows you to retrieve and display data without impacting the display of the page you're on. This gives the end user a much more modern user experience.
- *Theming*—Easy theming using a no-code approach allows you to quickly change the colors and fonts within your sites. Many out-of-the-box themes are provided, but you can also quickly create new ones by using PowerPoint to create a theme and import it for use in SharePoint.
- *Cross-browser support*—Cross-browser web access is provided using Internet Explorer, Firefox, and Safari.
- *Ribbon*—The Office Ribbon is now a feature of SharePoint, as shown in figure 1.1. This is the toolbar that's displayed at the top of the page, exposing most of the commonly used commands.
- *Embedded rich media*—Embedded rich media, shown in figure 1.2, lets you display and watch videos directly from your SharePoint pages.

Figure 1.1 The Office Ribbon is now included in SharePoint.

Figure 1.2 Media web part, which can be embedded in SharePoint pages

○ *In-context collaboration*—With in-context collaboration, shown in figure 1.3, as you're reviewing items you can hover over the user information and quickly reach out to the user via instant messaging, send them email, schedule a meeting, or just check out their My Site. It also displays their presence information so you know whether they're available. As you see, I'm busy right now because I'm writing this section.

○ *Office Web Apps*—Integration with Office Web Apps, which is a browser-based version of Word, Excel, PowerPoint, and OneNote, allows users to review and make some edits to information through the browser, thus not requiring them to own Office.

○ *Mobile access*—You have easy access to your content via mobile devices through Office Web Apps and SharePoint libraries.

○ *Cloud-ready*—Cloud offerings are available with SharePoint Online. If you don't have the IT support or infrastructure, let Microsoft host them for you.

Figure 1.3 In-context collaboration lets you quickly collaborate with your peers.

Figure 1.4 Ratings configured for a document library

⊙ *Co-authoring*—Co-authoring enables multiple users to work on the same document at the same time.

⊙ *My Site enhancements*—My Site is enhanced with activity feeds, status update capability, a note board, and a rich Silverlight organization browser.

⊙ *Rich content management*—Rich content management capabilities allow you to quickly tag and rate media. Ratings are shown in figure 1.4.

⊙ *SharePoint Designer*—SharePoint Designer (which is free) allows you to easily build no-code solutions to automate business processes through workflow tools, enhanced page-modification capabilities, and ease of access to external data.

These are just a few of the many commonly used new and great features of SharePoint 2010. You'll get to see the rest of them in real scenarios as you read through the book. Each scenario comes from my own experience working at Microsoft based on internal applications we built, requests from customers I've worked with, and sites I've built for my own personal use. The goal is to exercise your imagination so you can see the possibilities and see how easy it is to use, even if you're not a developer. Okay, I'm getting ahead of myself here. So you've met SharePoint, you know what it is, why it's important, and what it can help you do. Now let's see some of SharePoint's core concepts in action.

1.2 SharePoint sample (Hello World)

Let's go over some of the core concepts of a SharePoint site. We'll cover the components available once you create a site page, where the content is stored, and how permissions work. This intro is primarily a visual exercise so you can see and understand SharePoint if you're not familiar with it.

Why Hello World?

I anticipate that not all of the readers have been exposed to technical books in the past. For those of you who fall into that category, I'll explain this commonly used techie term. In the development world, it's common to have the first introductory tutorial for creating a program display the text "Hello World!" It's done with a simple bit of code that helps users get an understanding of some of the basic syntax. To keep with the theme, I've chosen to call our first site Hello World.

If you wish to build this site, you'll find the instructions for doing so in appendix B. In appendix A you'll find the steps to set up a test Share-Point environment. Many users reading this book will likely have access to SharePoint through a hosted service or through their employer. If that's the case for you, you can just use that. If you're not so lucky, don't worry; the appendix goes over the process for setting up a test SharePoint environment on your PC, and it has lots of pictures and additional details to make it easy for you to follow. If you're a visual learner, you'll most likely not need to follow this example step by step. You can get the core concepts from the visuals, and you'll get plenty of opportunities to do these steps in the following scenarios. So let's get started by introducing you to your Hello World website.

1.2.1 The Hello World site

Figure 1.5 is the result we're after. I've created a blank site, with the Hello World sample implemented. What you're looking at is the homepage of that site. I've rendered a logo of a fake company called

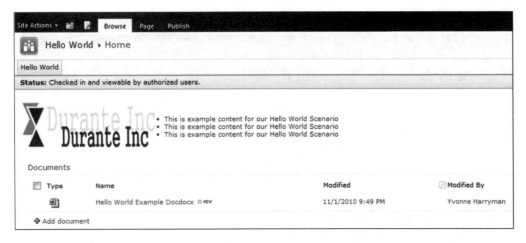

Figure 1.5 Hello World site that we'll use as our first example of a SharePoint site

Durante Inc and added some text to the right of the image. I've also displayed a document.

To give you a bit of background about what's going on, the text is the only thing stored directly on this page. You have the capability to create many pages for each site, and each page has a shared set of libraries and lists that you can access to render data via web parts on the page. For example, the Hello World Example Doc is pulling from a library on that site and is being displayed via a web part. This web part can be modified to filter out certain documents by the properties. I could filter it to show only documents that have been modified or created within the past seven days. To access additional site functionality, you can select the Site Actions menu shown in the upper-left corner of your screen. In the next section we'll cover some key links on the Site Actions menu.

Site Actions menu

On every page of your SharePoint site you'll always see the Site Actions menu, shown in figure 1.6. Two key links to become familiar with as you get started are the View All Site Content and the Site Permissions links. The other links are important, and we'll cover those in detail in the later chapters, but to get started you need to understand these two.

All Site Content page

This page provides you with links to all the lists and libraries associated with this site, as shown in figure 1.7. Here you can also access the Recycle Bin for deleted content and click links to associated sites. If you wish to create a new library or list, you can select Create and choose from a variety of options.

The All Site Content page is the hub for all the information that you can use on your pages. Do you recall the Durante logo shown in the example page? That image is stored in the images library, which you access through the All Site Content page. This allows you to have one central location for your information, with lots of options on how to display different views of that data on your site.

The next key link we're going to discuss that's available via the Site Actions menu is the Site Permissions link.

Site Permissions page

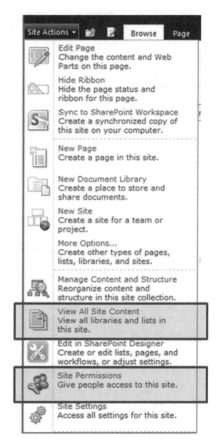

Figure 1.6 The Site Actions menu is found on all pages of a SharePoint site. Highlighted are two key links: View All Site Content and Site Permissions.

The site that you just created will have default permission groups set up, as shown in figure 1.8. The key groups that you need to understand are the Hello World Owners, Members, and Visitors. Each group is associated with a permission level. As a site owner who has the ability to manage permissions and modify the page, you should be in the Hello World Owners group, which has the Full Control permission. Your site collaborators, those

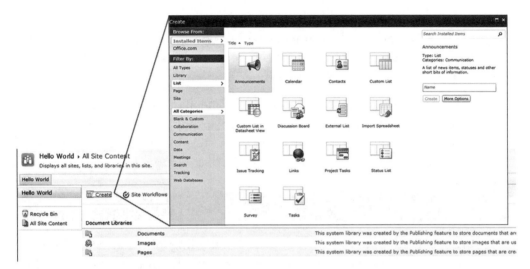

Figure 1.7 The All Site Content page is the hub for all content that you can use on your pages.

who should be able to add content to the libraries and lists, should be in the Hello World Members group, with the Contribute permission. The Hello World Visitors group is for the end users who consume the data in a read-only format and can't make any modifications to the site; they have the Read permission.

To add a user to one of these groups, you select the name of the group, and it will display the current users and provide you a New option, which links to a lookup tool for selecting users to add. We'll cover

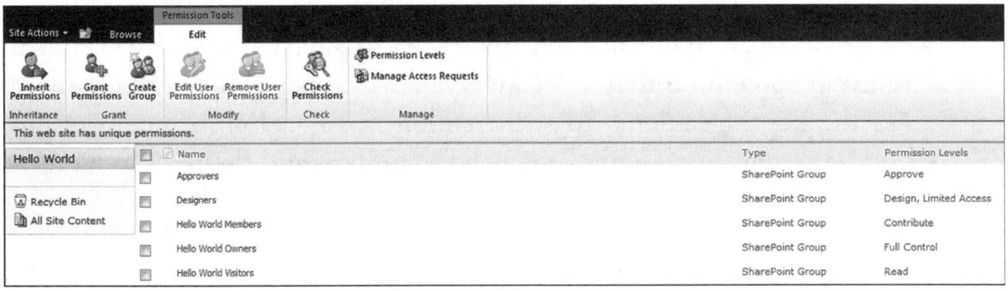

Figure 1.8 Site permissions groups and permission levels

other key topics regarding permissions in the governance sections, such as inheritance, item-level permissions, custom permissions, and authentication options. This brief section introduced you to the core aspects when first working with permissions.

You now have a good overview of the mechanics behind a SharePoint site, at least the main bits. The steps we took were very basic. If you need to see this process broken down step by step, you can get that from appendix B. Let's quickly summarize what you've learned.

1.3 Summary

You should now have a good understanding of what SharePoint is even if you've never worked with it before. If you have, hopefully I've interested you with a glimpse of some of the new functionality offered with SharePoint 2010, and most of all you should be excited about the possibilities of quickly and easily building robust sites with rich functionality without having a development background.

The next two chapters cover core terminology, out-of-the-box functionality, and features of the different versions. It's basic information, but it's important to understand so you know what's available out of the box. Don't feel compelled to read it all in one go; you can skim the material and jump to the scenarios in part 2 if you learn best by doing hands-on exercises. You can always refer back to these chapters later. I do ask that prior to creating your own sites you make sure you understand these chapters. I see on a regular basis site owners hiring developers or figuratively banging their head against a wall by trying to reinvent something that's already available. Imagination and creativity are the key ingredients to site creation in SharePoint, but to ensure your creativity is effective, you need to understand the tools at hand.

2

A deeper dive into SharePoint capabilities

This chapter covers

- Collaboration overview
- SharePoint capabilities
- SharePoint functionality

Before you read the other chapters or sections of this book, you need to understand what SharePoint is. In this chapter we'll briefly touch on the major components of building SharePoint sites. Once you've completed this chapter, you should have a broad overview of what SharePoint is and what out-of-the-box components it offers you for building sites.

Let's go ahead and begin looking at what the SharePoint 2010 capabilities are, along with a summary of the functionality associated with the different releases. After that I'll explain/review the terms that you'll continue to see throughout this book.

2.1 Introducing SharePoint 2010

For us to be on the same page and to move forward in the book, I need to define some key terminology. Some people refer to the technology as SharePoint, SharePoint Server, MOSS, SharePoint Foundation, and Office Portal Server. So let's start up front and get the terms straight. To begin, look at table 2.1 to see the product terminology defined. In section 2.1.5 of this chapter I'll provide additional tables that define terminology regarding SharePoint sites, the components within a site, and permissions. Let's get started with the product terms that have been used over the years.

SharePoint 2010 comprises three main editions: SharePoint Foundation, SharePoint Server Standard, and SharePoint Server Enterprise. From a licensing perspective there are variants of these if you're buying for an intranet or internet deployment on premises or if you're considering a deployment using Microsoft's cloud offerings. We won't focus on this from a licensing perspective but instead from a basic

Table 2.1 Product terminology

Term	Meaning
WSS 2.0	Windows SharePoint Services for 2003.
SharePoint Portal Server 2003	Extension of WSS 2.0 with portal functionality for 2003.
WSS 3.0	Windows SharePoint Services for 2007.
MOSS/Microsoft Office SharePoint Server	MOSS is an extension of WSS 3.0 for SharePoint 2007 technologies. The term *portal* was dropped because it provides greater capabilities than what many users expect from a portal.
SharePoint Foundation	Windows SharePoint Services for 2010. SharePoint Foundation 2010 is the core functionality of SharePoint 2010 technologies.
SharePoint Server	SharePoint Server 2010 is an extension of SharePoint Foundation for SharePoint 2010 technologies. The term *Office* was dropped because it isn't part of the Office client.

Table 2.1 Product terminology *(continued)*

Term	Meaning
SharePoint	Umbrella term used for all of the above technologies. If a user says *SharePoint*, it's important to clarify what they mean. You can start by asking if they're using 2003, 2007, or 2010 and then further clarify if it's just SharePoint Foundation/WSS or one of the server solutions: SharePoint Server 2003, MOSS, or SharePoint Server 2010.

explanation of the core functionality associated with each edition regardless of the license type you're purchasing. The basics of the relationship among the three editions are shown in figure 2.1.

As you can see, some editions include the functionality of another edition. For example, SharePoint Foundation is included in SharePoint

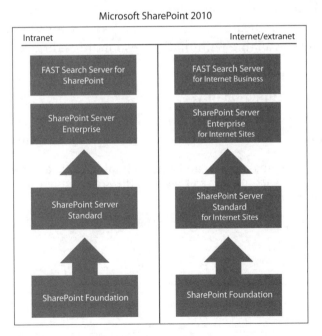

Figure 2.1 *SharePoint* is an umbrella term, which can include one or more of the editions listed. It's important to know what version you have in order to understand the functionality that's accessible to you.

Server Standard, and SharePoint Server Standard is included in Share-Point Enterprise. SharePoint Server extends the functionality of Share-Point Foundation. Therefore, if you're running either version of SharePoint Server, you have SharePoint Foundation. But if you're running SharePoint Foundation, you may not have SharePoint Server. This might sound confusing at first, but by the end of the chapter it should make perfect sense to you.

Let's look at some examples of SharePoint and go over the six core capabilities that make up SharePoint. Each edition contains aspects of these six core capabilities, with functionality increasing as you go from SharePoint Foundation to SharePoint Server Standard to SharePoint Server Enterprise.

2.1.1 SharePoint's six core capabilities

SharePoint is broken into six major categories of functionality that I'll refer to as capabilities. These capabilities are broken out in table 2.2. The following letters indicate the amount of functionality associated with each capability available with that corresponding edition:

- F = Full level of functionality.
- P = Partial level of functionality.
- IP = Increased Partial indicates more functionality than P but still not the full amount of functionality associated with that capability.

Table 2.2 Six major capabilities make up SharePoint technologies. SharePoint Foundation has core components of each of these areas, but they're extended with SharePoint Server Enterprise and Standard.

	Sites	Communities	Content	Insights	Composites	Search
SharePoint Server Enterprise						
	F	F	F	F	F	F
SharePoint Server Standard						
	F	F	F	IP	IP	IP
SharePoint Foundation						
	P	P	P	P	P	P

Now let's look at each of the six capabilities in more detail:

- *Sites* — This capability covers the components that make up a site to manage information. Features that compose this component are web-editing capabilities, the Ribbon UI, multilingual capabilities, audience targeting and personalization, web parts, standards compliance, Office Web Apps, and SharePoint Workspace.

- *Communities* — This capability covers the social computing aspects of SharePoint that empower people to connect. Features that compose this component are My Sites, social tagging, blogs, and wikis.

- *Content* — This capability covers the management of content throughout its entire lifecycle, from creation to deletion. Features that compose this component are managed metadata, unique document IDs, document sets, advanced routing, in-place records management, and web content management.

- *Insights* — This capability covers our Business Intelligence (BI) story. This component comprises Excel Services, PerformancePoint Services, and Visio Services.

- *Composites* — This capability covers solutions using out-of-the-box SharePoint tools to create robust sites without the need of IT. Some components that implement this are SharePoint Designer, InfoPath, and Access.

- *Search* — This capability covers the functionality to locate information. The searching components in 2010 have many enhancements on how to sift through the information, including refiners for easy exploration, phonetic searches, document thumbnails and preview pane, and much more depending on the level of search you've selected to implement.

Now that you understand the capabilities, we're going to look at the functionality of these core capabilities in relation to SharePoint Foundation and SharePoint Server.

2.1.2 SharePoint Foundation functionality

SharePoint Foundation is free and runs on Windows Server. Specific examples of functionality that you'll find in this version in relation to their capability are as follows:

Sites

- Cross-browser support.
- Contextual Ribbon interface.
- Mobile connectivity.
- Offline options for working with the data though SharePoint Workspace.
- More than 40 out-of-the-box web parts.
- Support for Office Web Applications.

Communities

- Blogs with many new content-editing features make it easy to upload pictures and provide rich formatting options for the content.
- Wiki functionality is now available for all pages in SharePoint, allowing rich inline page-editing capabilities.
- Discussion boards allow users to create discussion topics and respond using a threaded format.
- Presence allows those who have Microsoft's instant messaging tools installed to see a person's status and be two clicks from communicating with them. This will appear anywhere you see a person's name.

Content

- Microsoft Office integration so that users can quickly create documents and save them directly to libraries in SharePoint that they commonly use.
- Support for accessibility standards.

Insights—Business Connectivity Services (BCS) to connect to external data

- Business Data Connectivity (BDC) Services allow connectivity to external systems.

- External Data column lets you show the data in SharePoint using lists.
- External Data lists let you read and write the external data the same way you would a SharePoint list.

Composites

- Browser customizations by adding web parts such as calendar or task views.
- SharePoint Designer customizations such as reusable workflows, external content types, and rich design customizations to list views.
- Sandboxed solutions so you can deploy custom code in a controlled environment.

Search

- Site search to locate information in SharePoint.

Now that you understand the functionality that's in SharePoint Foundation, we can build on these functionalities and show what you'll get in addition to the SharePoint Foundation functionality if you have SharePoint Server.

2.1.3 SharePoint Server functionality

Microsoft SharePoint Server 2010 is an extension of SharePoint Foundation, which includes the previously discussed features and offers a more comprehensive solution for collaboration. SharePoint supports most intranet, extranet, and web application requirements, enabling your data to be maintained within one integrated platform, making it a truly robust solution for your enterprise information system.

There are two main editions of SharePoint Server available, Standard and Enterprise, with the Enterprise release having the most comprehensive functionality across the six capabilities. Following is a breakdown of the major pieces of functionality offered in SharePoint Server Standard, followed by the components associated with Enterprise.

Standard SharePoint offers all of the SharePoint Foundation functionality and the following additional functionality:

Sites

- Enhancements in scalability, so you can now have 30 million items in a single library.
- Audience targeting so you can change the content that individual users see when they access a site.

Communities, My Sites

- User profiles contain people's bios, contact information, interests, and previous projects. When you do a people search, this will be the information you get when you select a user.
- Status updates allow you to let people know what you're doing.
- Ask Me About is a feature that allows end users to identify their areas of expertise.
- You can create a colleague network by adding end users that you select or colleagues that were suggested via the colleague suggestion feature based on distribution lists, outlook emails, communicator contacts, and so on.
- Community memberships include such things as SharePoint sites or distribution lists.
- Note Board allows other users to post comments.
- My Content gives the end user a central location to keep their documents.
- My Newsfeed allows you to track updates of people you're following and interests you're tracking.
- Recent Activities shows different activities you've been involved in such as membership changes, note postings, and profile updates.
- Enterprise Wikis allow the categorization and grouping of pages with structured and unstructured data.
- Organization Browser is a Silverlight control that lets you navigate the organization structure to find peers, managers, and direct reports.

- Ratings is a five-star rating system that you can enable for pages, libraries, or individual items so users can rate the quality of the material.
- Social bookmarks are a way to share internal or external URLs.

Tags are available to help classify information. Features associated with tags are as follows:

- Tag clouds are key tags that are commonly used on content; their appearance is determined by how much that content has been tagged with the associated keyword. Selecting a tag will show you the associated content.
- Tag Profiles is a communities page that allows users to track content that gets tagged with keywords of interest.
- Tags and Notes is the "I like it" and notes feature that you can turn on for all of your pages within SharePoint. It's part of the social bookmarks mentioned previously.

Content

- Compliance Everywhere enforces records management via features such as retention, legal holds, file plans, and content types.
- Document sets let you manage a group of documents as a single entity.
- Metadata-Driven Navigation provides you the option to navigate documents in a library using key terms.
- Multistage disposition allows you to define multiple stages of content lifecycle retention policies.
- Rich media management is available for videos, audios, and images.
- Shared content types allow defined metadata for certain content types to be shared across site collections.
- Managed Metadata Service allows you to create term sets that can be shared across site collections.
- Content Organizer automates the classification of a document based on metadata values or content type.

- Unique document IDs allow you to easily find content, even if it has been moved, via search or permalinks, which are URLs that are independent of the location.

Insights—Business Connectivity Services (BCS) to connect to external data

- External Data Search shows the external content alongside your search results.

- Business Connectivity Services (BCS): Profile pages show information about an external item and its relationship to other items.

- Business Connectivity Services (BCS): Secure Store holds user credentials needed to access an external system.

Composites

- Customization of the forms associated with the out-of-box workflows.

Search

- Best Bets allow the search administrator to recommend a link based on commonly used keywords for that link.

- Duplicate results are collapsed to reduce clutter.

- Federated Search shows information from other search sources.

- Metadata-Driven Refinement Panel allows you to narrow search results based on metadata.

- You have the ability to search content from your mobile phone.

- You can locate people by searching for their expertise.

- Phonetic search is available.

- Query suggestions are offered: "Did You Mean...?"

- You can search up to 200 million documents and get sub-second responses.

- Search scopes allow you to search a subset of content, such as a search scope set up to return only results from blog sites.

- Enhanced search algorithms improve the quality of your search results.

- You have the ability to sort results on certain properties such as modified date.
- You have the ability to preview a document in the browser.

Enterprise SharePoint includes all of the above SharePoint Server and SharePoint Foundation functionality and the following additional functionality:

Insights

- Business Data web parts help you to display information from line-of-business or enterprise-resource planning (ERP) systems.
- Chart web parts allow you to quickly create charts using data in SharePoint lists, data in Excel documents, or data pulled via business connectivity services.
- Excel Services allows you to share your interactive reports created using Excel via the browser.
- Filter Framework lets you change filters that can be passed as parameters to many web parts on a page.
- Performance Point Services allows you to create rich dashboards and scorecards, pulling data from multiple systems.
- Status indicators let you monitor important metrics and use indicators based on the measurements.
- Visio Services allows you to share your interactive diagrams created using Visio via the browser.
- Web analytics customizations let you modify existing reports, tracking how SharePoint is being used.

Composites

- Access Services allows you to publish and share Access databases on your SharePoint site.
- InfoPath Forms Services lets you create forms-based SharePoint applications.
- Business Connectivity Services (BCS) lets you connect to external data.

- External Data web parts let you show external content in a web part.
- Office Client Integration lets you connect external lists to Outlook in a SharePoint workspace.

Search

- You can create ranking profiles for search results, so you can weight attributes differently to impact the order in which results are returned.
- Business Intelligence Indexing connector lets you search business intelligence reports such as reporting services reports along with the data behind the scenes.
- Contextual search allows search administrators to define results specific to a user's profile value such as a location or title.
- Deep Refinement gives you exact counts.
- You can search up to 500 million documents and get sub-second responses.
- Similar results will be returned based on your current search.
- You have the ability to sort results on custom properties.
- Thumbnails and previews are provided.
- Visual best bets are offered.

You should now understand the different pieces of functionality that compose SharePoint Foundation and SharePoint Server Standard and Enterprise. In the next section, I'm going to break down some of the key terms to make sure we're all on the same page.

2.1.4 SharePoint site terminology plain and simple

Now we're ready to move on to some more advanced topics and to discuss components that make up the site architecture of SharePoint. To start I'm going to go over some core terminology with you. I've broken the terms into three different tables. Table 2.3 covers the logical breakdown of sites. I then show the components that define a site in table 2.4. The last table, table 2.5, covers the core SharePoint groups for each site and what their permissions are.

Table 2.3 Product terminology

Term	Meaning
Web application	Web applications contain site collections.
Site collection	A site collection can't contain another site collection, but it can have many subsites. A site collection is where you would access core elements across the subsites, such as security, navigation, content types, and galleries for master pages, site templates, list templates, and the like.
Portal	Generic term that's often linked to a single site collection.
Subsite	A site or collection of sites that link to a site collection.
Site	Site is a generic term that can mean subsite, top-level site, or site collection.
Workspace	There are six types of workspaces: Document, Basic Meeting, Blank Meeting, Decision Meeting, Social Meeting, and Multi-page Meeting. Workspaces are generally considered ad hoc or temporary. A workspace is a place to quickly work on a document or organize meeting information, but any final deliverables will typically be stored on another site for long-term access.

Table 2.3 covers the logical components for sites. It defines what's needed for the creation of a site and the relationship between those components.

Figure 2.2 will help to explain and show the relationship of the logical components to one another.

Based on the diagram, you can see that a SharePoint deployment can consist of many site collections, which are top-level sites that can host many subsites. The top-level site of the site collection is only one site, but each subsite within the site collection can continue to build out and have additional subsites. Subsites that are within the same site collection can share certain core elements, such as security for people management, navigation, and content types, as well as style components, such as master pages and page layouts.

Learning the main components that cover the logical breakdown of sites and site collections is a good start, but you also need to

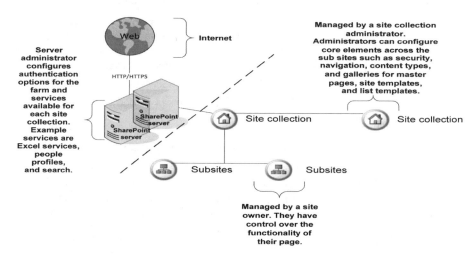

Figure 2.2 Logical structure for SharePoint. This diagram displays the breakdown of components and their hierarchical relationships. To start, users will access the World Wide Web or intranet, which connects to SharePoint servers. Hosted on those servers will be a series of site collections broken into subsites. Anything above the dotted line will be managed by your server administrator and networking team. This book covers the components that you can access below the dotted line.

understand some of the core site components for building your sites. Table 2.4 covers some of the core site tools that are critical to understand in order to effectively build out SharePoint sites.

Table 2.4 Site components

Term	Meaning
Web part	A web part is like a mini application or view of a list or other data source.
List	Lists are broken into libraries, communication, tracking, and custom. They provide users with different views and functionality for managing information.
View	A view allows users to access items in a list using different columns, filters, and styles.

Table 2.5 covers some of the core groups and permissions that are created by default for your top-level site and subsites. I'll go into much more detail about permissions later in this book, but as a start, these terms will help you understand how to administer security for your sites.

Table 2.5 Core groups and permissions

Term	Meaning
Site collection administrator	A site collection is created by server administrators. A site collection administrator manages core elements across the subsites such as security, navigation, content types, and galleries for master pages, site templates, list templates, and so on.
Site owners	Subsites can be assigned site owners. The site owner has full control of the site and can manage the permissions, design, lists, and the like.
Site members	Subsites can be assigned site members. The site members can contribute content to the site.
Site visitors	Subsites can be assigned site visitors. The site visitors can read content on the site.

Creating custom groups and permissions

Permissions can involve much more detail than just site owners, members, and visitors. These are the default groups. But you have the ability to create different groups and permission levels, getting as detailed as deciding who can add, edit, delete, or view versions. This will be covered in detail in chapter 11.

That's it! Now that you know the core terminology, I'll quickly summarize what you've learned. In the next chapter you'll get the opportunity to see and understand some of the out-of-the-box functionality of SharePoint.

2.2 Summary

You now have the foundation of SharePoint sites and what you can get out of the box. You should have a good understanding of the following:

- Six core capabilities of SharePoint
- Functionality you'll find in SharePoint Foundation versus SharePoint Server
- What the umbrella term *SharePoint* covers
- Easy reference tables for term lookups
- Logical structure for SharePoint
- The differences between SharePoint Foundation and SharePoint Server

Now we can get into the muscle of SharePoint and discuss what you can do as a power user to customize and create your own site templates. In this chapter you created a site and learned many of the core components that make up the site-creation process. In part 2 of this book you'll continue learning the fundamentals of SharePoint through a scenario-based approach. This will help you envision the different possibilities and get you on your way to creating customized sites for your own use. The next chapter will go over the out-of-the-box site templates. This is important to understand so you know what's already available before you create a customized site.

3

Creating sites using site and list templates

This chapter covers

- *Core list and library templates*
- *Web parts*
- *Site templates and their association with the SharePoint editions*

e'll now discuss core components of SharePoint that you can leverage with minimal configuration.

It's good to understand what components are provided out of the box. Once you have a solid understanding of that, you can begin to build your own if one of these doesn't meet your needs. In the scenarios where you build out custom sites, you typically start from a blank site template or a publishing site template. If you find that what you'd like to implement is similar to one of the out-of-the-box templates, you could always leverage one of these site templates, customize it, and save it as a custom site template based on your modifications. Before we get into site templates, let's discuss some of the core components that make up a site: lists.

3.1 Building templates with the different SharePoint editions

SharePoint Foundation and SharePoint Server sites are combinations of components. Think of a site as a holder that encompasses many different lists and web parts that can be accessed on web pages. When a user creates a site, it opens to the homepage. This is like the front page of a newspaper. Often the full stories aren't shown on the front page of a newspaper, just snippets of information, and you'll need to go to another page to get the full story. Well, a site is similar; the homepage often comprises web parts that contain summary views of information, and to get the full story you need to select the header of the web part to navigate to the web page that has all of the functionality and details. Users with the required permissions can move around the web parts and change their order within the different zones. The web parts are customizable, and users have many options for modifying their appearance. SharePoint Foundation and SharePoint Server provide a base set of list templates and site templates that users can leverage to quickly build out their sites. An example of a site with four web parts is shown in figure 3.1.

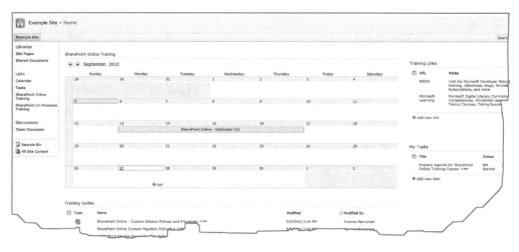

Figure 3.1 An example site that displays four web parts that each display snippets of data from the lists that compose the site

Figure 3.1 displays four web parts. These are web parts with views into the following types of libraries or lists: a calendar, a document library, a links list, and a task list. Each header of the web part gives you an idea of what that web part is filtered to show you. For example, the task list header reads *My Tasks*. If you were to select My Tasks, it would take you to all the tasks assigned to all users of this site. The view displayed in this web part has been configured to show the user only the tasks assigned to them that have not been completed. That is an example of how you'd use a web part to show snippets of data held within a list.

In addition, individual sites are combined and connected via a site collection. Sites within a site collection share navigation, permissions, and content. You can typically tell what site collection a site is part of by examining the URL. If it's similar to the following, http://portal.durante .com/sites/SiteA or http://portal.durante.com/sites/SiteA/SubSiteB, you should note that SubSiteB is part of SiteA. You can be certain by going to the top site, selecting View All Site Content, and seeing if the site is listed under Sites and Workspaces. This will show you only one level down, so if the site is nested further, the easiest way may be to look at the breadcrumb trail when you select the folder from the subsite to see what parent sites it has.

In the next few sections we'll cover some of the core list and library templates and then explain all of the site templates. It's important to have a good understanding of what's already available to you before creating your own site templates. In part 2 of this book, we'll cover how you can take the out-of-the-box site templates and develop your own site templates. Let's start by explaining some of the core list and library templates.

3.2 Core list and library templates

A variety of templates are provided for lists within SharePoint Foundation and SharePoint Server. A breakdown of all the lists and libraries associated with SharePoint Foundation and SharePoint Server will be covered in appendix A, so for this section I'll focus on introducing you to some of the more popular list templates that are available. It's important to understand these because they're the functionality that makes up sites and site templates. Each is powerful and can be configured many different ways to meet the site owner's specific needs. The templates we'll go over are the Document Library, Picture Library, Asset Library, Announcements, Contacts, Links, Calendar, Tasks, Discussion Board, and Survey templates.

Let's start by going through some of the core features that are included in all lists and libraries regardless of what template you're using.

Each list and library is formatted to meet a specific functionality. In the next section I'll provide a screen shot of the lists and libraries we're discussing and a brief explanation of some of the functionality specific to that item. List and libraries, likes sites, can be saved as templates. You can take a list or library and save all of your customizations for reuse on other sites.

3.2.1 Document Library template

The Document Library is one of the core components of a collaboration system. This allows users to manage their documents and enable other users to access them. Beyond the functionality described in the introduction of section 3.2, this list is unique because of the ability to check in and check out documents. This prevents other users from making modifications to a document while you're working on it. A full list of functionality that's available to you is displayed in figure 3.2. Note that this is a view of the SharePoint Server Enterprise license. Depending on the edition of SharePoint that you're using, you may or may not have all of these capabilities.

Note that you have two ways to work with the items in the list. You can do so through the tools provided in the Ribbon or via the context menu tied to the list item. Using the Ribbon, you can quickly create and upload new documents as well as organize your information using

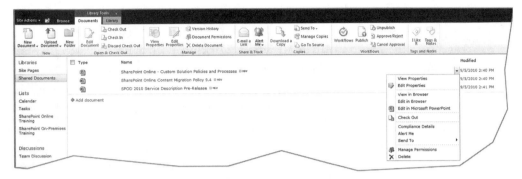

Figure 3.2 Document Library functionality for an item

folders. For each document added, along with options shown in the Ribbon you'll have a context menu, which is the drop-down menu shown for each item. Here you can view additional properties, choose different options to edit the document, or check it out so others can't make modifications. You also have the ability to set an alert on the item so you'll be notified of any changes or send a link to the item to your colleagues who have access to the site. The approval and workflow features are grayed out in this figure because they haven't been configured, but if you turn these on you'll see additional options to approve, publish, or manage the task requested by the workflow.

Lastly, there's a set of options associated with all of the documents, which can be found under the Library tab. This is shown in figure 3.3.

Along with item- and document-level functionality there are options at the library level. The most powerful features on this menu are the library settings and the ability to create and modify views. Let's quickly discuss the latter; right now you're looking at the default view. If you

Figure 3.3 Document Library functionality for the library

were to create a view, you'd get options to select which columns are displayed, set filters to see only certain items, and group and sort the results. This can be powerful when working with web parts to display snapshots of the data. The library settings are how you'd get to the configuration settings explained in table 3.1. Here you'll also see similar options explained in the previous paragraph, such as alerts. This will enable you to set an alert on the entire library, so you'll be notified if a document is ever created, deleted, or edited. There are many additional options, and we'll cover those in more detail in chapter 4, when we begin our first scenario, going through an example of building a site.

Table 3.1 Common settings for libraries and lists

Feature	Description
Web-based access	Web-based access means that each list is hosted on a web page so users can access them via the intranet or internet.
Version control	Version control allows users to modify items without the concern of losing any information. It can track the history of the previous items so you can view or roll back to a previous version.
Columns	Columns are metadata, information that can be captured and used to search and sort information pertaining to the document, such as author and status (draft/final).
Validation	Validation is a new feature in the SharePoint 2010 release; it uses formulas that can be configured to validate information captured in the columns.
Content types	Content types are containers of columns that can be shared across lists and libraries.
Views	Views can be used to provide your users with different ways to access the information. For example, you can have a view for all draft documents that only certain users can access and a view for final documents that all users can see.

Table 3.1 Common settings for libraries and lists *(continued)*

Feature	Description
Item-level permissions	Item-level permissions can be applied to each item in your list. An example of how this can be used is to allow users the ability to modify only their own items and not those of others.
Workflows	Workflows are available for all lists and can provide a lot of power for approval or other task-related items that you want triggered when new items are modified or added.
Ratings	Ratings is a new capability with SharePoint 2010 that allows end users to rate the individual list items (0–5).
Enterprise keywords	This setting helps users enter keywords, providing suggestions to autocomplete the word, based on similar keywords that users have entered into other keyword fields.

These capabilities are similar to all libraries and lists. For the next section we're going to discuss only those items that are unique to that list or library. Because the focus of this one is documents, we'll now discuss a library whose purpose is pictures.

3.2.2 Picture Library template

What makes the Picture Library unique is the additional capability to easily manage images by displaying thumbnails. An example of a Picture Library is shown in figure 3.4.

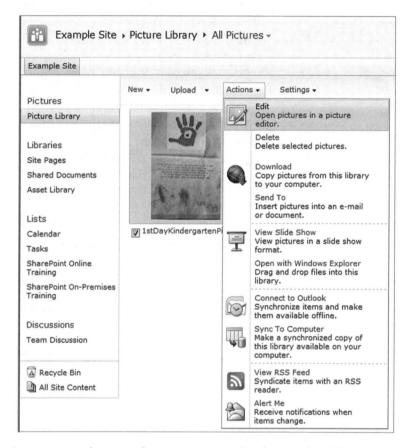

Figure 3.4 Picture Library with context menu displaying the different options

As you can see from figure 3.4, you get different options with a Picture Library, such as viewing the picture in a slide show format. These options make it easy to upload and organize your photos to share with others. When looking at the photos in slide show format, they'll appear as shown in figure 3.5.

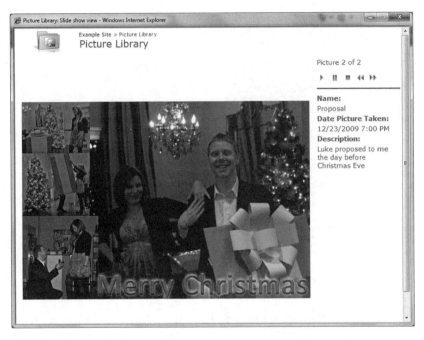

Figure 3.5 You can select certain pictures in a Picture Library and present them in slide show format.

You also have the ability to add a Picture Library slide show web part to the pages of your sites. This web part is shown in figure 3.6.

Picture libraries were critical in SharePoint 2007 because uploading an image had to be done by providing a web URL. In SharePoint 2010, you can often share an image that's stored on your computer, in a SharePoint library, or by providing a web URL. We'll talk about that more when we get to the Blog template, in the section covering site templates. The next list we'll discuss is the Asset Library.

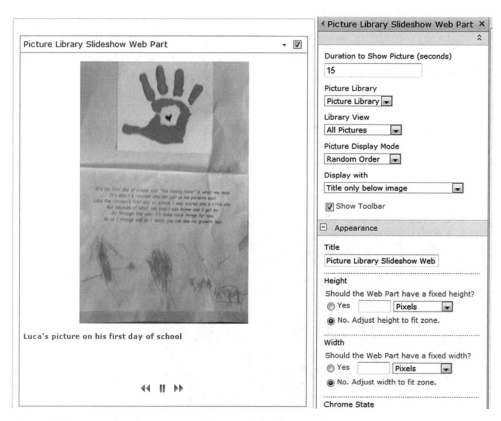

Figure 3.6 Example of a Picture Library slide show web part with the configuration options

3.2.3   Asset Library template

The Asset Library is new to SharePoint 2010. Its purpose is to help in the sharing of digital assets such as audio or video files. In figure 3.7 I show an example of the Asset Library being used in a scenario to share training videos.

A common web part used in conjunction with the Asset Library is the Media web part, which allows you to display embedded video files on a page. To see the Media web part in action, look at figure 3.8; the options for configuring the web part can be seen in the Ribbon.

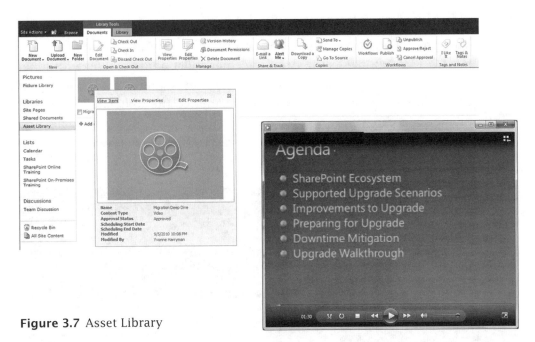

Figure 3.7 Asset Library

Now that we've discussed some of the common libraries that you can use, let's talk about common lists, starting with the Announcements list.

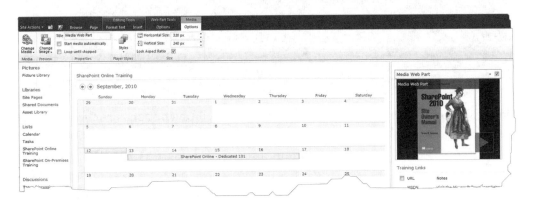

Figure 3.8 Media web part

3.2.4 Announcements list

The Announcements list has the core functionality of a list described in table 3.1. What makes the Announcements list unique is the additional capability to set an expiration date for the announcement that you enter. For example, if you want to announce the upcoming company picnic, you can set it to autoexpire on the day of the event. This will help keep your information up to date. In the example shown in figure 3.9, I'm creating an announcement and adding a picture to it.

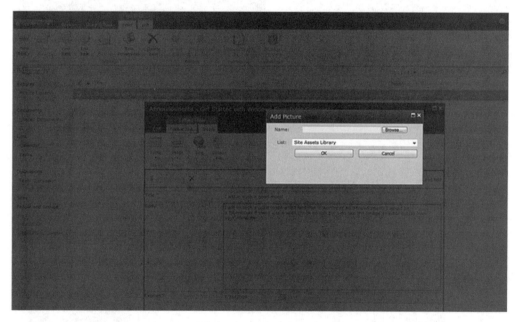

Figure 3.9 Announcements list with rich Silverlight editing options in action

You can leverage the Content Query web part (CQWP) to roll up announcements from subsites if you want to create a central location for users to see all of the announcements. The Announcements list will help you distribute and communicate important information. Next list we'll discuss the Contacts list, which will help you manage information about people.

3.2.5 Contacts list

The Contacts list has the core functionality of a list described in the introduction. What makes the Contacts list unique is the metadata for capturing information about individuals associated with that site and the ability to sync with your Outlook contacts. In addition, if you have SharePoint Server, you'll also have the ability to create a Contacts web database that leverages Access Services. We'll talk more about this in the section covering site templates. To start, let's see what a Contacts list can do, as shown in figure 3.10.

Figure 3.10 Contacts list

Note that you have many ways to work with this list. One way that's specific to this list is the capability to synchronize with Outlook. This will allow you to access these contacts offline or manage the contacts using Outlook, or you can do so in a SharePoint workspace. The next list we'll discuss is the Links list. The Links list is one of the more common lists used, because almost everyone has a need to organize and display links on a page.

3.2.6 Links list

The Links list, shown in figure 3.11, has the core functionality of a list described in the introduction. What makes the Links list unique is the additional capability to create and display a list of links, which provides the description and links to the web address.

Although many times you'll work with links using a Links list and adding a view of that list on a web page, there's another common way to work with links. When you design pages, several templates may contain summary links. This is a common way to use or create a page

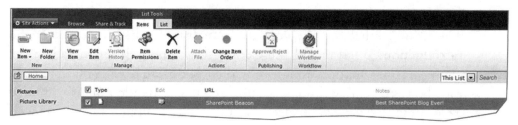

Figure 3.11 Links list

layout so that all pages will have links in a common location across the pages of a site.

The next list we'll discuss will help you to manage events and share them in various formats; this is a Calendar list.

3.2.7 Calendar list

The Calendar list has the core functionality of a list described in the introduction. What makes the Calendar list unique is the additional capability to display the items using a calendar format, as shown in figure 3.12. Notice that you can also create a workspace for the new events. This is essentially the equivalent of a site but with the expectation that it's temporary.

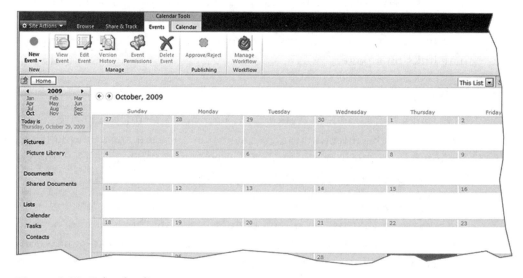

Figure 3.12 Calendar list

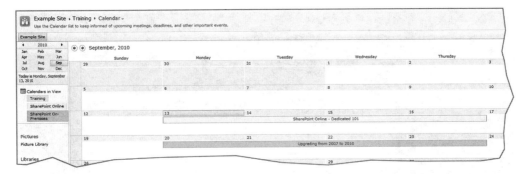

Figure 3.13 A calendar overlay combines the events from multiple calendars and color codes them.

A new capability is the ability to set up calendar overlays, as shown in figure 3.13. This allows you to see multiple calendars in a view and to configure style changes so you can easily identify the type of calendar events you're viewing.

Also note that although the calendar view is very popular, there are many other options where you can show events, based on how current they are, in a textual format, as shown in figure 3.14.

Figure 3.14 Example of textual format of current events

Now that you have a good understanding of how to handle events and calendars, the next list we'll discuss will help you to manage items that require an action.

3.2.8 Tasks list

The Tasks list helps you to manage action items. What makes the Tasks list unique is the additional capability to manage and assign tasks to different people associated with the site. Notifications will automatically be sent so that the assigned person will know to begin working on the task. When you create a new task, by default you'll get the options shown in figure 3.15.

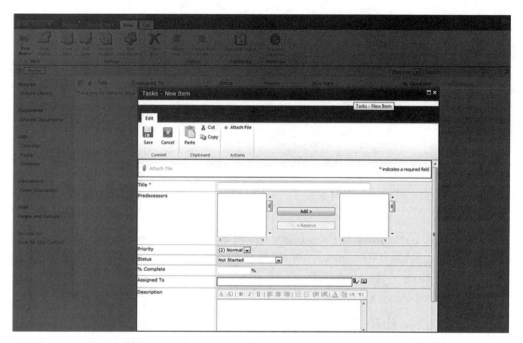

Figure 3.15 Tasks list with rich Silverlight editing options in action

Notice the many data points that help you keep track of the task. One of my favorites is the ability to link it to other tasks that may require completion in order to finish this task. If other tasks are present in the list, they'll show up in the Predecessors box so you can add them upon entry of a new task if they require completion first. As an example, if you need to buy gas before leaving on a trip, create the buy gas task first. Then when you create the leave on trip task, add *buy gas* as a predecessor. The next list we'll discuss is the Discussion Board list, which is great for informal group collaboration.

3.2.9 Discussion Board list

The Discussion Board list enables end users to carry on a casual conversation with other users and have the discussions organized by topic. It also provides the ability to manage threaded topics so you can respond to users throughout the thread and see which comment you're referring to. Another tool that's commonly used for casual discussions

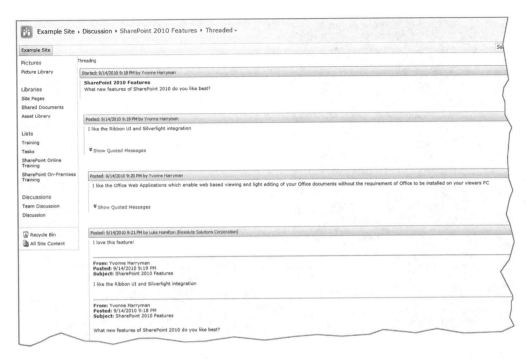

Figure 3.16 Discussion Board list

is the Blog template. One key advantage that the Discussion Board has is threaded comments. Comments in a blog are flat, and it can be difficult to tell to whom you're responding. Users can post discussion topics, and replies will be nested within each topic. An example of a threaded discussion on SharePoint 2010 features is shown in figure 3.16.

The next list we'll discuss is the Survey list. This list is commonly used in a polling scenario or when you want to put out a series of questions to your end users.

3.2.10 Survey list

What makes the Survey list unique is the additional capability to create a series of questions and format the survey with page separators and branching logic. The Survey list also supplies a graphical summary of all the responses. In figure 3.17 you can see the graphical summary

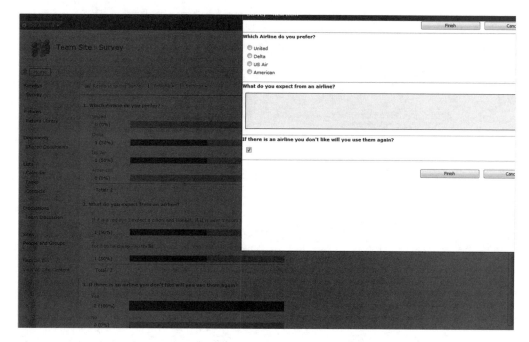

Figure 3.17 Survey list with rich Silverlight editing options in action

response on a survey for a consulting company where the employees travel quite often. The company is gathering feedback on the different airlines to provide advice to employees when they travel in the future.

If we had integrated branching logic or page separators, you might see an additional option to save or go to the next screen. This can be confusing to end users because they may click Save and think they've submitted their response. So be wary when using those features, and make it clear to your end users that saving is not submitting.

Now that we've covered some of the core libraries and lists, let's discuss how SharePoint Foundation and SharePoint Server provide a base set of site templates. Note that there are additional libraries and lists, but I wanted to cover the ones that are more extensively used so you can get a good introduction to what SharePoint can do out of the box. Each of the site templates that we'll cover in the next section comprises lists and libraries that we just discussed; combined with web parts and some customizations, they can support a common scenario and essentially be used as a business application. In part 2 of this book, you'll build your own sites that can be made into templates for reuse, similar to the site templates we're about to discuss. You'll create these templates to solve various business problems, but before you do that, we'll explore what's already available so we don't try to reinvent the wheel. We'll begin to define these in the following section.

3.3 Learning about the site templates

This section will cover all the out-of-the-box site templates that you can use as a starting point when you create a site. I'll provide scenarios for each site template along with what edition of SharePoint it's associated with. For example, certain templates apply only to SharePoint Server Enterprise, and they may not be available for use if you have Share-Point Server Standard. In part 2, you'll build similar sites to these, and we'll go into detail on how to configure these sites using web parts, lists, and other tools such as SharePoint Designer. Prior to doing that, though, you need to understand what options you have out of the box. Imagine how great it would be if you were sitting in your boss's office and he was discussing contracting with a company to help build and manage all internal records. He needed records to be routed to various locations based on metadata and to have the ability to look up a record based on a document ID. Wouldn't it be great if you had read this section and could tell him not to contract with a company for this because your company can do it with its SharePoint implementation without custom development?

Before we dive into the different site templates, I want to highlight the new site templates for SharePoint 2010:

- Group Work Site
- Visio Process Repository
- Assets Web Database
- Charitable Contributions Web Database

- Contacts Web Database
- Issues Web Database
- Projects Web Database
- Business Intelligence Center
- Enterprise Search Center
- Basic Search Center
- FAST Search Center
- Enterprise Wiki

If you're already familiar with the standard site templates for Share-Point 2007, this list will help you identify those that are new. Another thing to note is that several site templates have been deprecated, and these include the following:

- Wiki Site
- Site Directory
- Report Center
- Search Center with Tabs
- Search Center
- Collaboration Portal
- News Site

Now that you know which site templates are new and which ones have been deprecated, let's get started with discussing those site templates that are included with SharePoint Foundation.

3.3.1 SharePoint Foundation

SharePoint Foundation is the base of any SharePoint installation, so regardless of what version of SharePoint you're running, SharePoint Foundation technology underlies it. Because of that, the site templates shown in table 3.2 are included in all versions of SharePoint. The following sections will give a brief description along with a picture of each of the different SharePoint Foundation site templates.

Table 3.2 SharePoint Foundation site templates

Template	Description
Team Site	Team sites enable groups of end users to easily collaborate by sharing documents, tasks, events, and announcements and creating discussions.
Blank Site	A blank site has nothing configured on it, so you truly have a clean slate to begin creating your site.
Document Workspace	A document workspace is similar to a team site, but it limits the capabilities to focus on enabling end users to collaborate on the completion of a document by means of a document library, tasks, and a list of links associated with the documents.
Blog Site	A blog site allows contributors to post ideas and let the end users comment on those ideas.
Group Work Site	The group work site is a groupware option to allow end users to organize and circulate resources.
Basic Meeting Workspace	A basic meeting workspace helps end users organize meetings.
Blank Meeting Workspace	The blank meeting workspace is configured to provide a clean slate on which to begin creating your site.
Decision Meeting Workspace	The decision meeting workspace helps you to manage and track items and decisions made in a meeting.
Social Meeting Workspace	The social meeting workspace helps you organize and share pictures associated with a social event.
Multipage Meeting Workspace	The multipage meeting workspace helps you to manage a meeting and provides tabs so you can create many pages to capture action items, tasks, agendas, and the like.

Now that you have an idea of the different templates we'll be covering, let's dive deeper into each template so you can see it in action. We'll discuss them in the order listed in the table. I've tried to group them based on similarities. We'll start with some of the core general collaborative templates, such as the Team Site template.

3.3.2 SharePoint Foundation collaborative site templates

I've grouped the SharePoint Foundation templates into a series of collaborative templates that have various purposes, mostly organized around team collaboration and social collaboration. The following section includes those that are focused on meeting organization and collaboration.

Team Site template

A team site is a site for teams to quickly organize and share information. For example, if you'll be working with a team over the next few months to define IT policies for you company, you'd most likely start a team site so you could share your thoughts and ideas via the web. It provides important pieces of functionality, such as a document library and lists for managing announcements, links, calendar items, tasks, and team discussions. An Image web part set to the Windows SharePoint Services logo is also available for you to customize and replace with your team's logo. An example of a team site is displayed in figure 3.18.

Figure 3.18 Out-of-the-box SharePoint Foundation site template for a team site

SharePoint Foundation web part components shown in this template are the Announcements web part, Calendar web part, and Links web part. The Windows SharePoint Services image is displayed in an Image web part. Notice that it doesn't have a header like the other web parts. You can modify this by editing the web part and then switching the chrome type under the Appearance group. Web parts are easily customized. You can change this image by uploading another image and adding the new link to the web part properties.

The next template we're going to discuss is the Blank Site template.

Blank Site template

A blank site has all the same functionality as other sites, but nothing is precreated. For example, you won't have a Document library or Announcements list. About the only thing you'll see on a blank site is the Image web part with the SharePoint Foundation logo. This is good when you're planning to create your own custom site. An example of what a blank site looks like is shown in figure 3.19.

The next template we'll discuss is the Document Workspace template, whose sole focus is collaboration on a document.

Document Workspace template

This site enables a group of users to collaborate on a document or documents. It offers a Document library to use for uploading and storing the files. Additional lists are provided to facilitate collaboration. These include calendar, discussion board, announcements, and task lists. On

Figure 3.19 Out-of-the-box SharePoint Foundation site template for a blank site

Figure 3.20 Out-of-the-box SharePoint Foundation site template for a Document Workspace site

the right side of the site is the Members web part, which is useful for seeing other users associated with this workspace. If the site is so configured, you'll also have access to members' presence and contact information. By default, this shows the groups, but it can easily be configured to show individual users. This template is displayed in figure 3.20.

Presence information

In a SharePoint site you'll often see Messenger-style icons in front of people's names corresponding with their IM status. When you place the mouse pointer on the icon, additional functionality becomes available, such as the ability to send an email to that person or plan a meeting with them. For users to see this, they would need to have a compatible instant messaging client installed such as Lync, Communicator, Windows, or MSN Messenger.

SharePoint Foundation web part components shown in this template are the announcements, shared documents, tasks, members, and links. Notice that the Quick Launch navigation displays links to calendar and team discussions. You can easily modify Quick Launch to display your choice of links and lists. We'll discuss this further in the *Quick Launch* section in chapter 4.

The next template we're going to discuss is the Blog Site template.

Blog Site template

A blog is a site for users to share information with other users and provide them with a forum so that they can comment on the different posts. It provides easy ways for you to categorize your post and manage the site. Blog sites are commonly used with SharePoint Foundation for public-facing sites by SharePoint techies to post their ideas and guidance in relation to SharePoint. You'll often see executive blogs in corporations, and individual employees may even create one and tie it into their personal site if they're running SharePoint Server. The Blog Site template is displayed in figure 3.21.

Figure 3.21 Out-of-the-box SharePoint Foundation site template for a blog site, with sample data

The image denotes the ability to categorize your posts and archive them. Also, many people like to post their picture on their blog.

The next template we'll discuss is the Group Work Site template.

Group Work Site template

This template, shown in figure 3.22, is new to SharePoint Foundation. It's a groupware solution that teams can use to create, organize, and share information. It includes a group calendar, which allows you to schedule members and reserve resources. It has a Whereabouts section so you can update the group as to your status. A Circulations list lets you post either public or confidential memos to members and get a confirmation that the memo was read. It also includes a Phone Call Memo, which can also be set to confidential and be available only to the specified members. In addition to these great new features you'll find the core list, such as the Document library, task, links, discussions, and surveys.

Working remotely never got any easier than this! Make sure you mention this new site template when you're trying to make a case to your boss as to why you should be allowed to work remotely.

Next, we'll discuss the different meeting templates starting with the Basic Meeting Workspace template.

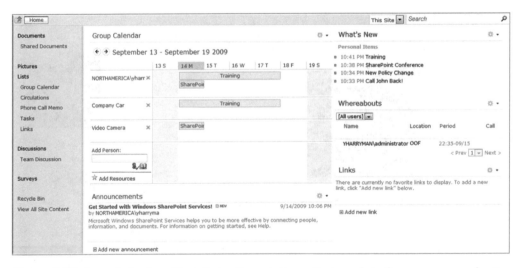

Figure 3.22 Out-of-the-box SharePoint Foundation site template for a group work site

3.3.3 SharePoint Foundation meeting site templates

The rest of the templates included in SharePoint Foundation are meeting templates. There are five of them, all with a slightly different purpose for the organization and continuing collaboration of meetings. We'll start by discussing the Basic Meeting Workspace.

Basic Meeting Workspace template

A meeting workspace is a site for organizing and capturing the actions in a meeting. It provides lists for managing the objectives, agenda, meeting attendees, and documents. It's a great site to use when setting up a meeting, and you really can't go wrong with an acronym like BMW. An example of a Basic Meeting Workspace template is shown in figure 3.23.

SharePoint Foundation web part components shown in this template are a custom list for objectives, attendees, and agenda and an out-of-the-box Document library web part. Notice that a web part is highly customizable. For example, if you were to select Add New Item for the Agenda web part, you'd see that a lot of other data is captured besides what's displayed in the web part. Web part customizations will be covered extensively throughout all of the scenarios. Now we'll discuss another meeting template: the Blank Meeting Workspace template.

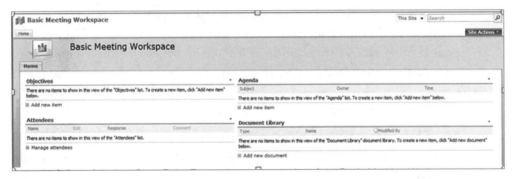

Figure 3.23 Out-of-the-box SharePoint Foundation site template for a Basic Meeting Workspace

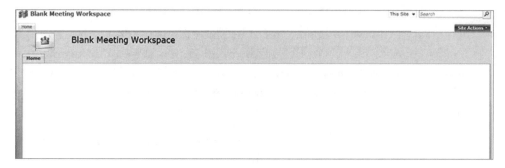

Figure 3.24 Out-of-the-box SharePoint Foundation site template for a Blank Meeting Workspace

Blank Meeting Workspace template

Need I say more—a picture is worth a thousand words, as shown in figure 3.24. As you can see from the image, this meeting workspace is blank and available for a site owner to customize it as they wish.

Whereas this site template is set up so you can design it to your heart's content, the next template has a specific focus—capturing decisions and the execution of those decisions that are sometime made in a meeting (if it's a productive one).

Decision Meeting Workspace template

A Decision Meeting Workspace expands the previous meeting site. It provides additional lists for creating tasks and recording decisions. The goal of this site is to provide a bit more structure for a meeting to ensure that outcomes of the decisions are tracked. As you can see in figure 3.25, this site is configured to capture objectives, tasks, a detailed agenda, and any decisions that were made.

The SharePoint Foundation web part components shown here are the same as for the previous template with the addition of tasks and decisions.

The next template we'll discuss is the Social Meeting Workspace template.

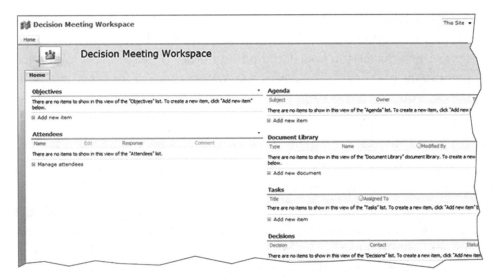

Figure 3.25 Out-of-the-box SharePoint Foundation site template for a Decision Meeting Workspace

Social Meeting Workspace template

A Social Meeting Workspace is a site for planning social occasions. It provides lists for tracking attendees, providing directions, instructions for what to bring, discussion boards, and storing pictures of the event. Notice how it organizes the information through the use of tabbed navigation, as shown in figure 3.26.

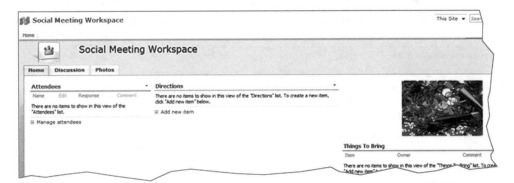

Figure 3.26 Out-of-the-box SharePoint Foundation site template for a social meeting workspace

The SharePoint Foundation web part components shown here are the custom lists Attendees, Directions, and Things To Bring. The other tabs offer a discussion board and photo library. I've seen several implementations of the tabbed meeting workspaces reused for other site purposes. You can always remove the custom web parts associated with the meeting from the template and customize it to make it your own.

Now let's discuss the last meeting template, which is another tabbed template for the Multipage Meeting Workspace.

Multipage Meeting Workspace template

A Multipage Meeting Workspace is similar to the Basic Meeting Workspace with the addition of two blank pages for you to customize based on your requirements. The tabs are shown in figure 3.27. I commonly see this template reused and renamed for other purposes because people love to have the tabbed web part to display multiple pages.

The SharePoint Foundation web part components shown here are a customized list for objectives, agenda, and attendees. Two blank pages have already been added for further customization. Even though there are only three pages displayed, you can add extra pages and delete existing pages using the Site Actions menu.

Before we dive into the next section, let's recap what you've learned. You now understand the core templates that come with the free version of SharePoint Foundation, but what you haven't seen yet are some of the more powerful site templates that come with SharePoint Server.

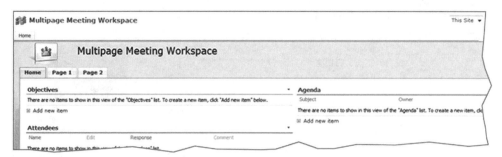

Figure 3.27 Out-of-the-box SharePoint Foundation site template for a Multipage Meeting Workspace

The next section will dive into the details of those templates. This is where you'll begin to learn about the business automation and application capabilities of SharePoint along with enhanced collaboration. Remember that users who have SharePoint Server can also use the templates we just reviewed.

3.3.4 Out-of-the-box site templates for SharePoint Server

The following sections will give a brief description along with a picture of each of the different SharePoint Server sites. To get started we'll cover those templates included in SharePoint Server Standard; in the next section we'll cover those in SharePoint Server Enterprise.

3.3.5 SharePoint Server Standard templates

In table 3.3 I provide a brief description of the templates that can be found in SharePoint Server Standard and follow it up with a detailed description and image of each.

Table 3.3 SharePoint Server Standard templates

Template	Description
Enterprise Wiki	The Enterprise Wiki template's goal is to provide you typical functionality that you'd find in a wiki site. It helps you to share information by allowing the easy creation of multiple web pages that can be interconnected.
My Site Host	The My Site Host template is a site-collection template that can be created for each person who uses SharePoint to share information about them.
Personalization Site	The Personalization Site is a site within the My Site Host template that's available for each person who uses SharePoint to store their own documents, links, and the like.
Publishing Portal	This is a site-collection template that's typically used for an internet or intranet site. It has built-in processes for content approval and security measures to ensure anonymous users can access only certain content.

Table 3.3 SharePoint Server Standard templates *(continued)*

Template	Description
Publishing Site	The Publishing Site enables content authors to modify the page in a draft format prior to publishing to the end users.
Publishing Site with Workflow	The Publishing Site with Workflow is the same as the Publishing Site, with the additional of a workflow process built in for the approval of the content prior to publishing to end users.
Visio Process Repository	The Visio Process Repository is set up to help end users manage and share Visio documents.
Basic Search Center	This enables users to search for content within SharePoint along with various external sources, if configured.
Enterprise Search Center	The Enterprise Search Center provides the same search functionality as the Basic Search Center, but it has an additional tab so you can also do people searches.

Now that you understand at a high level the different site templates associated with SharePoint Server Standard, I'm going to go through each one in detail and provide a visual so you can see how it works. I'll start with the Enterprise Wiki template.

Enterprise Wiki template

One unique thing to note about the Enterprise Wiki is that all pages in SharePoint are now termed *wiki pages*. This new functionality was added to the SharePoint 2010 release, and it allows you to select any site page that you're editing and add content. Figure 3.28 shows an example of an Enterprise Wiki in edit mode, so you can see the different editing options available. All SharePoint pages can be edited in a similar manner.

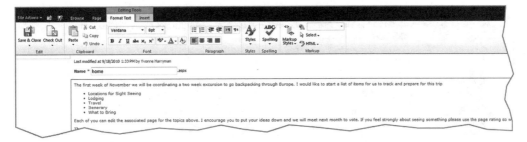

Figure 3.28 Out-of-the-box SharePoint Server site template for an Enterprise Wiki

The Enterprise Wiki template introduces some additional capabilities such as the ability to comment, rate, and categorize on the wiki page.

The next site template we're going to cover focuses on My Sites.

My Site Host template

If My Sites are configured in SharePoint Server, you'll have the ability to provide each of your end users with a site collection, which allows them to share information about themselves or organize their personal content. The My Site Host template is the public page that's tied to people search and allows users to share information. An example of my public page that I have up for Microsoft is shown in figure 3.29. Certain information is blocked out because I don't want to publicly distribute all of my details, but you can get a good idea of how it works from the information shown.

The next site template we're going to discuss is also tied to My Site. It's specifically focused on the end user's personalized view of their content.

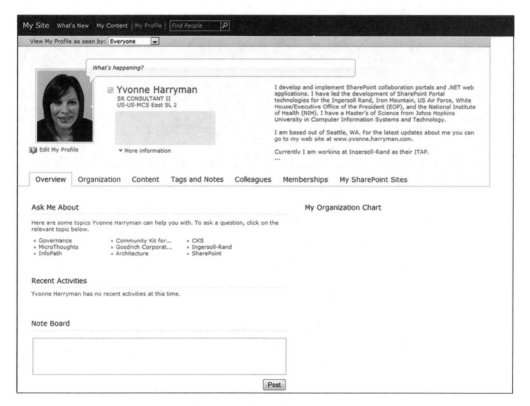

Figure 3.29 Out-of-the-box SharePoint Server site template for a My Site host

Personalization Site template

A Personalization Site is often added to a user's My Site. It's good for delivering personalized views of information for the user who accesses it. It includes personalization-specific web parts and navigation so you can track your colleagues, interest, sites, and the like. The Personalization Site is shown in figure 3.30.

Now that we've covered My Sites and you understand how to organize and share end-user information, let's discuss the most popular set of templates for sharing read-only content.

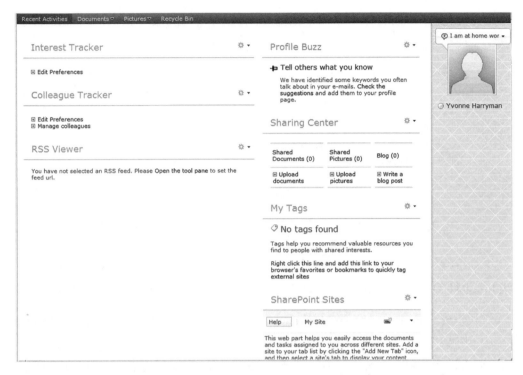

Figure 3.30 Out-of-the-box SharePoint Server site template for a Personalization Site

Publishing Portal, Site, and Site with Workflow templates

A publishing site is typically used if the process of sharing information needs to be formalized. A publishing site, regardless of it being a publishing portal, a publishing site, or a site with the publishing workflow added, will work and look like figure 3.31. A portal just means it's a site collection with a series of publishing sites as subsites; this is typically used for public-facing SharePoint sites or internal company portals. A publishing site or a publishing site with workflow is an individual site configured with publishing rules, which allows you to work on the content in draft format before enabling end users to see the information. This is the power of a publishing site, because it allows the content editors to work on draft versions of pages, which are not visible to readers until it's published. The page's editing toolbar is visible in the screen

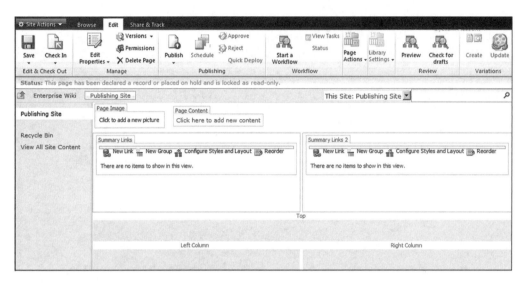

Figure 3.31 Out-of-the-box SharePoint Server site template for a Publishing Site

shot. The site does include some lists, such as a Document and Image library for storing web-publishing assets.

The key difference between the Publishing Site and the Publishing Site with Workflow templates is an approval process that's built into the Publishing Site with Workflow template. This template allows you to have a multilevel approval process for publishing a site and schedule when it can be displayed to the end users.

When you start part 2 and begin to build out the scenarios, you may want to consider starting from a Publishing Site rather than a blank site.

The next site template we're going to discuss is specific to Visio and organizing your process diagrams.

Visio Process Repository template

The Visio Process Repository template was added because of a common request regarding storing organization diagrams. The solution was a SharePoint site template where Visio users can leverage the SharePoint capabilities such as check in and check out, associating metadata with diagrams that are uploaded, and workflow for any required approval. To see the Visio library in action, take a look at figure 3.32.

Figure 3.32 Out-of-the-box SharePoint Server site template for a Visio Process Repository

Wow, we've almost finished reviewing the site templates associated with the standard version of SharePoint. Without ever installing or playing with SharePoint, you should have a pretty good idea of what SharePoint has to offer. For our last two site templates, we're going to discuss search.

Basic Search Center template

This is your template for a basic search site. Here you'll have the basic search options, which display results to your end users based on keywords they enter. There'll also be some options for advanced search and the ability to filter your search results using the refinement panel on the left, as shown in figure 3.33.

The next template we'll discuss is an additional search center template.

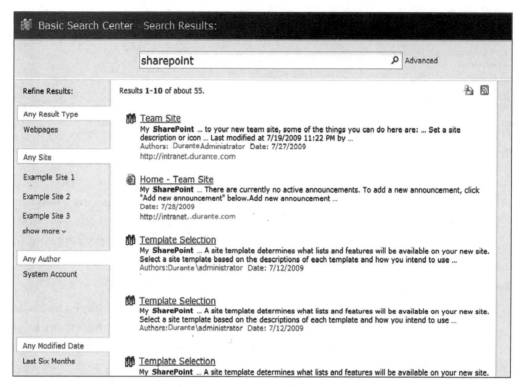

Figure 3.33 Out-of-the-box SharePoint Server site template for a Basic Search Center

Enterprise Search Center template

The Enterprise Search Center, shown in figure 3.34, is similar to the Basic Search Center with the exception that it has a People tab so you can search for people.

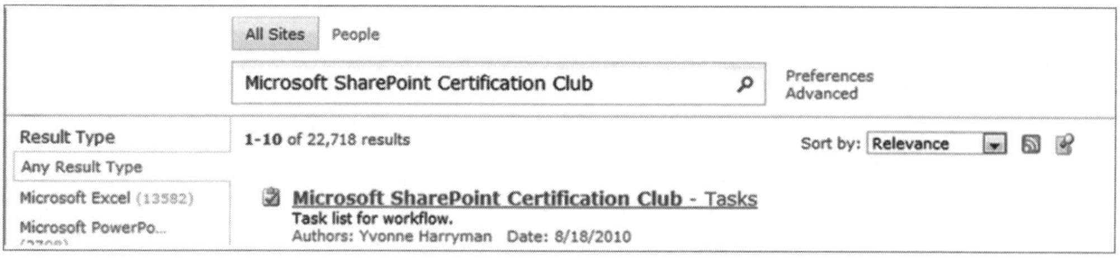

Figure 3.34 Out-of-the-box SharePoint Server site template library for an Enterprise Search Center

We have one more set of templates to go through, and then you'll know what's available to you out of the box. This is important to understand before diving into the instructions for creating your own custom site templates. The last series of templates we're going to discuss is associated with the Enterprise version of SharePoint Server.

3.3.6 SharePoint Server Enterprise templates

The highest version of SharePoint that you can have is Enterprise. This will give you access to all the functionality and all the site templates that we've already covered in the previous templates. To begin, I'll list in table 3.4 the site templates that are unique to Enterprise and provide a brief description of their purpose. I'll then dive into each one and show a visual example it. These templates have been organized into Enterprise templates and followed by templates specific to Access Services.

Table 3.4 Enterprise templates

Template	Description
Business Intelligence Center	The Business Intelligence Center is known for hosting information that we refer to as BI. It also has the capability to link to content from Performance Point Services.
Document Center	If you need one central repository for documents across the enterprise, you can use the Document Center.
Records Center	The Records Center helps route and store files in compliance with the company's records management policy.
FAST Search Center	The FAST Search Center enables some enhanced search capabilities and provides document previews.
PowerPoint Broadcast Center	The PowerPoint Broadcast Center is a site collection that allows presenters to create a link for viewers to watch a slide show with them as they flip through it.
Assets Web Database	The Assets Web Database enables you to manage your active and retired assets along with their value.

Table 3.4 Enterprise templates *(continued)*

Template	Description
Charitable Contributions Web Database	The Charitable Contributions Web Database allows you to manage many different campaigns and the events associated with them along with any fundraising goals and donations received.
Contacts Web Database	The Contacts Web Database helps you to manage your contacts.
Issues Web Database	The Issues Web Database helps to track issues, their status, and resolution of the issues.
Projects Web Database	The Projects Web Database helps you track multiple projects and the tasks and status of those tasks associated with the project.

Now we'll go though each of these templates, and I'll provide an image of them so you can get a better idea of how they work. To begin, we'll discuss the Business Intelligence Center.

Business Intelligence Center template

The Business Intelligence Center can be tied to Performance Point Services or it can be used standalone. It allows you to track status indicators to measure performance. We'll step though an example of configuring status indicators in chapter 9. You can publish and share your Excel spreadsheets using Excel Services or create rich dashboards pulling from Performance Point and Excel Services. The Business Intelligence Center is shown in figure 3.35.

If you need to do some knowledge mining on data you have, the BI features included in SharePoint and grouped together in the Business Intelligence Center template are a good place to start.

The next set of templates we'll discuss is focused on the centralized storage of documents and records.

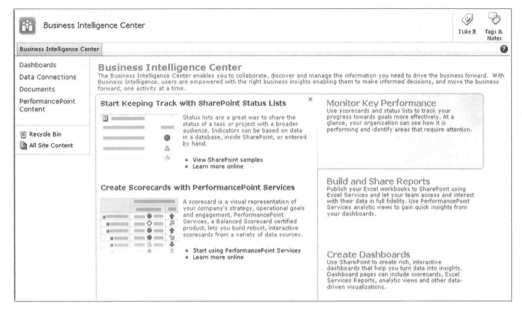

Figure 3.35 Out-of-the-box SharePoint Server site template for a Business Intelligence Center

Document Center template

The Document Center is a site you'd create if you chose to create a central repository for the documents in your enterprise. It provides tree-view navigation, and you can use the relevant document web part on this site to help you manage a large number of documents. Certain document-management features are enabled on this template such as versioning and required checkout. New features since 2007 include the creation of a unique ID upon creation, which can be used to look up documents, enterprise metadata, ratings, and document sets. The Document Center homepage is shown in figure 3.36.

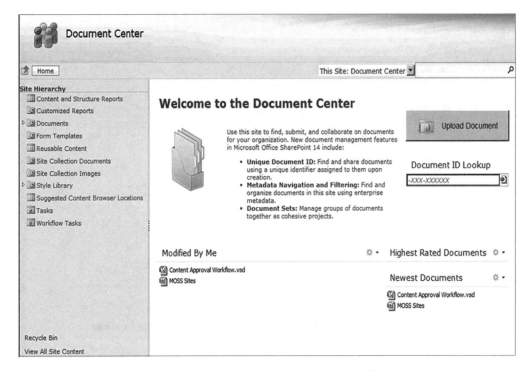

Figure 3.36 Out-of-the-box SharePoint Server site template for a Document Center

If you go into the Document Center you'll see some additional features such as the enhanced capabilities to filter though documents. This is shown in figure 3.37.

Similar to the Document Center template is the Records Center template, which is focused on capturing any documents that are considered records.

Records Center template

The Records Center is a site for records management and storage of documents that require long-term archival; it isn't meant for collaboration. Records managers can configure the routing table to direct incoming files to specific locations based on the type of record. Records can't be modified after they're added to this repository. The Records Center is shown in figure 3.38.

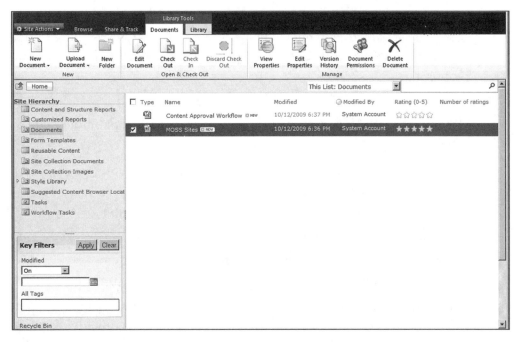

Figure 3.37 Document Center enhanced features

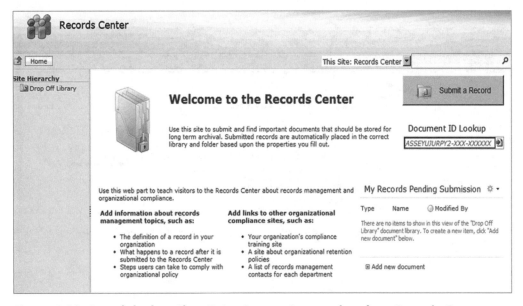

Figure 3.38 Out-of-the-box SharePoint Server site template for a Records Center

You should have a good idea now of your enhanced capabilities for centrally storing documents. The next template that we're going to discuss, the FAST Search Center template, will help you to later find that content.

FAST Search Center template

If you license FAST, it offers you additional search capabilities such as these:

- Search enhancements to return items based on your prior search history and email content
- Perform a new search based on certain search results
- Sort results based on managed properties
- Refine results based on metadata for all returned items
- Display document previews, as shown in figure 3.39

You now have lots of new knowledge of the capabilities to manage documents and records and search on your content. Let's quickly discuss a new template that helps you to broadcast your content using the PowerPoint Broadcast Center.

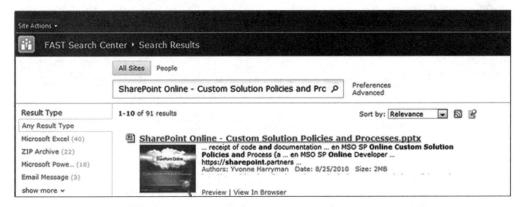

Figure 3.39 Out-of-the-box SharePoint Server site template library for a FAST Search Center

PowerPoint Broadcast Center template

The PowerPoint Broadcast Center is a site-collection template. You can configure this so that you can share a presentation with end users by selecting in PowerPoint that you'd like to broadcast the slide show. PowerPoint will then go through a series of steps in which you can select the Broadcast Center, and it will generate a link for you that you can send out to end users. The PowerPoint screen will appear, as shown in figure 3.40, which is how you know you're broadcasting your presentation via the PowerPoint Broadcast Center. Any end users who go to the site will be watching the presentation with you as you go through the slides.

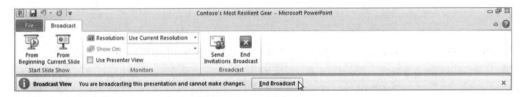

Figure 3.40 PowerPoint Broadcast Center

The next series of templates that we're going to discuss is associated with Access Services.

3.3.7 SharePoint Server Access Services templates

These templates use Access to create an application that maintains the information in an Access database versus a SharePoint list. In chapter 11 we'll walk through a scenario where you set up an Access database and use Access Services. To begin, let's see what's already configured and set up for you using the site templates.

Assets Web Database template

The first Access Services site template that we'll discuss is the Assets Web Database template, as shown in figure 3.41. There are four main tabs to help you manage and track current assets. In this image we're focused on the reports of the assets that have been entered. If you needed to track your assets and their value, this is a great application to use.

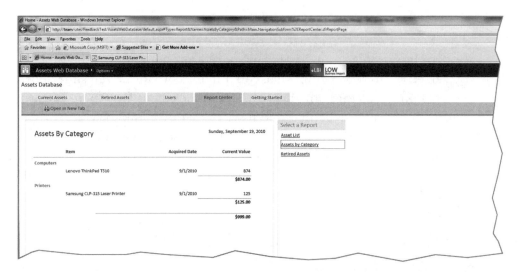

Figure 3.41 Out-of-the-box SharePoint Server site template library for an Assets Web Database

The next Access Services template we'll discuss is focused on the management of charities.

Charitable Contributions Web Database template

The Charitable Contributions Web Database allows you to track various charity campaigns and associate multiple events with each campaign. An example of entering the details of a campaign is shown in figure 3.42. Here you can enter the fundraising goal and track donations received in association with the various events.

This is a great and easy way to manage a nonprofit without have to buy or design and build an application. The next site template we'll look at is the Contacts Web Database template.

Contacts Web Database template

The Contacts Web Database is useful for tracking contacts that need to be shared with a team. For example, if your company has many clients, this would be good to use to track and share information about your clients. There's a Notes section as well, so you can enter specific information about a person to share with the team. I've entered myself as an example contact in figure 3.43, so you can see the Contacts Database in action.

Figure 3.42 Out-of-the-box SharePoint Server site template library for a Charitable Contributions Web Database

Figure 3.43 Out-of-the-box SharePoint Server site template library for a Contacts Web Database

Figure 3.44 Out-of-the-box SharePoint Server site template library for an Issues Web Database

The next Access Services template we'll discuss is the Issues Web Database template.

Issues Web Database template

The Issues Web Database can help you track active and closed issues. They can be assigned and categorized. An example of entering issues is shown in figure 3.44. This would be a great template to use for a help desk to log problems and track their status.

The last Access Services template that we'll cover is the Projects Web Database template.

Projects Web Database template

The Projects Web Database can help you track multiple projects and the tasks associated with each project. If you were to use this, I'd suggest tracking key milestones for each project and using the Project Site template, which we discussed earlier, for the details. This is a good template to use for tracking at a high level the status of many projects. I've entered an example project with tasks in figure 3.45. I'm tracking tasks associated with the completion of my SharePoint 2010 book. If you were to continue building out that scenario, I'd recommend having Manning enter all of their books in production and having each chapter be a key milestone. The editors could then update the chapters as they're completed, and the publishers could check this site at any point to see the overall status of the many different books being prepared for publication.

You now have a really good idea of most of the capabilities of Share-Point out of the box, and you've never even opened SharePoint. This

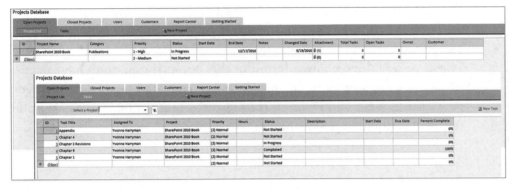

Figure 3.45 Out-of-the-box SharePoint Server site template library for a Projects Web Database

chapter is great for showing you what SharePoint can do without any customizations. If you read only this chapter, I'd say you're well versed in what SharePoint is. Let's summarize what you've learned.

3.4 Summary

You now have the foundation of SharePoint sites and what you can get out of the box. You should have a good understanding of the following:

- The different lists and libraries that are available
- What a web part is
- Out-of-the-box site templates for SharePoint Foundation
- Out-of-the-box site templates for SharePoint Server Standard
- Out-of-the-box site templates for SharePoint Server Enterprise
- Meeting site templates
- Access Services site templates
- Search site templates
- How you can leverage this functionality

Now we can get into the muscle of SharePoint and discuss what you can do as a power user to customize and create your own site templates. The rest of the book will continue teaching the fundamentals of

SharePoint through a scenarios-based approach. This will help you envision the different possibilities and get you on your way to creating customized sites for your own use. So let's get started with the fun part. Part 2 covers the scenarios found in this book. If you don't have access to an environment to build out these scenarios, appendix A has been provided to walk you through the steps to create your own SharePoint test or development environment.

Implementations using real-world scenarios

Part 2 discusses the various components of SharePoint: sites, content, communities, insights, composites, search, and governance. Here you'll not only learn and implement the functionality in a hands-on approach, but you'll also get an understanding of the possibilities that SharePoint offers. Because each scenario is drawn from the real world, you may find a reason to keep using each solution you build.

4

Setting up a document collaboration site

This chapter covers

- Site branding
- Document libraries and the collaboration features
- Custom lists and lookup fields
- Library and list web parts
- Connected web parts
- Publishing sites

In the previous part of this book we covered SharePoint terminology, capabilities, and the out-of-the-box features. What I didn't do was exercise your imagination for designing and creating powerful sites. The chapters in this part are going to guide you through a step-by-step process of how to configure and deliver a site.

In this chapter you'll build out a scenario for meeting the requirements for managing a proposal and resume document workspace. Why would you want to do that? This scenario touches on the common problems associated with organizing associated documents. There are many options to do this, and the implementation that follows will go over one of the possibilities.

4.1   Managing business proposal resources

This topic is broken up into three sections: situation, business priorities, and solution. The first section, situation, will give a detailed explanation of a request that you've received. The next section, business priorities, will extract a list of requirements based on priority to accomplish your goals. It's important when gathering information such as this to not mix technology with the requirements. Business process, not technology, should drive the requirements. The third section will give you an overview of the solution that we will spend the rest of the chapter walking through and building.

4.1.1   Situation

You are a resource manager for Durante Inc. You're responsible for tracking employees, employees' resumes, and the proposals they're associated with. You're often asked to provide information on the employees associated with a proposal. Currently this is a time-consuming task for you because you have the data dispersed and unassociated. The proposal team keeps the proposals on a file share. You manage the resumes by having the employees keep them up to date and send them via email to you if there are changes. You then store them in a folder in Outlook. When you are requested to provide their resumes for a proposal, you go the proposal file share, look up the resources listed, and then locate their resumes in your resumes folder in Outlook. You compile the data and send it to the requester. You're certain there's an easier and more efficient way to handle this data.

Because you now understand the situation at hand, let's extract the requirements. Several practices to keep in mind when doing this are as follows:

- Keep the technology separate from the requirements.
- List the requirements by priority.
- Provide daily updates and let the requester know what challenges you're facing. Oftentimes you'll find that the business priorities

will change once they understand the complexity behind meeting such a request.

4.1.2 Business priorities

You understand the current situation, so let's discuss what the business priorities are so you can put together an appropriate solution for Durante Inc:

- Create a central repository to manage the resumes, employees, and proposals.
- Ensure the resumes and proposals can still be managed by the employees.
- Provide an easy way to sort the data so you can quickly access
  - The employees associated with a proposal
  - The employees' latest resume

The next section will highlight the solution you're going to build in this chapter. In this case I know what the best solution should be. It didn't hurt that I created the requirements. If you were gathering the requirements beforehand, I'd advise that you do a proof of concept prior to proposing a solution to the business. Many times you'll have an idea of how you can solve a problem with SharePoint, but there are always limitations, especially when you're planning on using the out-of-the-box functionality with no customization. It's important to brainstorm and test your ideas first and then let the requester know how you plan to move forward.

4.1.3 Solution

Once you complete the steps in this chapter, you'll have a site that meets the situation and business priorities specified to you. Your final solution will look like figure 4.1.

Notice in figure 4.1 that when I selected a specific proposal, it showed the resources associated with that proposal in the web part beneath labeled Human Resources. When I selected one of the people assigned to that proposal, it filtered out the other resumes to show me that

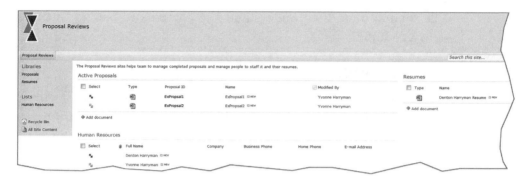

Figure 4.1 The solution that will be implemented in this chapter is based on the requirements specification and business priorities.

person in the web part to the right, under Resumes. Now that you understand what you're building, let's get started by implementing it. Don't worry; I'll make it easy and guide you step by step.

4.2 SharePoint Foundation features

To begin you'll need to create a site by choosing Site Actions > New Site. Depending on what version of SharePoint you're running, you should select Blank Site or Publishing Site and choose More Options. Remember, if you're running SharePoint Server, you may want to consider the publishing site as an option, which is covered in section 4.3. You'll want to enter the following for Title, Description, and Web Site Address:

Property	Value
Title	Proposal Reviews
Description	The Proposal Reviews site helps teams to manage completed proposals and manage people to staff it and their resumes.
Web Site Address	ProposalReviews

NOTE   It's a good practice to not enter spaces into your Web Site Address; for example, instead of entering ProposalReviews you could enter Proposal Reviews but the URL will then have %20 added into it to denote the space.

Now that you've created your initial site, whether it's a blank or a publishing site, we'll discuss branding. This is useful to understand as you build out any of your scenarios. It's quick and easy to apply a bit of style to your site. It can help you make sure your site stands out and is different from the other more commonly used portal or team site.

4.2.1 Branding

I'm going to help you become familiar with the options available to you for customizing your site. We'll discuss some of the tools for doing this such as site themes and the Look And Feel options under Site Settings. Additional options for branding will be covered later in this chapter when we discuss the Content Editor web part and the SharePoint Server features for a publishing site. This will help you to further create a unique look and feel to help users identify the site.

Site themes: a quick way to switch the color scheme

One of the easiest ways to make an impact is to switch the theme. You can do this by completing the following steps:

Step	Action	Result/Notes
1	Go to Site Actions > Site Settings.	

Step	Action	Result/Notes
2	Under the Look And Feel section, select the option called Site Theme.	Here you will see a list of different themes you can select from and a preview window to give you an idea of what each one does.
3	Select Azure and click Apply.	Navigate back to the homepage of your site to see the changes you've made.

If you have some spare time, I recommend playing around with the different themes and applying them. It's amazing the difference it can make on the impression a user gets when they come to the site. In the next section you'll create an Image library to help you manage your images. These images will be used later to help you further brand the site.

Image library: managing your images

To add a logo to your site you need to have a URL with an image to point it to. If you have an image on the web you could use that, but another easier way for you to manage it is to create an image and upload the image into a library in the Durante website. I have a dummy image that I'm using to complete this scenario; you can grab any small image or create one to test in your environment. Once you have your image, follow these steps to create your first library. This library will be the location for all of your image files:

Step	Action	Result/Notes
1	Choose Site Actions > More Options.	A dialog box will appear and present you with a list of options.
2	Select Picture Library. You can filter by library to narrow your list of options.	For the name enter SiteImages.
3	Select More Options.	For the description enter This library contains all the images used for this site.

Step	Action	Result/Notes
4	Select No for displaying the picture in the Quick Launch bar. Because this is an administration list and won't be necessary for general use, we'll opt to exclude it from the main navigation.	
5	Select Create.	

You should now be looking at the main page for the Site Images library, as shown in step 1 of the following table. You'll notice a toolbar under the library's name with different options to help you manage the Picture library and the uploaded content:

Step	Action	Result/Notes
1	Select Upload > Upload Multiple Pictures.	A dialog box to upload your pictures will appear, as shown in figure 4.2.
2	Under Upload Settings select Send Pictures Optimized for Viewing on the Web.	This will reduce the size of the picture to ensure better performance for your page loads that need to render the image.
3	Press Ctrl-A to highlight all the pictures.	
4	Click Upload and click Close.	

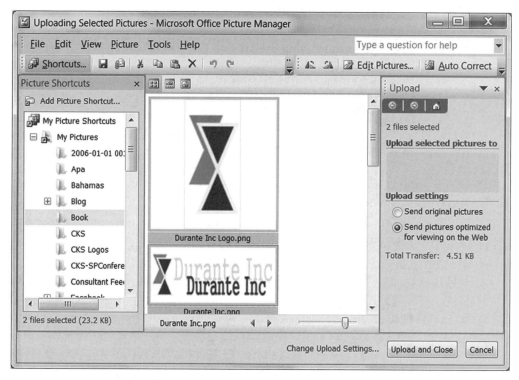

Figure 4.2 Uploading Selected Pictures dialog box

> **Adding a picture shortcut**
> If you downloaded the pictures to the My Pictures folder, you'll now see the book images that you'll need to upload. If you don't see the pictures, you'll need to add a picture shortcut. To do this, select Add Picture Shortcut, locate the folder for your images, and click Add.

Now that you have the images uploaded to the site, you can easily reference them in other areas. In the next section, you'll use the Durante_Inc_Logo image to modify the site's default icon, so you won't have the default icon used for other out-of-the-box sites.

Site icon: personalizing your site with a logo

You should now be back at the homepage of the Site Images library. The next few steps will demonstrate how to get the reference URL for the image:

Step	Action	Result/Notes
1	Select Go Back to "Site Images."	Proposal Reviews — Libraries / Lists / Discussions — Recycle Bin / All Site Content — "If you have not finished up / Go back to "Site Images""
		After uploading your picture, you'll need to navigate back to the Site Images library to see them.
2	Select the Durante_Inc_Logo image by clicking it.	This will take you to a page with the image properties.
3	Select the Durante Inc Logo in the Preview section.	Name — Durante Inc Logo / Preview
		You should now be on a page with only the image displayed.
4	Copy the URL from this page to use in the next few steps.	
5	After you've copied the URL, click your browser's Back button to get back to the Properties page.	
6	Choose Site Actions > Site Settings.	

Step	Action	Result/Notes
7	Select Title, Description, and Icon under Look and Feel.	**Look and Feel** Title, description, and icon Tree view Site theme Navigation
8	In the URL box paste the logo and select Click Here to Test to verify that your logo appears.	URL: /Site%20Images/Durante%20Inc%20Logo.jpg Click here to test
9	Click OK.	Site Actions ▾ **Proposal Reviews** You should now see this logo at the top of your site next to the name.

It's important to understand some of the core features for branding your sites. You can use this skill on any site that you build to help create a unique identity. Similar to branding, navigation for quick access to important information is also important to understand. These both help your end users quickly identity the purpose of your site. We'll cover navigation now.

Quick Launch: modifying the site's navigation

The Quick Launch bar displayed on the left side of your site is often used as the main navigation source for users to access the resources available to them. In this scenario you're going to provide your users with two document libraries for managing proposals and resumes and a custom list to track the human resource data, such as name and contact information. In order to reduce the clutter that's displayed by default when a user logs onto the site, you're going to remove some of the items.

Once you've finished, select Proposal Reviews from the breadcrumb navigation trail (found in the upper-left corner of your screen) to

Step	Action	Result/Notes
1	Choose Site Actions > Site Settings.	
2	Under Look and Feel select the Navigation option.	**Look and Feel** Title, description, and icon Tree view Site theme Navigation
3	In the Navigation, Editing, and Sorting section select Discussions, click Delete, and click OK.	Move Up · Move Down · Edit... · Delete · Add Heading... · Add Link... — Delete the selected item from navigation Global Navigation Current Navigation Libraries Lists Discussions

navigate back to the main page. Verify that your Quick Launch looks like figure 4.3.

This covers the basics of site branding and navigation modifications that are available for a blank site. Remember that in this book we're not discussing any of the branding techniques that will require server-side access or the use of development tools, because we're taking a no-code approach and focusing on site owners' capabilities. If you're interested, you can look into additional branding techniques through the use of SharePoint Designer to create master pages and

Figure 4.3 Quick Launch bar after the modifications have been applied

page layouts and to modify the CSS files. Now that you have the shell of your site created, you'll need to start creating your data sources to track human resources, resumes, and proposals. To do this we'll dive into how to use a list.

4.2.2 Contacts list: tracking the human resources

To get started we're going to walk through the steps to use a standard Contacts list and customize it for tracking people and their resumes.

Lists within SharePoint are powerful because they're easy to modify to meet your specific requirements. In this example you're using the Contacts list because it already has columns that you can use, such as Email Address, Business Phone, and so on.

Contacts list: creating a list to manage your resources

You'll start by creating a Contacts list. When you complete step 1 to create the list, you'll see many other options. While here you may want to take the time to hover your mouse over some of the other lists available under Communications, Tracking, and Custom Lists. If you click a type, a description is displayed on the right side of the page to help you understand some of the other options available to you:

Step	Action	Result/Notes
1	Choose Site Actions > More Options.	A dialog box will appear and present you with a list of options.
2	Select Contacts. You can filter by list to narrow your options.	For the name enter Human Resources.
3	Click Create.	

You should now see the Human Resources list in your Quick Launch bar under Lists. Also notice that you're now on the main page of the Human Resources list library. A series of control options have been provided to help you manage these items. We'll focus on the List Settings control, shown in the Ribbon on the far-right side, to customize the list's metadata; see figure 4.4.

List settings: disabling attachments

By default when you create a Contacts list, a paper clip icon will display attachments associated with an item. For our scenario there's no need for a user to upload an attachment because all the information needed can be captured in the columns, so you're going to disable the feature.

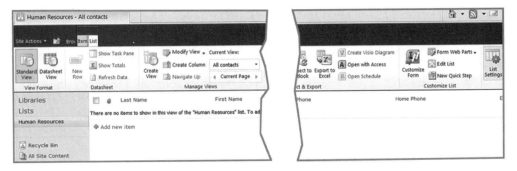

Figure 4.4 Customization options for a list in SharePoint that are available

Step	Action	Result/Notes
1	Choose List Settings under the List tab located in the Ribbon.	
2	Select Advanced Settings under General Settings.	**General Settings** Title, description and navigation Versioning settings Advanced settings
3	Click the radio button to disable attachments to list items.	Attachments to list items are: ○ Enabled ◉ Disabled
4	Click OK.	

Your users will no longer have the ability to add an attachment. Now we'll discuss how to customize the rest of the columns in the list.

List columns: customizing the data captured

This section will deal with modifying the columns associated with the Human Resources list under List Settings. You're going to require your users to always enter their full name, so instead of breaking the name into first name and last name, which is how it's configured by default, you'll require maintenance of only the full name:

Step	Action	Result/Notes
1	Select Full Name and click Delete.	You'll later update the Last Name column to be the Full Name column. The Last Name column, unlike other columns, is required, and you don't have the option to delete it, but you can rename it. This process will help you remove it.
2	Select Last Name under Columns.	Change the Column Name value to Full Name.
3	Click OK.	
4	Select First Name and click Delete.	

When updating this list you should now only need to enter the user's Full Name; the other data will be optional. So you now have a list to track all the employees who would have associated resumes and would be assigned to a proposal.

4.2.3 Document libraries: managing the proposals and resumes

You'll want to create a Document library to hold the proposal and resumes, which will allow end users to access them in one central location. By enabling version control and item-level permissions for editing rights, all end users will be able to work in a single library while maintaining security and historical records. To do this you need to complete the following steps.

Document library: managing the proposals

To get started you'll create the Proposals library:

Step	Action	Result/Notes
1	Choose Site Actions > More Options.	A dialog box will appear and present you with a list of options.
2	Select Document Library. You can filter by library to narrow your list of options.	For the name enter Proposals.

Step	Action	Result/Notes
3	Select More Options.	For the descriptions enter The following library is for proposal documents.
		Click Yes in response to Create a Version Each Time You Edit a File in This Document Library?
4	Click Create.	

Once the library is created, you'll want to add additional columns to prompt your end users to enter metadata when they create or upload a new proposal, such as the status of the document.

Library columns: customizing the metadata associated with the proposals

This section will guide you through the steps for creating custom columns to associate metadata with each document that's added to the library:

Step	Action	Result/Notes
1	Choose Library Settings under the List tab located in the Ribbon.	
2	In the Columns section select Create Column.	For Column Name enter Proposal ID.
		Choose Single Line of Text.
		Click Yes under Require That This Column Contains Information.
3	Click OK.	

Now you're going to add a Status column. This will be important for you to manage the proposals and indicate whether they're inactive, active, or still in the draft phase. In the following section you'll use this column to help you create views of the proposals that are uploaded.

Step	Action	Result/Notes
4	In the Columns section select Create Column.	For the Column name enter Status. Under The Type of Information in This Column Is, select Choice. Click Yes under Require That This Column Contains Information. In the section labeled Type Each Choice on a Separate Line, replace Enter Choice #1 with Active Enter Choice #2 with Archived Enter Choice #3 with Draft
5	Click OK.	

You should probably update the column order. This will impact the user when entering the information, and it creates a much better user experience if they see the required items at the top of the list. This will help your users understand the priority for entering information:

Step	Action	Result/Notes
1	Under Columns select Column Ordering.	Create column Add from existing site columns Column ordering Indexed columns
2	Modify Proposal ID to be the first position from the top.	Field Name — Position from Top Name — 1 Title — 2 Proposal ID — 3 Status — 2 3 Prop 4
3	Click OK.	

Your users will now be able to upload proposals and take advantage of the great features that a SharePoint document library provides, such as co-authoring, versioning, and item-level permissions, to name a few. Also, unique metadata is captured to help identify and find the document.

Next, we're going to discuss how to modify the view of the data.

Library views: modifying the management view

When users navigate to the Proposals list, they'll be looking at the All Documents view. This is where they can go to see all of the proposals without any filters applied. The only modifications you'll want to make are to ensure that the new columns are displayed in the desired order:

Step	Action	Result/Notes
1	Select Modify View under the Library tab shown in the Ribbon.	
2	Change Position from Left for Proposal ID to 2.	
3	Change Position from Left for Status to 4.	
4	Click OK.	

Congratulations! You've created the Proposals document library. You have one more key data source to create, and then you'll have all the pieces to start building out the web parts on your site. You'll now do the same for Resumes.

Document library: managing the resumes

It's great to have access to the proposals and information on the people assigned to the proposal, but you can take it a step further by also managing their resumes:

Step	Action	Result/Notes
1	Choose Site Actions > More Options.	A dialog box will appear and present you with a list of options.
2	Select Document Library. You can filter by library to narrow your list of options.	For the name enter Resumes.
3	Select More Options.	For the description enter The following library is for human resources resumes. Click Yes in response to Create a Version Each Time You Edit a File in This Document Library?
4	Click Create.	

You should now have a Proposals library to manage the resources' resumes. Now that you have your libraries and list created, you'll need to assemble the main page of the site with views into the data of these libraries and list to help the users access the information. How will you do this? You'll use web parts with a unique view and connections.

4.2.4 Web parts: customizing the Proposal Reviews homepage

To complete this next section you'll need to navigate back to the Proposal Reviews homepage. Once there you'll begin by placing the page in edit mode and examine the concept of zones. You'll need to do the following:

Step	Action	Result/Notes
1	Select Edit Page located under the Page tab in the Ribbon.	

NOTE   The Publishing page will give you some additional options for managing the modifications of a page and working with page layouts.

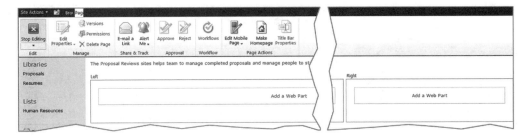

Figure 4.5 Proposal Reviews homepage in edit mode

You'll notice that your page is broken up into different zones. In figure 4.5 you see a Left zone and Right zone. In each of these zones you can add different web parts that are customized views of the data in the libraries and list that you created in the previous sections. I often use the front page of a newspaper as an analogy when explaining the concept to my customers. It's a way to give your readers the pertinent information, and they can then drill down into the individual sections to get the full details:

Step	Action	Result/Notes
2	Click Add a Web Part in the Left zone.	
3	Select the Proposals web part and click Add.	If it ends up in the wrong place, you can hover your mouse over the title and drag and drop it onto the correct location.
4	Do the same for Human Resources.	
5	Click Add a Web Part in the Right zone, select the Resumes web part, and click Add.	

A dialog box will display the different options for web parts that you can add to your page, as shown in figure 4.6.

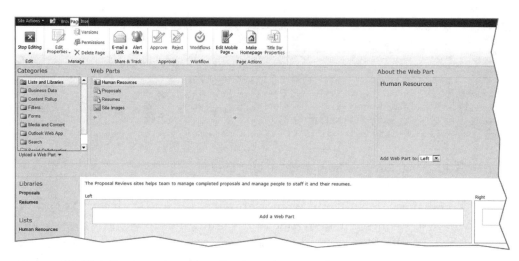

Figure 4.6 Web Parts options that display when you begin to customize the home-page of a site

A view of the information in the Human Resources list and the Proposals and Resumes libraries is now available on your main site, as shown in figure 4.7.

Now that you have the web parts arranged and displaying the appropriate information, you're going to add some additional functionality to help the users manage the information by connecting the web parts and adding filters. This is important to help users navigate the information.

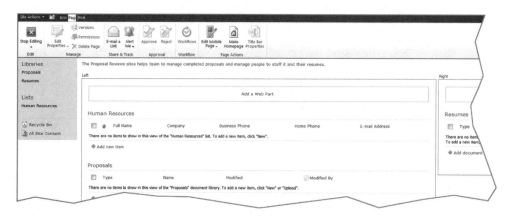

Figure 4.7 How the web parts should be displayed after being reorganized on the page

4.2.5 Linking resources and resumes with proposals

Connecting web parts is a powerful feature that allows you to switch the data that's displayed in different web parts by applying a value filter from an item selected in a different web part. In this section we'll walk through the steps for setting up the Proposals, Human Resources, and Resume web parts so that they're connected. For example, if a user selects a proposal, the team that's assigned to that proposal will appear in the Human Resources web part. If a user then selects one of the team members, their resume will then display in the Resumes web part.

Lookup columns: associating data from one list to another

To begin you'll need to create a lookup column in the Human Resources list. The lookup column will display a list of the proposals when a user goes to enter a human resource. Without completing this step, you won't have an association between the resources and the proposals:

Step	Action	Result/Notes
1	Select the Human Resources list.	This will take you to the default view of the Human Resources list.
2	Choose List Settings under the List tab located in the Ribbon.	
3	Select Create Column under Columns.	Create column Add from existing site columns Column ordering Indexed columns
4	For Column Name enter Proposals.	
5	Select Lookup (information already on this site) for The Type of Information in This Column Is.	
6	Under Get Information From, select Proposals.	Get information from: Proposals In this column: Proposal ID ☐ Allow multiple values

Step	Action	Result/Notes
7	Under In This Column, select Proposal ID.	
8	Select Allow Multiple Values.	
9	Click OK.	

Now that you've successfully created and understand a lookup column, let's create another one, to create an association between the human resources and the resumes. The lookup column will display a list of the human resources that a user can associate with a resume when it's added to the library:

Step	Action	Result/Notes
1	Select the Resumes list.	This will take you to the default view of the Resumes list.
2	Choose Library Settings under the Library tab located in the Ribbon.	
3	Select Create Column under Columns.	Create column Add from existing site columns Column ordering Indexed columns
4	For Column Name enter Human Resources.	
5	Select Lookup (information already on this site) for The Type of Information in This Column Is.	
6	Under Get Information From, select Human Resources.	
7	Under In This Column, select Full Name.	Get information from: Human Resources ▾ In this column: Full Name ▾ ☑ Allow multiple values

Step	Action	Result/Notes
8	Select Allow Multiple Values.	
9	Deselect Add to Default View.	☐ Add to default view
10	Click OK.	

Congratulations! All of your web parts now have associations. In the next section you'll modify the web parts and more specifically the fields that are displayed in the web parts. This is a required step in order for the web parts to apply filtered connections.

Web parts properties: modifying the display options

You have the core components added now, but you should flesh out what's displayed in each web part. You're going to do this by modifying the web parts' display columns, header, and view:

Step	Action	Result/Notes
1	Navigate back to the Proposals site homepage.	
2	For the Proposals web part, select Edit Web Part by selecting the Edit menu options, via the dropdown arrow in the header of the web part.	Proposals — Minimize / Close / Delete / Edit Web Part
3	Select Edit the Current View.	

Additional options for making modifications to the web part will appear to the right of the screen, as shown in figure 4.8. Over the next few steps you'll be making modifications to the view that's displayed in the web part and the title of the web part.

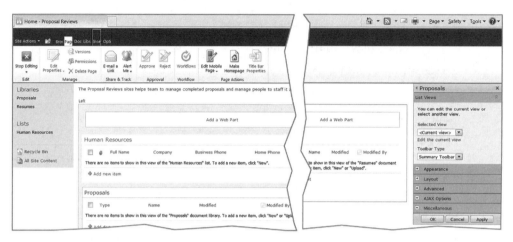

Figure 4.8 Additional options to modify the Proposals web part are displayed to the right after selecting Edit Web Part.

What's the difference between editing the current view using the web part menu versus doing it through the list settings?

When you modify or add a public view through the list settings, it will be accessible when users navigate to the list. A view of the data through a web part will often be structured differently because it's a glimpse of the data and has a limited amount of space depending on the number of other web parts on the page. If you modify the view by editing the current view using the web part menu, it won't appear in the list of views when a user navigates to the list.

Step	Action	Result/Notes
4	Select Proposal ID and change the Position from Left to 2.	☑ Proposal ID 2 ▼ ☐ Status 19 ▼ ☐ Title 20 ▼ ☐ Version 21 ▼
5	Deselect Modified.	

Step	Action	Result/Notes
6	Scroll down to the Filter section and select Show Items Only When the Following Is True. Set Show the Items When Column Status Is Equal to Active.	
7	Scroll to the bottom and click OK.	

You've now modified the view of your web part to display only the proposals that are active. How do you indicate that to the end users? You'll want to make this clear to the users by modifying the title of your web part:

Step	Action	Result/Notes
1	Select Edit Web Part by selecting the Edit menu options via the dropdown arrow in the header of the web part.	
2	Expand Appearance, and for Title enter Active Proposals.	
3	Click OK.	

Next, you'll modify the columns in the Resumes list:

Step	Action	Result/Notes
1	Select Edit Web Part by selecting the Edit menu options via the dropdown arrow in the header of the web part.	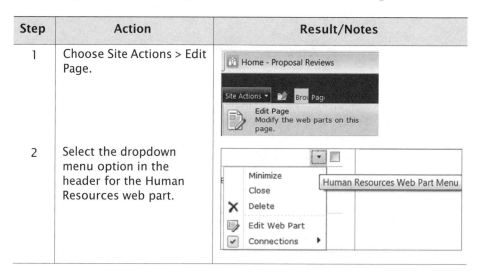
2	Select Edit the Current View.	
3	Deselect Modified and Modified By.	
4	Click OK.	

The web parts look good now, so you can start connecting the data.

Sort/filter connection: connecting the proposals, resources, and resumes

To create your connections you'll need to follow these steps:

Step	Action	Result/Notes
1	Choose Site Actions > Edit Page.	
2	Select the dropdown menu option in the header for the Human Resources web part.	

When you select the dropdown from the upper-right menu bar of the web part in edit mode, you'll find an additional option for connections, as shown in step 2 and in figure 4.9.

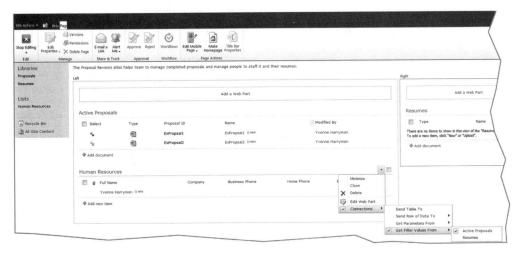

Figure 4.9 Web part menu options that are available when you're in edit mode

Step	Action	Result/Notes
3	Choose Connections > Get Filter Values From > Active Proposals.	
4	In the Provider Field Name box, select Proposal ID.	A dialog box will appear prompting you to enter the information for configuring your connection. You may need to allow pop-ups to see the dialog box.
5	In the Consumer Field Name box, select Proposals.	

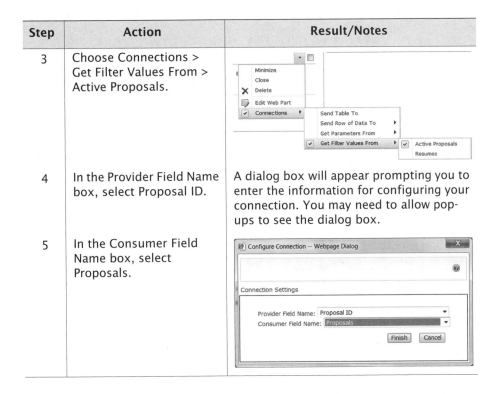

Step	Action	Result/Notes
6	Click Finish.	You should now see a Select option in the Active Proposals web part. Once you have uploaded a proposal it will look like this: 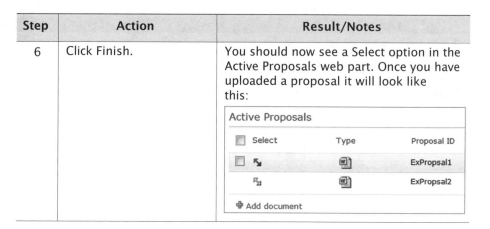

The next series of steps will walk you through connecting your Resumes web part with the Human Resources web part:

Step	Action	Result/Notes
1	If you're not still in edit mode, choose Site Actions > Edit Page.	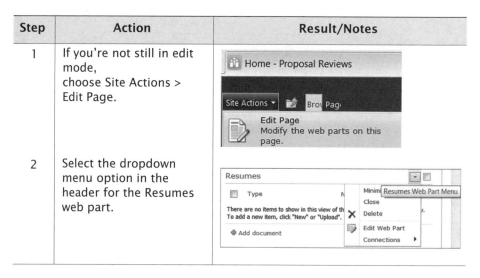
2	Select the dropdown menu option in the header for the Resumes web part.	

Step	Action	Result/Notes
3	Choose Connections > Get Filter Values From > Human Resources.	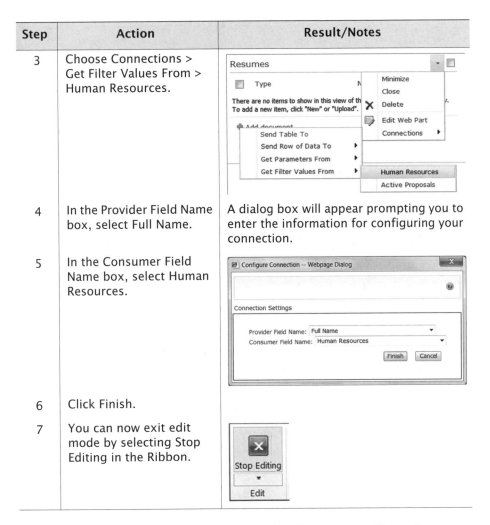
4	In the Provider Field Name box, select Full Name.	A dialog box will appear prompting you to enter the information for configuring your connection.
5	In the Consumer Field Name box, select Human Resources.	
6	Click Finish.	
7	You can now exit edit mode by selecting Stop Editing in the Ribbon.	

To really see the power of the connected web parts, you'll need to enter some data. The following images demonstrate what the connected web parts will do once data has been entered. If you look closely at figure 4.10, you'll see that there are now Select buttons that you can use to filter the data.

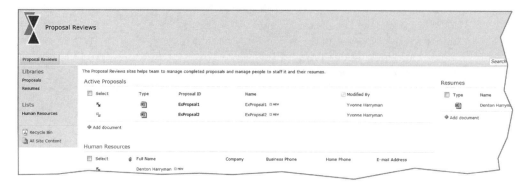

Figure 4.10 Proposal Reviews site with data entered into the web parts.

The next image demonstrates how the data in the web parts will change when a different item is selected. In figure 4.11, I've changed my selection to ExProposal2 and requested to see the resume of Lorena Tinsley.

Good job! Now you should have a good understanding of some of the core components of site design and web part configuration. If you wanted to, you could stop here and you would have met the core requirements of our scenario. If you have SharePoint Server, I'd like to go over with you how you can take this a step further by using a publishing site.

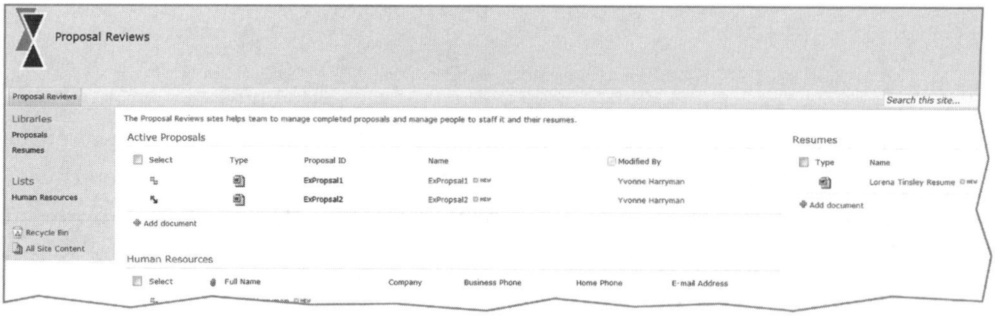

Figure 4.11 Proposal Reviews site with filters applied to the connected web parts

4.3 SharePoint Server features

This section will demonstrate the additional functionality of using a publishing site. SharePoint Server is an extension of SharePoint Foundation, so you'll find that many of the steps are similar. The most significant difference is not in how it works but in the additional functionality.

4.3.1 Publishing: working with publishing sites

An alternate option to creating a blank site is to create a publishing site, as shown in the site-creation options displayed in figure 4.12.

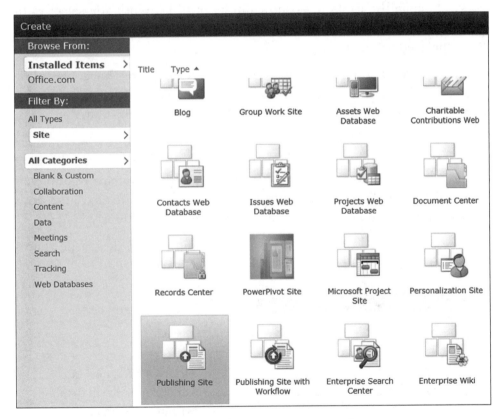

Figure 4.12 Site template options when creating a new site

Figure 4.13 Different options available for editing the page within the Ribbon

When you choose a publishing site, you'll get different options for editing the page and the Publish tab in the Ribbon, as shown in figure 4.13.

A new tab to publish your page once you've made the changes is now available in the Ribbon, as shown in figure 4.14. Until you select Publish, the end users will not see the changes you've made, unless they're authorized to see them.

Even more options will be available to you if you have workflow enabled by selecting a publishing site with workflow, as shown in figure 4.15. This will force an approval process to be instantiated when you go to publish a page.

When you're making your changes now or in the future on a publishing site, the users of the site will not be impacted by your changes until you publish them. So until you either publish or check in to share the draft with authorized users, only you will see the modifications you make.

You're now well on your way to understanding site design in SharePoint. Let's quickly summarize what you've learned.

Figure 4.14 A new tab called Publish will display within the Ribbon.

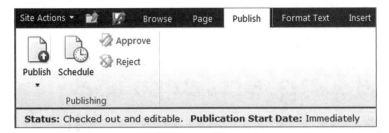

Figure 4.15 Different options are available for publishing when you create a site based on the Publishing Site with Workflow template.

4.4 Summary

Following is a summary to help you understand the functionality that you should now be comfortable with implementing for this scenario:

- Creating a blank or publishing site
- Working with different libraries and lists, specifically the Document and Image libraries and the Contacts list
- Branding a site using site themes and site icons
- Customizing the navigation
- Adding and customizing web parts
- Connecting your web parts to create filters on the information

Congratulations! Now you have a good understanding of web parts and site design. The next scenario will discuss how you can create a site that's published on the web for anonymous access along with a customized view for users who log in to look at the same site. We'll also briefly talk about hosted solutions, which is a great option for users who are interested in using SharePoint for personal use.

5

Leveraging enterprise content management features

This chapter covers

- Content types
- Information management policy
- Retention schedules

This chapter will guide you through the process of configuring a site for meeting the requirements of corporate records management policies. Records management is important to corporations that might be audited. If auditing is a concern, these companies need to secure and store all pertinent data that would be considered records. But content management features can also be used for other purposes, such as clearing out the junk! So let's start clearing it out. First, we'll discuss some of the technology that you're going to use to build out our scenario.

5.1 Managing business proposal resources

This section covers three areas: situation, business priorities, and solution. The first area, situation, provides a detailed explanation of the request that you've received. The next area, business priorities, extracts a list of requirements based on priority to accomplish your goals. It's important when gathering information such as this to not mix technology with the requirements. Business process, not technology, should drive the requirements. The third area gives you an overview of the solution that we'll spend the rest of the chapter walking through and building.

5.1.1 Situation

This scenario is a continuation of chapter 4. Now that you have a way to track employees, their resumes, and the proposals they're associated with, you're asked to ensure these proposals are removed after one year to clear out any of the clutter that remains after the completion of the project.

5.1.2 Business priorities

Now that you understand the current situation, let's discuss the business priorities so you can put together an appropriate solution for Durante Inc:

- Ensure that all proposals capture required metadata, such as start and end date of the project.
- Ensure that the document is removed exactly one year after the project is completed.

The next area highlights the solution you're going to build in this chapter.

5.1.3 Solution

Once you complete the steps in this chapter, you'll have a site that meets the expectations of the situation and the business priorities specified. Your final solution will look like figure 5.1.

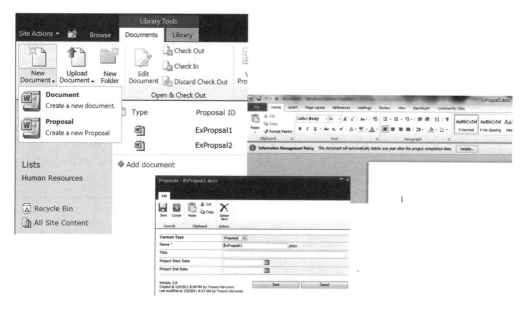

Figure 5.1 The solution that will be implemented in this chapter is based on the required specifications and business priorities.

From left to right, the figure displays a Document library with a proposals content type. If a user were to associate a document with that content type, additional properties would need to be filled in. This is shown in the lower image with the project start and end dates. The window to the right clearly displays the information management policy to inform the user that this document will be deleted within one year of project completion. This is a good thing, because you don't want the site to get stale with old documentation. To set this up, you'll start with features that can be found in SharePoint Foundation.

5.2 SharePoint Foundation features

To begin, navigate to the Proposal Reviews site that you created in chapter 4. I'm going to use that site to detail the enterprise content management features discussed in this chapter. I'll begin with SharePoint Foundation and show how you can use content types to capture metadata. The retention of the documents will require SharePoint Server, so to get the full solution you'll need SharePoint Server. If you don't have

SharePoint Server, you can do the first part of the scenario, but you won't be able to use the information management policy options.

5.2.1 Content types: associating metadata with certain content

Let's get started by defining a proposal content type at the site level. This will ensure that when your end users create a document on this site, they can mark it as a proposal and therefore get prompted for additional information that you want to gather about all proposals. You're going to associate project start and end dates with this content type so that anytime a user identifies a document as a proposal they'll be requested to also enter this information:

Step	Action	Result/Notes
1	Choose Site Actions > Site Settings.	**Site Actions ▾** **Sync to SharePoint Workspace** Create a synchronized copy of this site on your computer. **New Document Library** Create a place to store and share documents. **New Site** Create a site for a team or project. **More Options...** Create other types of pages, lists, libraries, and sites. **View All Site Content** View all libraries and lists in this site. **Edit in SharePoint Designer** Create or edit lists, pages, and workflows, or adjust settings. **Site Permissions** Give people access to this site. **Site Settings** Access all settings for this site.

Step	Action	Result/Notes
2	Under Galleries, choose Site Content Types.	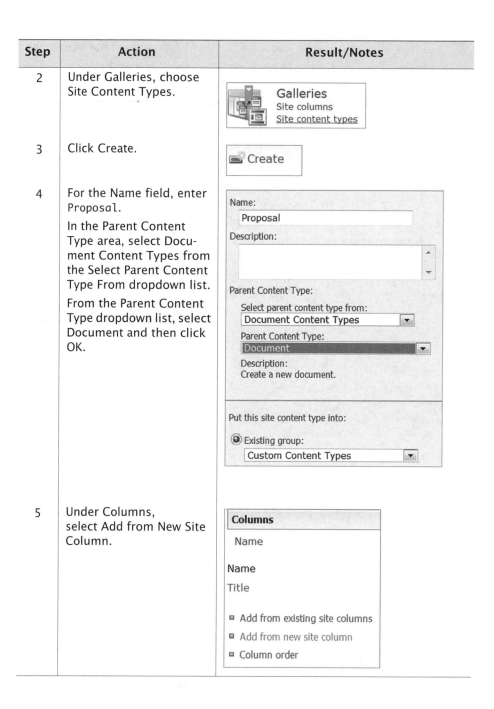
3	Click Create.	
4	For the Name field, enter Proposal. In the Parent Content Type area, select Document Content Types from the Select Parent Content Type From dropdown list. From the Parent Content Type dropdown list, select Document and then click OK.	
5	Under Columns, select Add from New Site Column.	

Step	Action	Result/Notes
6	For the Column Name field enter Project Start Date. For the type of information choose Date and Time. Click OK.	Column name: Project Start Date The type of information in this column is: ○ Single line of text ○ Multiple lines of text ○ Choice (menu to choose from) ○ Number (1, 1.0, 100) ○ Currency ($, ¥, €) ◉ Date and Time
7	Repeat steps 5 and 6 to create a site column named Project End Date.	

You now need to go back and update the Proposals library so you can see that documents uploaded here should be associated with the content type proposals.

Associating the content type with your library

You now have a proposals content type and want to ensure that every document uploaded to the Proposals library will get tagged with this content type and will have the required metadata entered. If you don't do this step, the pertinent data to track your proposal's beginning and end won't be captured. In your case that's start and end dates for the project. To associate this content type to the library, you need to complete the following steps:

Step	Action	Result/Notes
1	Navigate to the Proposals library, and under the Library tab in the Ribbon select Library Settings.	Library Settings Library Permissions Workflow Settings ▾ Settings

Step	Action	Result/Notes
2	Select Advanced Settings under the General Settings section.	**General Settings** Title, description and navigation Versioning settings **Advanced settings**
3	Click Yes to allow management of content types, and then click OK.	Allow management of content types? ⦿ Yes ⦾ No
4	You should now see the option Add from Existing Site Content Types. Prior to step 3, this option wasn't available.	**Content Types** This document library is configured to behavior. The following content types Content Type Document Add from existing site content types
5	Locate the Proposal content type, add it, and click OK.	Select site content types from: All Groups Available Site Content Types: List View Style Master Page MSIT Page Content Type Exam Page Page Layout Picture Project Page Publishing Master Page Redirect Page Report Add > < Remove Content types to add: Proposal

At this point if you were to navigate back to the Proposals library, you'd see two options for creating a new document, as shown in figure 5.2. In this case you'll remove the document content type to ensure everything that gets added to this library is a proposal. An alternate option, not related to this scenario, would be the creation of many content types that are associated with the library.

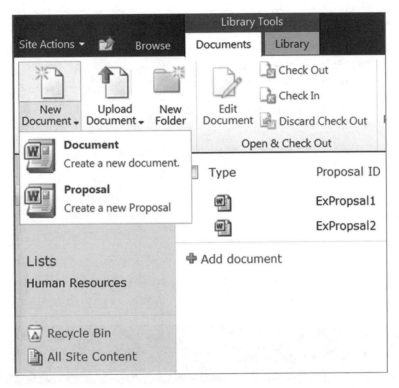

Figure 5.2 The library with two content types: document and proposal. You can have many more if you choose.

In our scenario you want end users to upload only documents of type proposal, so you're going to delete the default document type:

Step	Action	Result/Notes
6	Select Document under Content Type.	Content Type Document Proposal

Step	Action	Result/Notes
7	Select Delete This Content Type. **NOTE:** If you already have documents in the library, you'll need to change their current content type by editing the properties prior to doing this step.	**List Content Type Information** Name: Document Description: Create a new document. Parent: Document **Settings** ▫ Name and description ▫ Advanced settings ▫ Workflow settings ▫ Delete this content type

All documents that are now uploaded to this library will request the end users to enter project start and end dates, as shown in figure 5.3.

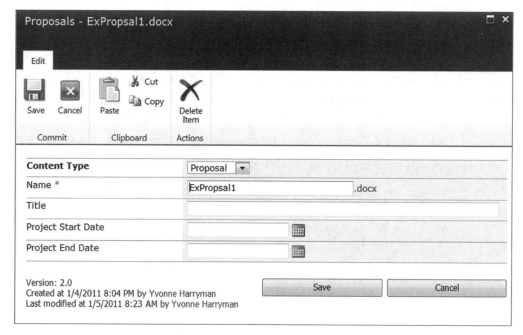

Figure 5.3 If you look at the properties of a document identified as a proposal, you'll see that it also requests project start and end dates.

Now you can centrally manage the proposal's content type and add or change the columns that are associated with the proposal's content type. You can also use this content type in other libraries, as long as they're in that same site. If you were to do that, you'd have one location where you could go to modify the data that's captured on content across many sites. We'll cover site collection administration for managing content types across sites in chapter 11, when we discuss governance topics. Let's take the content management capabilities to the next level by discussing some of the capabilities that are made available to you if you have SharePoint Server.

5.3 SharePoint Server features

Now we're going to discuss the information management policy options that are available with SharePoint Server. For this scenario we'll talk about enabling a retention plan on the proposals content type. But as you can see in figure 5.4, there are other options you can associate with an information management policy.

You should spend some time experimenting with the different capabilities for creating an information management policy. They can be powerful for meeting your content management requirements. In this scenario you're going to delete proposals so the content doesn't go stale. You'll use the metadata that you captured for your proposals to define when it can be deleted.

Policy Statement

The policy statement is displayed to end users when they open items subject to this policy. The policy statement can explain which policies apply to the content or indicate any special handling or information that users need to be aware of.

Retention

Schedule how content is managed and disposed by specifying a sequence of retention stages. If you specify multiple stages, each stage will occur one after the other in the order they appear on this page.

Note: If the Library and Folder Based Retention feature is active, list administrators can override content type policies with their own retention schedules. To prevent this, deactivate the feature on the site collection.

Auditing

Specify the events that should be audited for documents and items subject to this policy.

Barcodes

Assigns a barcode to each document or item. Optionally, Microsoft Office applications can require users to insert these barcodes into documents.

Labels

You can add a label to a document to ensure that important information about the document is included when it is printed. To specify the label, type the text you want to use in the "Label format" box. You can use any combination of fixed text or document properties, except calculated or built-in properties such as GUID or CreatedBy. To start a new line, use the \n character sequence.

Figure 5.4 This screen shows a list of all the information management policy settings that you can work with.

5.3.1 Retention plan: creating an information management policy

In this scenario you need to ensure a document is removed after one year to avoid clutter. To do this you'll associate an information management policy with any documents that are marked as a proposal using the content type. This policy will enable the retention feature to ensure all project proposals are deleted one year after project completion:

Step	Action	Result/Notes
1	Choose Site Actions > Site Settings.	Site Actions ▾ **Sync to SharePoint Workspace** Create a synchronized copy of this site on your computer. **New Document Library** Create a place to store and share documents. **New Site** Create a site for a team or project. **More Options...** Create other types of pages, lists, libraries, and sites. **View All Site Content** View all libraries and lists in this site. **Edit in SharePoint Designer** Create or edit lists, pages, and workflows, or adjust settings. **Site Permissions** Give people access to this site. **Site Settings** Access all settings for this site.
2	Under Galleries, select Site Content Types.	**Galleries** Site columns Site content types
3	Locate Proposal under the Custom Content Types section and select it. **NOTE:** Notice that Share-Point Server has additional settings that you can configure for your site content types. The one you're going to work with is Information Management Policy Settings (click it now).	**Custom Content Types** Proposal SiteCollectionInformation SubWebInformation **Settings** ▫ Name, description, and group ▫ Advanced settings ▫ Workflow settings ▫ Delete this site content type ▫ Document Information Panel settings ▫ Information management policy settings

Step	Action	Result/Notes
4	For the policy statement enter This document will automatically delete one year after the project completion date.	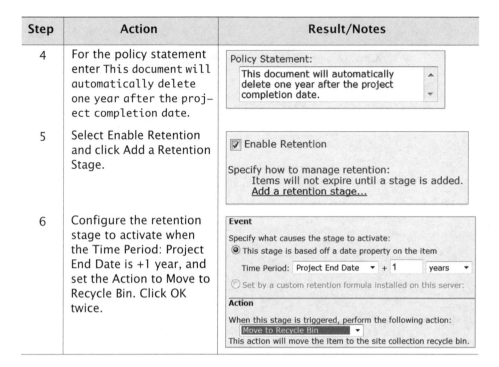
5	Select Enable Retention and click Add a Retention Stage.	
6	Configure the retention stage to activate when the Time Period: Project End Date is +1 year, and set the Action to Move to Recycle Bin. Click OK twice.	

Now when you go to view this document, you'll see the policy statement shown, as displayed in figure 5.5.

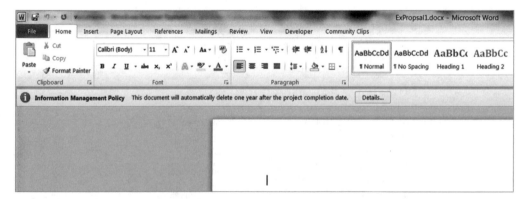

Figure 5.5 Once you've associated the information management policy with the content type, all documents that are tagged as a proposal will now show the disclaimer that notifies the user that this document will automatically delete one year after the project completion date.

Note that this policy will move the document to the Recycle Bin, where it will stay (assuming the default has not been changed) for 30 days, before permanent deletion.

Good job! You're on your way to understanding some of SharePoint's advanced capabilities for document management. Imagine how much less junk you would have if you stored all your data in SharePoint versus file shares or on your hard drive and you categorized your data and set up policies to automatically clean it out. Ironically for most of us, the opportunity cost of the time spent cleaning files off our hard drive is very high, but not if we automate it!

5.4 Summary

Let's quickly summarize what you learned from completing this scenario to help you understand the functionality that you should now be comfortable with implementing:

- Leveraging content types to capture metadata
- Creating an information management policy
- Defining retention schedules to schedule deletion of the documents

Congratulations! Now you have a good start at understanding the enterprise content management features. We'll go over additional features such as the records center in chapter 11, which covers features that span sites and site collections. The next scenario will discuss how you can create a site that is published on the web for anonymous access. In addition, you'll create a secured view for users who log in so they can get more detailed information. We'll also briefly talk about hosted solutions, which is a great option for users who are interested in using SharePoint for personal use.

Let's test your knowledge. A few of the questions that you should be able to answer are these:

- Can you have more than one content type associated with a document library?
  Yes.

- Is a content type defined at the library level?
  No, you associate it at the library level, but it's defined at the site or site collection level (the latter will be discussed further in chapter 11).
- Can you define an information management policy in SharePoint Foundation?
  No, this feature is specific to SharePoint Server.

6

Publishing information to the web

This chapter covers

- *Hosted internet-facing sites*
- *Blogs*
- *Lists such as discussion boards and surveys*
- *Permissions*
- *Embedded video (Option for SharePoint Foundation and SharePoint Server)*

In the last chapter I introduced you to a standard site that can be used to manage documents and associated information. In this chapter you're going to do something a bit more fun; the scenario that you're going to implement is for publishing a site to the World Wide Web with details for an upcoming wedding. Almost all of the scenarios in this book are slight modifications to real sites I've created and this one is no exception, because it was my own wedding website! To get started I'll walk you through the scenario you've been given and show how you'll attain the solution utilizing SharePoint.

6.1 Determining what information to make available for your guests

Let's discuss the three core parts of our scenario: situation, business priorities, and solution. The first part, situation, provides a detailed explanation of the request that you've received. The next part, business priorities, extracts a list of requirements based on priority to accomplish your goals. The third section gives you an overview of the solution that we'll spend the rest of the chapter walking through and building.

6.1.1 Situation

You're coordinating a wedding and you'll have guests attending from all around the world. You want to notify them as early as possible about travel information and details so they can prepare for their trip. Because there'll be over 200 guests, you decide the best way to do this is via a website, but you don't want to learn HTML or any other web design technology. You also want to ensure that certain information can be viewed only by your guests.

Business priorities

Let's discuss the business priorities so you can put together an appropriate solution:

1   You want to have a part of the site that's accessible by anyone and another part where your users have to log in to access the information.

2   You don't want to learn code or maintain a server.

3   You'd like to maintain a blog, survey, discussion board, images, and video on your site.

4   It needs to be easy to create new pages for highlighting information for your guests.

Based on those priorities, let's see what the solution will look like that you're going to build out in this chapter.

6.1.2 Solution

Once you complete the steps in this chapter, you'll have a site that meets the situation and business priorities specified to you. This scenario is based on an actual site that I created for my wedding; naturally, you won't want to use the same content. I'll lead you through the steps for adding embedded video and the appropriate verbiage or images to your pages, but I encourage you to use your own content when completing these steps. When you've finished, you'll have a site that's very similar to that shown in figure 6.1.

> **Do it yourself**
> To do this exercise without a public internet site, create a web application with anonymous access enabled. Then create a team site collection. After the site collection is created, go to Site Actions > Site Permissions and select Anonymous Access in the Ribbon. Select Anonymous Users Can Access: Entire Web Site, and click OK.

It's important to understand that this is just one type of site that you can create using the techniques shown in this chapter. You can easily

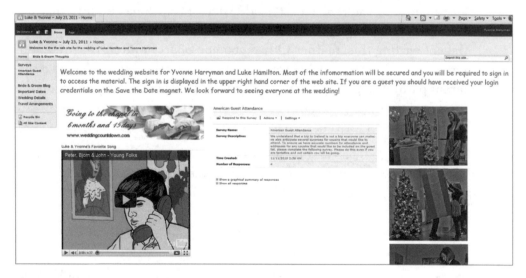

Figure 6.1 The solution that will be implemented in this chapter is based on the required specification and business priorities.

use the skills that you'll learn here for other types of sites, such as a personal website where you host your resume, one where you share personal interests with your friends, or a site for a school project.

It's time to get started. Now that you know the solution for our scenario, you can begin building out the site.

6.2 Setting up a SharePoint site for the internet

In this section you're going to look at options for setting up a SharePoint site that's available via the internet. Now, you can go out and purchase a server, configure SharePoint, and make it available via the web. This is a completely adequate approach, but for the purpose of this book, we're going on the assumption that you don't want to learn how to build out and maintain your own infrastructure to create your website. The next-best option would be to fire up Bing and start some basic research on hosting providers.

The site I'm going to demonstrate in this scenario is my personal site, and I chose to use ASPHostPortal. Microsoft also has an offering that I'd highly encourage you to consider, which is part of Office 365. At the time of writing this, neither Office 365 nor SharePoint 2010 with anonymous access was available for their online offering, so I selected a different path. Along with these two options, there are many others on the market, so do your research and select what's best for you. A few key deciding factors for this scenario were these:

- It needed to be a reasonable price. This is a personal site, so I didn't want to spend an arm and a leg. Prices have changed since the time I made my decision, so make sure you understand what you're paying for.
- I wanted SharePoint Server 2010 so I could maximize the functionality that's available for configuring my site.
- I wanted anonymous access to be available so my users would go to a landing page and know they were in the correct location before being required to sign in.

Once you make your selection, you'll need to fill out the required enrollment information and give them your credit card info. After that, you can go and enjoy a glass of wine as you wait for them to get back to you and confirm that your site is ready to be used. That's not too tough, eh? Pinot noir for me, please.

6.3 Configuring your site

By this point I assume you've been sent the information for your site, or if you're showing off, you've configured your server and have a site up and running that's available via the web.

Now that you have your site, let's get started with the fun part, which is changing it so it meets the purpose of this scenario. To get started you'll create pages for the information that you'd like to share. The pages will group certain information pertinent for the guest, such as travel details or logistics of the wedding.

6.3.1 Site pages: defining the information you want to share

Your homepage is already created for you. This is the first page that you see when you go to your site. You'll customize this page in the following steps. After that you'll create two more pages. One will be for communicating the wedding details, and the other will be to let the guests know what travel arrangements have been made. You'll get started by modifying the homepage. To begin you'll add some images and a quick intro paragraph for the guests to see when they land on it. Later on you'll add a survey and embedded video to make the page more interactive:

Step	Action	Result/Notes
1	Choose Site Actions > Edit Page.	Site Actions ▾ Browse Page Edit Page Edit the contents of this page.

Step	Action	Result/Notes
2	Place your cursor anywhere on the page and enter a welcome message for your guests to read, letting them know they've come to the correct site.	Because you'll make this page available to the public, you may want to indicate here that they'll need to select the sign-in option displayed in the upper-right corner to view all of the information.
3	Format the text to appear the way you'd like it to be viewed. The options for doing this can be found under Format Text in the Ribbon editing tools.	
4	Insert images of you and your loved one by going to the Insert tab and selecting pictures.	
5	When finished, click Save & Close.	

Good job! You've completed your homepage. You'll now create the Wedding Details page. The purpose of this page is to share with your guests any details regarding the wedding. Some people like to be secretive about this information, but I wanted to share with everyone who the band would be, among other details:

Step	Action	Result/Notes
1	Choose Site Actions > New Page.	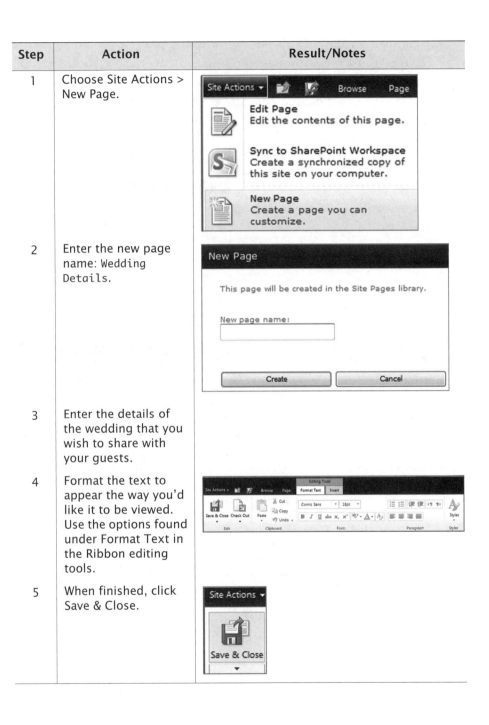
2	Enter the new page name: Wedding Details.	
3	Enter the details of the wedding that you wish to share with your guests.	
4	Format the text to appear the way you'd like it to be viewed. Use the options found under Format Text in the Ribbon editing tools.	
5	When finished, click Save & Close.	

Almost finished—you have one more page to create. Now that you have an introduction page and one to cover the wedding details, you'll start another that's focused on travel details for those guests who aren't local. This will enable your guests to know about any hotel blocks that you've reserved or transportation that you've arranged:

Step	Action	Result/Notes
1	Choose Site Actions > New Page.	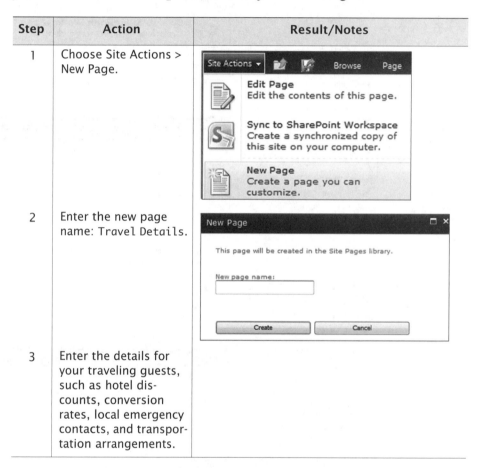
2	Enter the new page name: Travel Details.	
3	Enter the details for your traveling guests, such as hotel discounts, conversion rates, local emergency contacts, and transportation arrangements.	

Step	Action	Result/Notes
4	Format the text to appear the way you'd like it to be viewed, using the options under Format Text in the Ribbon editing tools.	
5	When finished, click Save & Close.	

Yay, you've now created the core pages! You can take this further and create additional pages such as information regarding your wedding registry. Use your imagination.

In the next section you're going to create some additional lists that will help supplement the site and add some additional content to these pages. To get started you're going to create a calendar.

6.3.2 Calendar

It wouldn't be a wedding website if you didn't keep track of all the important dates and events for your guests to attend. In this section you'll build out a calendar that your guests can easily access to find out when the different events will be held, such as the rehearsal dinner and bridal party fittings:

Step	Action	Result/Notes
1	Choose Site Actions > More Options.	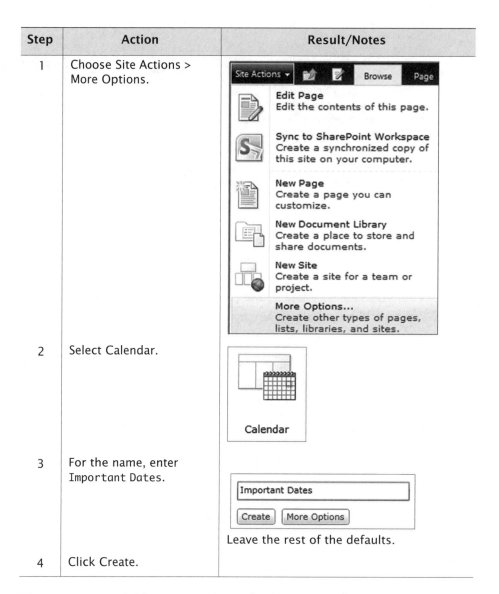
2	Select Calendar.	Calendar
3	For the name, enter Important Dates.	Important Dates Create More Options Leave the rest of the defaults.
4	Click Create.	

You can now quickly communicate the important dates to your guests, which is great. The next form of communication is more interactive and encourages your guests to participate in the discussion.

6.3.3 Discussion boards: let your audience communicate

Although many of you may be tempted to be a bridezilla or groomzilla, it's good to let your guests participate some! This section walks you through the process of creating a discussion board and adding it to the page. Much of the site is meant to have read-only content, but there may be certain sections where you'd like your guests to contribute to the content. This discussion board will enable your guests to communicate about travel deals that they find or other topics, such as credit cards with no foreign transaction fees:

Step	Action	Result/Notes
1	Choose Site Actions > More Options.	
2	Select Discussion Board.	

Step	Action	Result/Notes
3	For the name, enter Travel Deals.	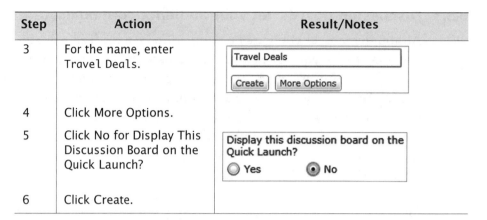
4	Click More Options.	
5	Click No for Display This Discussion Board on the Quick Launch?	
6	Click Create.	

You've created your discussion board, but now you need to display it in the appropriate spot for your end users. In this case, many of the guests won't need to travel to attend the wedding, so you won't want to make this discussion board part of the homepage. Because of this, you won't display the discussion board on the Quick Launch, as noted in step 6 above; instead you'll only add a view of it to the Travel Arrangements page:

Step	Action	Result/Notes
1	Navigate to the Travel Arrangements page and choose Site Actions > Edit Page.	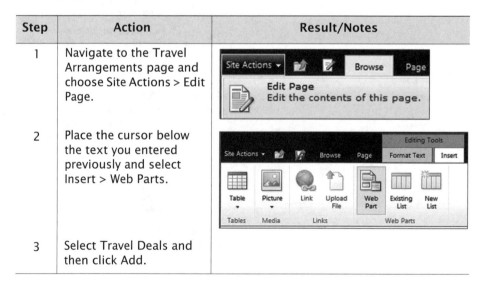
2	Place the cursor below the text you entered previously and select Insert > Web Parts.	
3	Select Travel Deals and then click Add.	

Step	Action	Result/Notes
4	Go to the Page tab in the Ribbon and click Save & Close.	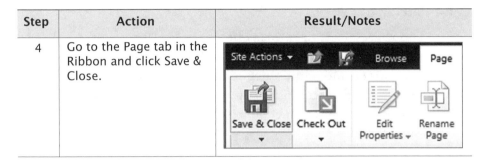

Your page should now be similar to figure 6.2.

Your guests can now locate the Travel Arrangements page from the homepage of the site. When they select the page, it will show them the verbiage that you wanted to highlight and a discussion board that they can use to share with others any details regarding their travel.

The next addition to your site will be the creation of a survey. This will help you determine how many of your traveling guests will attend the wedding. This can be used for any type of survey you want, such as whether your guests would like an Italian or French meal. In my case, we wanted to find out how many of our American guests were planning to travel to Ireland.

Based on our research the average cost of travel to Ireland will be around $1100 for a flight.

Hotels that we are recommending guest stay at is:

- Sandy Mount
- Clarion

If you find a good deal please post it on the discussion board below so others are aware of it.

The family of the bride will be arriving July 18th and departing July 25th.

Travel Deals

☐ Subject

Travel details for the family of the bride and bridal party, traveling from the US

✛ Add new discussion

Figure 6.2 Travel Arrangements page with the discussion board added at the bottom

6.3.4 Surveys

The survey feature in SharePoint is a great way to reach out to your end users and get interactive feedback from them. You'll build out a base survey and add branching logic to it, so the questions will change based on end users' answers to the previous questions. This is a powerful and easy piece of technology that I recommend you learn to use and understand:

Step	Action	Result/Notes
1	Choose Site Actions > More Options.	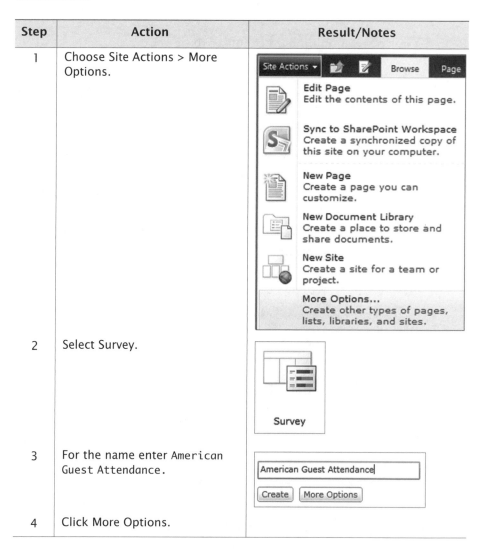
2	Select Survey.	
3	For the name enter American Guest Attendance.	
4	Click More Options.	

Step	Action	Result/Notes
5	For the survey options click No in response to Show User Names in Survey Results? Click Yes for Allow Multiple Responses?	Show user names in survey results? ○ Yes ● No Allow multiple responses? ● Yes ○ No
6	Click Create.	

Before we move on, I want to explain why the default settings were switched in step 5 to not show the user names and to allow multiple responses associated with the login. I'll go into this in more detail in section 6.5, once we cover permissions management for this site. In short, to easily communicate to the end users how to log in and access the information, we created one generic login for everyone to use. This was convenient as well for adding the information to the invitations. If each end user had their own login, you wouldn't need to change those settings.

Now let's discuss how to configure the questions. To start you should now be on the configuration page for new questions, which should look like figure 6.3.

Figure 6.3 Survey configuration page for new questions

Question:

Type your question here...

The type of answer to this question is:

○ Single line of text
○ Multiple lines of text
● Choice (menu to choose from)
○ Rating Scale (a matrix of choices or a Likert scale)
○ Number (1, 1.0, 100)
○ Currency ($, ¥, €)
○ Date and Time
○ Lookup (information already on this site)
○ Yes/No (check box)
○ Person or Group
○ Page Separator (inserts a page break into your survey)
○ External Data

Require a response to this question:

○ Yes   ● No

Enforce unique values:

○ Yes   ● No

Type each choice on a separate line:

Enter Choice #1
Enter Choice #2
Enter Choice #3

Display choices using:

○ Drop-Down Menu
● Radio Buttons
○ Checkboxes (allow multiple selections)

Allow 'Fill-in' choices:

○ Yes   ● No

Default value:

● Choice   ○ Calculated Value

In table 6.1 I provide example questions and the branching logic that I used for the survey on my site. Branching allows you to go to a different question in the survey based on the end user's answer. I assume for your site that you may want to focus on a different survey topic, and you may use this more as an idea for when you'd use branching logic or create different types for your questions.

Table 6.1 Questions for the survey

Question	Type	Additional Settings
Will you be attending?	Choice	– Required: Yes – Choices: Yes; No; Maybe
Will you bring a guest?	Choice	– Required: Yes – Choices: Yes; No
If you are an aunt or uncle of the bride or groom, would any of your children like to come to the wedding?	Choice	– Required: Yes – Choices: Yes; No
What is their preferred mailing address?	Multiple lines of text	
Because you used a generic login, please identify yourself by typing in your name.	Single line of text	– Required: Yes

Using these questions as an example, let's discuss some ideas of how you could use branching. To do this you'll need to add the example questions above. There are two specific example questions where branching would be useful:

- *Question 1*: Will you be attending?
  Logic: If our guest is not attending, we don't need to ask them if they will have a guest. So I decided to skip to the next question to see if they felt any of our cousins would like to attend. I have a big family, so instead of tracking down everyone's address, I decided to put the responsibility on their parents to let us know if their children would like to attend.

- *Question 2:* If you are an aunt or uncle of the bride or groom, would any of your children like to come to the wedding?

Logic: If they say No, then they should skip to the last question that asks them to identify themselves because they're using a generic login. If they say Yes, then I need to get my cousins' addresses so I can send them an invitation.

Now that you understand why you want to implement branching logic, let's discuss the steps required to do it:.

Step	Action	Result/Notes
1	Select the question: Will you be attending?	**Question** Will you be attending? Will you bring a guest?
2	For the branching logic select Jump To for the following choices: Yes: Will you bring a guest? No: If you are an aunt or uncle of the bride or groom, would any of your children like to come to the wedding? Maybe: Will you bring a guest?	**Possible Choices** / **Jump To** Yes — Will you bring a guest? No — If you are an aunt or uncle of the bride or groom, would any of your children like to come... Maybe — Will you bring a guest?
3	Click OK.	

The next series of steps will walk you through the branching logic for question 3: If you are an aunt or uncle of the bride or groom, would any of your children like to come to the wedding?

Step	Action	Result/Notes
1	Select the question: If you are an aunt or uncle of the bride or groom, would any of your children like to come to the wedding?	**Questions** A question stores information about each item in the survey. The follov **Question** Will you be attending? Will you bring a guest? If you are an aunt or uncle of the bride or groom, would any of your children like to come to the wedding?

Step	Action	Result/Notes
2	For the branching logic select Jump To for the following choices: Yes: What is their preferred mailing address? No: No Branching	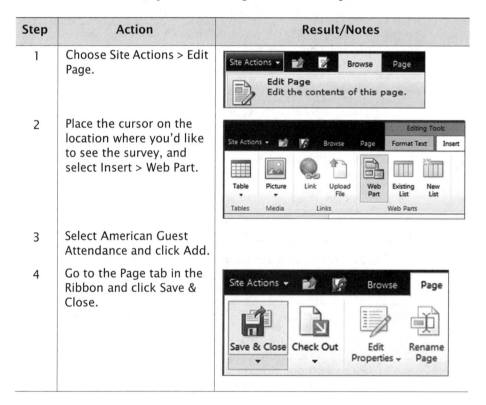
3	Click OK.	

You want to bring attention to this survey, so you'll achieve this by adding a web part to the homepage. This will ensure the guests see it and are aware that they should complete this survey:

Step	Action	Result/Notes
1	Choose Site Actions > Edit Page.	
2	Place the cursor on the location where you'd like to see the survey, and select Insert > Web Part.	
3	Select American Guest Attendance and click Add.	
4	Go to the Page tab in the Ribbon and click Save & Close.	

Once you've added the web part to the homepage, it will display as shown in figure 6.4.

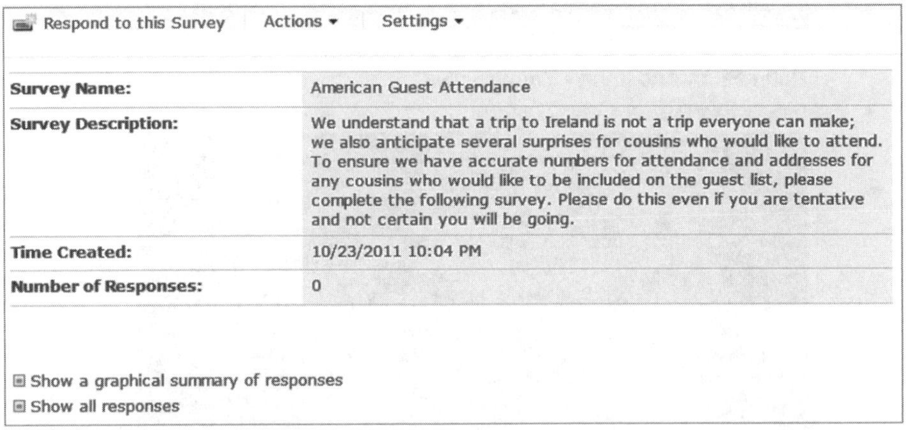

Figure 6.4 Survey web part to get an idea of attendance of the traveling guests

You're well on your way to being a savvy SharePoint site owner. Not only are you creating a site available via the web for personal use, but you are making it interactive so your users can participate in the information that's displayed on the site through the survey you created and the discussion board that you added to share travel deals. You'll take this even further in section 6.3.6, when you create a blog site. Before we jump to the creation of a subsite, you'll jazz up the site even more by adding an embedded video.

6.3.5 Embedded video

It's common in today's world to share a video that you found on YouTube. I'll share with you a little trick to show a video, even if you don't have a media player. It isn't as powerful as the rich media capabilities that SharePoint Server has to offer, and we'll discuss those capabilities in greater detail in section 6.6.

To get started, locate the video on YouTube that you want to display. In my case, I love the song "Young Folks" and wanted that to display when users went to the homepage. Once you locate your video, you should see the option buttons Like, Add To, and Share and the word Embed, as shown in the image in figure 6.5. You'll need to select Embed to copy this code and save it to a text file.

Figure 6.5 YouTube video with the options selected to get video embed code

Once you save the code to a text file, you'll need to add that document to the Shared Documents library or another library you have on the site. This is so you can easily reference the text file from a Content

Editor web part, which will be explained in a later section. To get started, let's quickly walk through the steps to upload the file:

Step	Action	Result/Notes
1	Copy the embedded code and save it to a text file on your hard drive.	In this scenario I called our text file Young-FolksSong.txt.
2	Switch back to your Share-Point site. Choose Site Actions > View All Site Content.	
3	Locate your Shared Docu-ments library and click the link to go to the main page.	
4	From here you can locate the upload document under the Documents tab in the Ribbon and follow the steps to upload your text file.	

Once your code has been uploaded in a text file, you'll add it to your homepage so your end users can see it. You're going to do this by using a Content Editor web part. The Content Editor web part was really popular in the SharePoint 2007 release because SharePoint 2007 didn't have the easy wiki page-editing capabilities that you saw in the examples earlier in this chapter where you easily made changes to the pages. As you'll see here, the Content Editor web part still has some good uses, such as the ability to easily display this embedded video in a friendly format:

Step	Action	Result/Notes
1	Choose Site Actions > Edit Page.	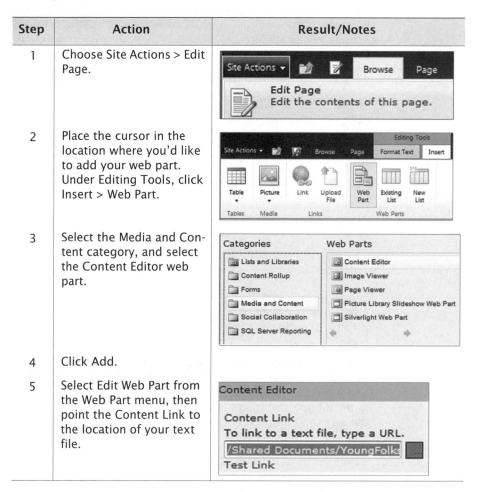
2	Place the cursor in the location where you'd like to add your web part. Under Editing Tools, click Insert > Web Part.	
3	Select the Media and Content category, and select the Content Editor web part.	
4	Click Add.	
5	Select Edit Web Part from the Web Part menu, then point the Content Link to the location of your text file.	

You should now see your video on the page. Notice that it has all of the controls down at the bottom to play, pause, fast forward, rewind, and enlarge your screen. When a user chooses one of these controls, it will perform the action and keep them on your site, not reroute them to YouTube.

Later on in this chapter, in section 6.6.1, we'll cover the media player and other media features associated with SharePoint Server, which you can use if you want to manage the videos from SharePoint. Although your current setup is good,

Figure 6.6 Embedded YouTube video

the capabilities get much better with SharePoint Server. For instance, you'll be able to set the video to autoplay. In the previous example, your end user has to request the video to play. But before we jump into SharePoint Server, I want to cover two additional core features of SharePoint Foundation: blogs and permissions.

6.4 Blogs: creating a subsite to blog

A blog is a great way to share ideas or news about what's on your mind and allows others to leave comments for a continued dialogue about your news. In this scenario we wanted to share with our guests information about us and the wedding-planning chaos. As you learn about this, think of other scenarios where you could use a blog. For example, one of the most common scenarios where I see the blog site template used is for company news. Each division creates its own blog post to share news and uses a Content Query web part (which will be discussed in the final chapter, *Pulling it all together with search, My Sites, and cross-site functionality*) to pull all of the latest new articles onto a central site. The point I'm trying to make is get creative with these technologies. You'll be surprised at the many ways you can use the functionality. So let's get started and create a blog site:

Step	Action	Result/Notes
1	Choose Site Actions > New Site.	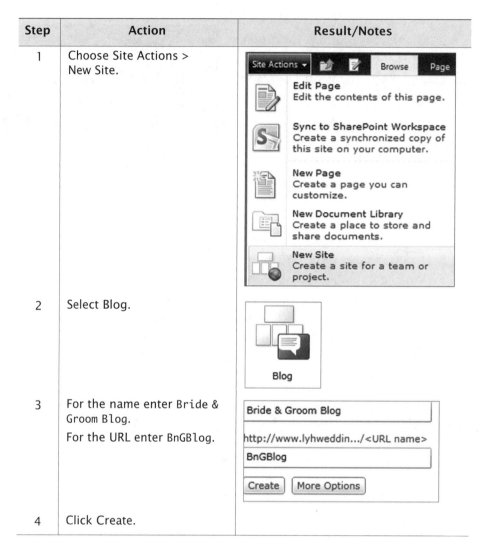
2	Select Blog.	
3	For the name enter Bride & Groom Blog. For the URL enter BnGBlog.	
4	Click Create.	

Congratulations! You're now the proud owner of a blog. Figure 6.7 shows you what this template looks like out of the box. It's pretty self-explanatory if you've ever worked with a blog before, but don't worry if you haven't. I'll walk you through the basics to start using it.

To start, you'll set up the categories. These are displayed in the upper-left corner, and the defaults are Category 1, 2, and 3. If you select a category, the blog will filter the posts that are displayed and show you

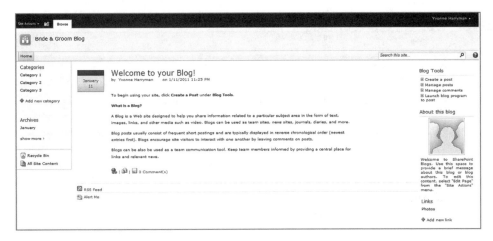

Figure 6.7 Out-of-the-box template for a blog site

only those that are associated with that category. The next series of steps walks you through adding and editing the existing categories:

Step	Action	Result/Notes
1	Select the Categories header.	Home Categories Category 1 Category 2 Category 3 ✛ Add new category
2	Here you'll see a list of all the categories; you can click the Edit button to modify the default categories. Some example categories could be The Groom or The Bride.	Edit

Now that you've defined your categories, you probably want to get started blogging. The default blog that's set up is an introduction to your blogging site. You probably don't want to your guests to read that blog post, so you'll change it. To get started select the title Welcome to

Figure 6.8 Post page for a blog site. Notice the commenting capabilities that are now displayed.

Your Blog. This will bring you to the post page, as shown in figure 6.8. Notice that when your end users are on the post page, they'll get the option to leave a comment.

To edit this post, you'll need to complete the following steps:

Step	Action	Result/Notes
1	Click Edit, shown in the upper-right corner of the blog post.	Edit

Step	Action	Result/Notes
2	Modify the existing blog post to show text that's relevant for you, add related categories, and click Publish.	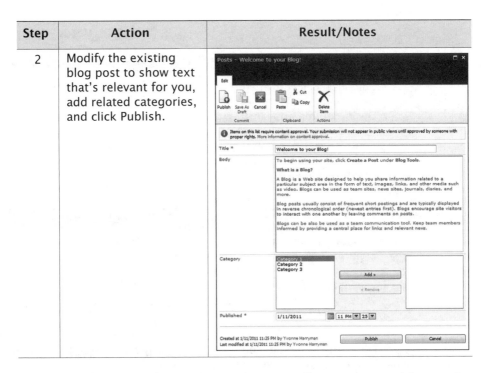

That wasn't too hard. The last bit that we'll go over is updating the homepage of your blog site so it has a picture of the person who owns it. If it's a topic-based blog, you could also insert a picture of the topic you intend to cover. To do this, you'll start by adding a photo to the page. This is easy with SharePoint 2010:

Step	Action	Result/Notes
1	Navigate back to the homepage and select Site Actions > Edit Page.	Site Actions ▾ Browse Page — Edit Page / Edit the contents of this page.

Step	Action	Result/Notes
2	The Blog Site template displays a demo photo for guidance. Select the demo photo, and you'll see a Design option appear in the Ribbon under Picture Tools. Click Change Picture, and upload the picture that you want from your computer.	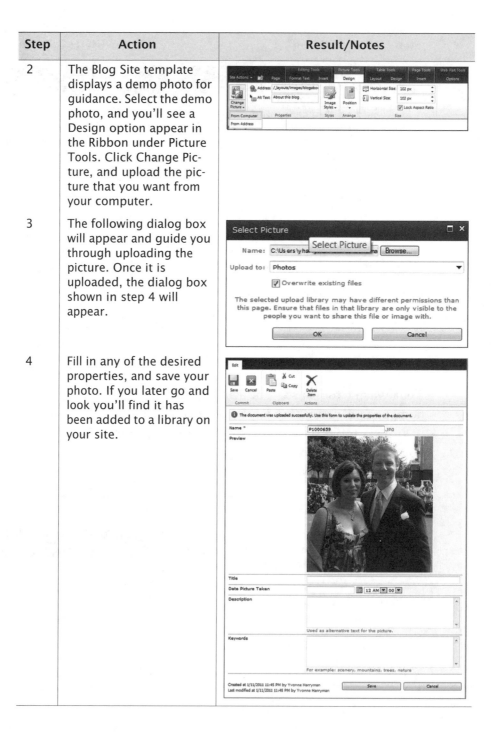
3	The following dialog box will appear and guide you through uploading the picture. Once it is uploaded, the dialog box shown in step 4 will appear.	
4	Fill in any of the desired properties, and save your photo. If you later go and look you'll find it has been added to a library on your site.	

Step	Action	Result/Notes
5	Finally, click Stop Editing in the Ribbon to see your completed work.	Site Actions ▾ [×] Stop Editing ▾ Edit

Good job! You now have a blog site. Based on the changes we made, figure 6.9 shows what my final version looks like. Yours should be similar, with slightly different content and the pictures that you selected.

Your site is visually complete, but now we'll discuss securing the content so people can see and do only what you want them to see and do. We'll go over how to secure certain information from anonymous users. Other information will need to be locked down so it can only be read, whereas you may want users to be able to enter information in other parts of it.

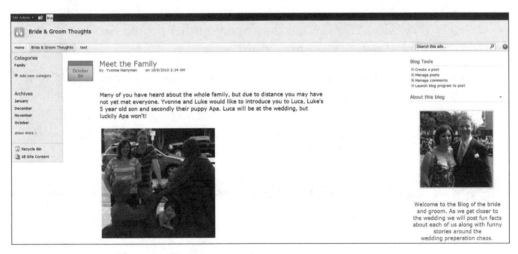

Figure 6.9 Final blog site after the modifications have been made

6.5 Permissions: managing access to your site

We're now going to discuss anonymous access and show how to enable all users on your intranet or via the internet to see the contents of the site. After we cover anonymous access, we'll then dive into list, item, and subsite permissions. You'll want to ensure that some of the information is locked down to prevent everyone from having access to all of your content.

6.5.1 Anonymous access

I'll get started by making sure you understand what anonymous access is. This is a published SharePoint, and anyone regardless of credentials has access to it. If it's an intranet scenario, such as at work, it will be open to anyone on the network. In this case, we're accessing it via the web, so it's available to anyone via the internet. Naturally, you don't want everyone to see all of the details, so I'll show you how to lock down certain aspects of the site in sections 6.6.2 and 6.6.3, so only authenticated users can get to the content. For example, in figure 6.10 you can see what an anonymous user would see if they were to navigate to my site. You can tell they're not authenticated because the Sign In prompt shows in the upper-right corner.

Figure 6.11 shows that the users whom I provided credentials to are able to access the site and get additional information, such as our favorite song and the survey. You can tell that it's the view of an authenticated user because their user name is displayed in the upper-right corner.

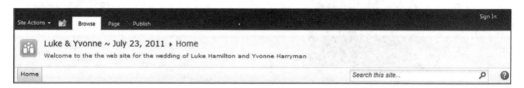

Figure 6.10 View of the homepage for an anonymous user

Figure 6.11 View of the homepage for an authenticated user

In order for you to allow anonymous access, your server administrator will need to have configured the capability via central admin. Once you complete the following steps, you'll have anonymous access configured:

Step	Action	Result/Notes
1	Choose Site Actions > Site Permissions.	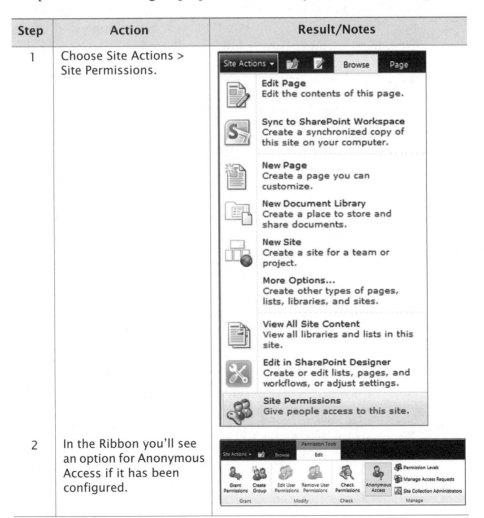
2	In the Ribbon you'll see an option for Anonymous Access if it has been configured.	

In this scenario, it's configured so that anonymous users can access the entire site. You'll now configure lists and items to have unique permissions if you don't want them accessible by anonymous users. You'll start at the list level.

6.5.2 List-level permissions

In our scenario , it makes sense to lock down the survey list so anonymous users don't see who is coming to the wedding. You may also want to lock down the Shared Documents library, where you uploaded your embedded video code. The latter isn't necessary, so we'll cover the steps for surveys. If you want to, you can complete the same steps listed here for other lists or libraries that you choose to lock down:

Step	Action	Result/Notes
1	From the homepage Quick Launch, select Surveys.	Home Surveys Bride & Groom Blog Important Dates Wedding Details Travel Arrangements
2	Select the survey that you created. In my case it will be American Guest Attendance.	Surveys American Guest Attendance
3	Under Settings choose Survey Settings.	Settings ▾ Add Questions Add an additional question to this survey. Survey Settings Manage questions and settings for this survey.
4	Under Permissions and Management select Permissions for This Survey.	Permissions and Management Delete this survey Save survey as template Permissions for this survey

Step	Action	Result/Notes
5	Select Stop Inheriting Permissions from the Ribbon. A dialog box will pop up and say, "You are about to create unique permissions for this list. Changes made to the parent site permissions will no longer affect this list." Click OK.	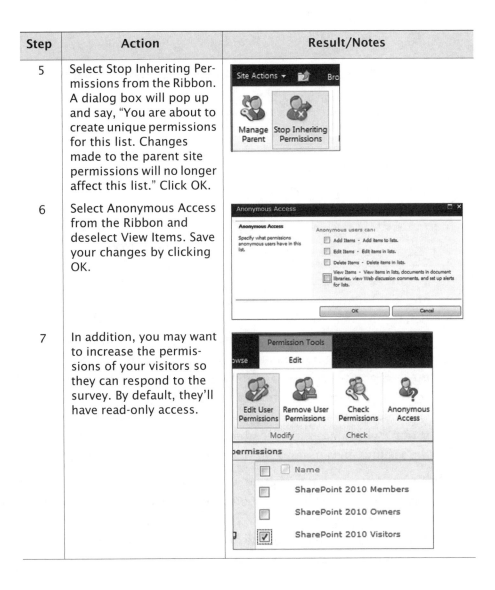
6	Select Anonymous Access from the Ribbon and deselect View Items. Save your changes by clicking OK.	
7	In addition, you may want to increase the permissions of your visitors so they can respond to the survey. By default, they'll have read-only access.	

Step	Action	Result/Notes
8	For the Visitors group, leave the default Read permission and add the Contribute permission. Click OK.	

I want to clarify a bit why you made the permission change in steps 7 and 8. When you add users to your site, you have three choices by default: Members, Owners, and Visitors. You could add your users to the Owners or Members group, but that would give them permission to modify the pages and add content to all of the lists and libraries. My guess is you want most of your end users to be consuming the data in a read-only format, with the odd exception, such as a survey or discussion board. In that case I recommend adding your users to the Visitors group, which has only Read access by default, and then later upping the visitors' permissions on that list to have Contribute access.

Now that you have a good understanding of permissions, consider what other lists or libraries you want to lock down, and follow the same steps for those lists. In my case I locked down Travel Deals as well as Shared Documents. Go ahead and lock those down, and then we'll jump into item-level permissions.

6.5.3   Item-level permissions

In this chapter you added a lot of different pages. I've decided that other than the homepage, I don't want anonymous users to have the ability to view the information on those pages. A page is essentially an item in a Pages library. You'll need to lock down most of the pages but not all of them, so you can't use the techniques listed in section 6.5.2. To apply security at the item level, you need to complete the following steps:

Step	Action	Result/Notes
1	Choose Site Actions > View All Site Content.	Site Actions ▾ **Sync to SharePoint Workspace** Create a synchronized copy of this site on your computer. **New Page** Create a page you can customize. **New Document Library** Create a place to store and share documents. **New Site** Create a site for a team or project. **More Options...** Create other types of pages, lists, libraries, and sites. **View All Site Content** View all libraries and lists in this site.
2	Select Site Pages.	**Document Libraries** Shared Documents Site Assets Site Pages Style Library
3	Select the dropdown menu of the page you want to change. In this example I selected the Travel Arrangements page. Select Manage Permissions from the menu.	Type Name Home Travel Arrangements Wedding Details View Properties Custom Edit Properties How To Use This Library Check Out ✛ Add new page Version History Alert Me Send To Manage Permissions ✕ Delete

Step	Action	Result/Notes
4	Select Stop Inheriting Permissions from the Ribbon. A dialog box will pop up and say, "You are about to create unique permissions for this list. Changes made to the parent site permissions will no longer affect this list." Click OK.	

This will prevent the Travel Arrangements page from inheriting the anonymous access permissions, locking it down so only your end users will see the page. If anonymous users click the links, they'll be prompted to enter their credentials. You'll now need to complete the same steps for all the pages you created with the exception of the homepage. The last sets of permissions we'll discuss are the permissions for a subsite. In this scenario we created one subsite, and that was for our blog.

6.5.4 Subsite permissions

This is an easy section and the final one we'll cover on permissions for now. I'll try my best to mix in the fun with the, well, not so much fun. It's a lot more exciting when you get to see a result at the end of your work. Modifying the subsite permissions is similar to step 4 in the previous section; you just get to it a slightly different way:

Step	Action	Result/Notes
1	Choose Site Actions > Site Permissions.	 Site Actions ▾	Browse	Page **Edit Page** Edit the contents of this page. **Sync to SharePoint Workspace** Create a synchronized copy of this site on your computer. **New Page** Create a page you can customize. **New Document Library** Create a place to store and share documents. **New Site** Create a site for a team or project. **More Options...** Create other types of pages, lists, libraries, and sites. **View All Site Content** View all libraries and lists in this site. **Edit in SharePoint Designer** Create or edit lists, pages, and workflows, or adjust settings. **Site Permissions** Give people access to this site.
2	Select Stop Inheriting Permissions from the Ribbon. A dialog box will pop up and say, "You are about to create unique permissions for this list. Changes made to the parent site permissions will no longer affect this list." Click OK.	Site Actions ▾ Manage Parent Stop Inheriting Permissions

We're finished with that. I know permissions are not the most exciting topic in the world, but it's important to understand them so you can secure your information when appropriate. In this chapter you modified the out-of-the-box permissions; in chapter 11, we'll cover the creation of custom permissions groups. Now let's look briefly look at the rich media features that are part of SharePoint Server. We discussed alternate options when you displayed a video from YouTube, but there are much more advanced options for doing this if you have SharePoint Server.

6.6 Taking it further with SharePoint Server

I'm going light covering the SharePoint Server functionality for our public-facing-sites scenario. Let's face it; hosting a site is expensive, and having to add the cost of server licensing to it only adds to that cost, at least for a personal site. If it's for a business, that's an entirely different scenario, and I would assume you'd be using some of the richer customization capabilities that SharePoint allows through code customizations. One really great feature that you should be aware of, though, is the SharePoint Media web part. We covered an alternate option for embedded video previously, but the features of the Media web part are much richer.

6.6.1 Embedded video: SharePoint Server's Media web part

A new feature of SharePoint 2010 is the ability to add video and audio to a page. This is something you can easily do through the wiki editing capabilities by editing the page. In the Ribbon you'll see additional options that you don't get with SharePoint Foundation for adding video and audio. For example, you can configure the media to start automatically when a user comes to the page and continuously loop, among many more options. An example of the Video and Audio option that you'll see in SharePoint Server is displayed in figure 6.12.

Figure 6.12 Video and Audio option that's displayed with SharePoint Server

If you select the Video and Audio option, you'll get a Media web part added to the page, as shown in figure 6.13.

You can then select it to get the configuration options. Here you can upload various types of media such as a video or an audio file. You'll get the same play, stop, increase screen size, fast forward, and rewind features as you've seen in the past as well as some additional options, as shown in figure 6.14.

Figure 6.13 Media web part

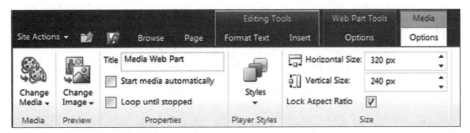

Figure 6.14 Additional options for configuring the Media web part

Notice that you can customize the image that's displayed and set the media to start automatically and continue to loop. Figure 6.15 shows a Media web part in action, once it has been configured.

Figure 6.15 Configured Media web part

You may have also noticed that when you upload the video, it will tell you that it's putting it into your Site Assets library. This is a library option that you get with SharePoint Server. It helps you organize your videos and images that are uploaded to a page. When you create a site page, it will create a folder for each page and add any images or videos that you associate with that page, leveraging the easy page-editing wiki technology.

Go get a cup of coffee/wine, whatever your poison is, and give yourself a break. Come back, and we'll do a quick summary and jump into the next chapter.

6.7 Summary

Following is a summary to help you understand the functionality that you should now be comfortable with implementing after completing this scenario:

- The creation of pages to organize the content on your site
- Understanding of the use of anonymous access for publicly available internet sites
- Hosted SharePoint and its advantages, if you're not good with server and networking technologies and/or you don't have the desire to maintain a server environment
- Leveraging blog sites to share ideas and news
- The use of discussion boards and surveys to encourage your end users to participate on the site
- Securing your site using the SharePoint permissions model
- Embedded video for SharePoint Foundation and SharePoint Server

Hopefully this chapter has given you some good ideas on how to use SharePoint for a public-facing site, although many of these same technologies can be used for other types of scenarios. In the next chapter, we're going to discuss business intelligence, often referred to as BI. This should be fun, because BI gets into the cool graphics.

Let's test your knowledge. A few of questions that you should be able to answer are these:

- What's the difference between a Site Asset library and other libraries?
  It creates a folder for each new page and stores any content such as images or videos that are added to the page via the wiki technology.

- How can you tell if you're viewing a site as an anonymous user?
  You'll see a sign-in option at the upper-right corner of the page.

- If you want to host a public-facing site using SharePoint, do you need to own and configure a server?
  No, there are lots of hosted solutions where someone else will do it for you.

7

Empowering users with business intelligence

This chapter covers

- *Office Web Access*
- *Excel Services*
- *Status list*
- *Key performance indicators*
- *Chart web part*
- *Dashboards*

In this chapter we're going to focus on the business intelligence (BI) capabilities that are part of SharePoint Server Enterprise. Only one of the items listed above can be tied to SharePoint Foundation and Share-Point Server Standard, and that's Office Web Access. This is available for SharePoint if you have a Microsoft Office 2010 volume license. The scenario that you're going to implement, following a step-by-step process, is for a sales advertising company tracking sales. To begin we'll discuss the scenario and how you'll attain the solution utilizing SharePoint Server.

7.1 Determining what information to make available for your guests

This section is broken up into three areas: situation, business priorities, and solution. The first section, situation, gives a detailed explanation of the request that you've received. The next, business priorities, extracts a list of requirements based on priority to accomplish your goals. The third section gives you an overview of the solution that we'll spend the rest of the chapter walking through and building.

7.1.1 Situation

You're the owner of an advertisement sales company. You currently track sales by commercial, cost, salesperson, show, and fiscal year. You want to mine this data and create performance indicators to track overall sales, profit per client, and personnel progress on sales delivery.

Business priorities

I'll now define the business priorities so you can put together an appropriate solution:

1. Sync up to an existing Excel spreadsheet that's currently used to track sales.
2. Graphically show the sales each employee has made.
3. Track against a quota for each sales employee.
4. Show what commercials are bringing in the most revenue.

Based on these priorities, I'll show the solution that you're going to build out in this chapter.

7.1.2 Solution

Once you complete the steps in this chapter you'll have a site that meets the situation and business priorities specified to you. When you've finished, you'll have a site that's similar to that shown in figure 7.1. The homepage of your BI site will display the Excel spreadsheet that you use to track the sales data.

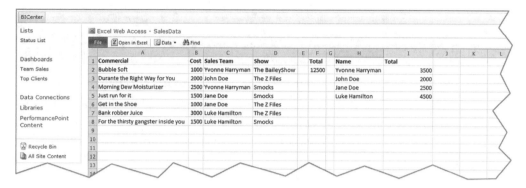

Figure 7.1 Homepage of the BI site you'll be creating for this scenario. This displays Excel data using Excel Web Access.

In addition, you'll create two dashboards, one named Team Sales and the second named Top Clients. The one for team sales will display a status list of key performance indicators (KPIs), which track the total sales goal and the status against each employee's quota. You'll also graphically display how each employee is doing. The dashboard will look like the one in figure 7.2.

The Top Clients dashboard will display graphically the sales for each commercial. You'll also render a subset of the data from your Excel spreadsheet to use as a lookup for client information. The dashboard will look like the one in figure 7.3.

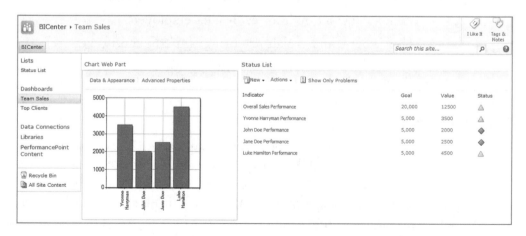

Figure 7.2 Team Sales dashboard, graphically displaying employee sales and KPIs

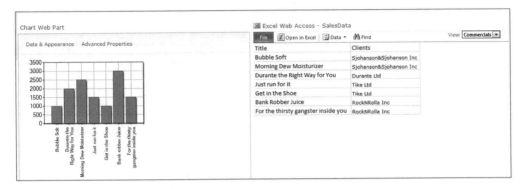

Figure 7.3 Top Clients dashboard, graphically displaying commercial data and a subset of information from Excel

It's important to understand that this is one type of site that you can create using the techniques shown in this chapter. Using the skills that you'll learn here, you can easily duplicate these steps to generate other types of reports.

It's time to get started. Now that you know the solution for your scenario you can start building out the site to reach that solution.

7.2 Setting up a SharePoint Business Intelligence Center

To get started you'll need to create a Business Intelligence Center. This will ensure that you have all the correct tools available for you to work with the functionality that you're going to configure in this chapter. When you first create the site, you'll notice some reading material, which you can read to help you understand all the capabilities that are available to you:

Step	Action	Result/Notes
1	Choose Site Actions > New Site.	**Site Actions ▾** **Browse** **Documents** **Edit Page** Modify the web parts on this page. **Sync to SharePoint Workspace** Create a synchronized copy of this site on your computer. **New Page** Create a page in this site. **New Document Library** Create a place to store and share documents. **New Site** Create a site for a team or project.
2	Filter by Site and select Business Intelligence Center. **Note:** SharePoint Server Publishing Infrastructure and Performance-Point Services Site Collection Features should be activated to see the Business Intelligence Center.	**Business Intelligence Center**
3	Enter a name and URL and click Create.	BICenter http://yvonneharryma.../<URL name> BICenter [Create] [More Options]

See how easy it is to create a Business Intelligence Center! Now comes the hard part—configuring it. Don't worry; I'll guide you step by step so it will seem like a piece of cake, and you'll wonder why you haven't used the business intelligence features of SharePoint before!

7.3 Creating your data source

This is an easy one. In the past chapters you typically used a list as your data source. In this chapter you're going to use Excel instead.

SharePoint 2010 offers some powerful capabilities with Office Web Access and Excel Services, which allow your end users to visualize and edit Excel data within SharePoint. They don't have to own Excel or even leave the site to do this. To get started, though, you need to create the initial spreadsheet with Excel, so go ahead and load Excel and create a new workbook and save it somewhere on your PC as Sales Data. Table 7.1 details how you're going to lay out the Excel spreadsheet. I've also entered the values of the dummy data that I'm using for this scenario. Feel free to copy my data or use your own dummy data.

Table 7.1 Spreadsheet data

Worksheet	Column	Dummy Data (enter in the same order)
Advertise-ment Sales	Commercial; Cost; Sales Team; Show	*Commercial:* Bubble Soft; Durante the Right Way for You; Morning Dew Moisturizer; Just run for it; Get in the Shoe; Bank Robber Juice, For the thirsty gangster inside you
		Cost: $1,000; $2,000; $2,500; $1,500; $1,000; $3,000; $1,500
		Sales Team: Yvonne Harryman; John Doe; Yvonne Harryman; Jane Doe; Jane Doe; Luke Hamilton; Luke Hamilton
		Show: The Bailey Show; The Z Files; Smocks; Smocks; The Z Files; The Z Files; Smocks
Sales Team	Name	*Name:* John Doe; Jane Doe; Yvonne Harryman; Luke Hamilton
TV Shows	Shows	*Shows:* The Z Files; The Bailey Show; Smocks
Commercials	Title; Clients	*Title:* Bubble Soft; Morning Dew Moisturizer; Durante the Right Way for You; Just run for it; Get in the Shoe; Bank Robber Juice; For the thirsty gangster inside you
		Clients: Sjohanson&Sjohanson Inc; Sjohanson&Sjohanson Inc; Durante Ltd; Tike Ltd; Tike Ltd; RockNRolla Inc; RockNRolla Inc
Clients	Name	*Name:* Sjohanson&Sjohanson Inc; Durante Ltd; Tike Ltd; RockNRolla Inc

For initial entry of the data, if you're Excel savvy, you may wish to turn on data validation features to create list dropdowns on certain cells. If you choose to do this, please note that you'll need to clear the data validation prior to uploading it to SharePoint and accessing it via Excel Services. Data validation isn't supported, and your information won't render if you don't clear the validations.

To begin, you need to upload your file to SharePoint. I won't detail these steps, because you should be familiar with uploading a file by this point. Make sure you locate your Documents library choosing View All Site Content from the Site Actions menu and upload the sales data. Notice that when you select the file, by default it will render in the browser using Excel Web Access, which is part of Office Web Access. Your spreadsheet should render and look similar to the one in figure 7.4.

You now have your data source and your BI site, so let's get started with the fun stuff and begin the configurations to start data mining.

BICenter ▸ Documents ▸ SalesData.xlsx

File   Open in Excel   Data ▾   Find

	A	B	C	D
1	**Commercial**	**Cost**	**Sales Team**	**Show**
2	Bubble Soft	1000	Yvonne Harryman	The BaileyShow
3	Durante the Right Way for You	2000	John Doe	The Z Files
4	Morning Dew Moisturizer	2500	Yvonne Harryman	Smocks
5	Just run for it	1500	Jane Doe	Smocks
6	Get in the Shoe	1000	Jane Doe	The Z Files
7	Bank robber Juice	3000	Luke Hamilton	The Z Files
8	For the thirsty gangster inside you	1500	Luke Hamilton	Smocks

Figure 7.4 What your newly created spreadsheet should look like once you've

7.4 Configuring your Business Intelligence Center

Now that you have your data connection and your data source uploaded to the BI site, the next step is to configure your BI site. First, you'll clear the homepage and display your Excel workbook by adding an Excel Web Access web part to the page. Then you'll configure your KPIs and create dashboards for viewing the data.

7.4.1 Excel Web Access

To begin you'll edit the homepage and render your data source for your end users using Excel Web Access. This will provide an easy way for everyone to see the data that's been entered and is driving the values in the dashboards. It will refresh automatically when the content is edited and saved to SharePoint, so you know you're always looking at the latest information:

Step	Action	Result/Notes
1	Navigate to the list of libraries by selecting Libraries from the Quick Launch bar. Go to the Pages library. You'll need to check out the default page to begin any edits.	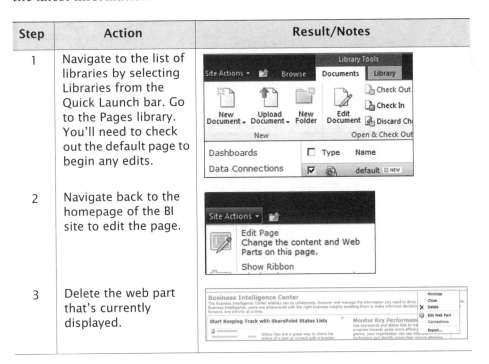
2	Navigate back to the homepage of the BI site to edit the page.	
3	Delete the web part that's currently displayed.	

Step	Action	Result/Notes
4	Now that you have the page, select Add a Web Part > Excel Web Access. You'll find this under the Business Data category.	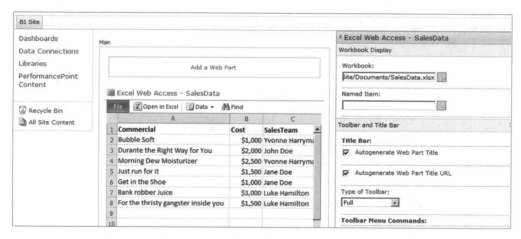
5	Next, you need to configure it to point to your Sales Data workbook in your Documents library.	Once completed, it will look like figure 7.5.

Figure 7.5 The Excel Web Access web part will appear, as shown, once configured.

Your homepage is created, and everyone can easily access the data in a read-only format. The next step is to configure your KPIs to track the sales goals. Let's get started.

7.4.2 Creating a KPI in a Status List

For this scenario I opted to use an Excel workbook, but you could complete this same scenario use SharePoint lists and you wouldn't need to do the additional steps that we're about to cover. I wanted to ensure we covered a new set of technologies, so I opted not to do the scenario leveraging SharePoint lists. When creating a KPI in Excel, you need to identify a cell address for your KPI. If you were pulling it from a SharePoint list, you'd have more configuration options to do these calculations via the SharePoint user interface. Quickly update Excel so it does some important calculations for you:

Step	Action	Result/Notes
1	Open your Sales Data workbook in edit mode and add the following in cell F1.	Total
2	For the formulas starting in cell F2 enter:	F2: =SUM(B2:B100) I1: Total I2: =SUMIF(C2:C100,H2,B2:B100) I3: =SUMIF(C2:C100,H3,B2–B100) I4: =SUMIF(C2:C100,H4,B2–B100) I5: =SUMIF(C2:C100,H5,B2–B100)
3	In cells H1–H5 enter the following values:	Name: Yvonne Harryman; John Doe; Jane Doe; Luke Hamilton
4	Save your changes back to SharePoint.	Your Excel workbook should now look like figure 7.6.

	A	B	C	D	E	F	G	H	I
1	Commercial	Cost	Sales Team	Show		Total		Name	Total
2	Bubble Soft	1000	Yvonne Harryman	The BaileyShow		12500		Yvonne Harryman	3500
3	Durante the Right Way for You	2000	John Doe	The Z Files				John Doe	2000
4	Morning Dew Moisturizer	2500	Yvonne Harryman	Smocks				Jane Doe	2500
5	Just run for it	1500	Jane Doe	Smocks				Luke Hamilton	4500
6	Get in the Shoe	1000	Jane Doe	The Z Files					
7	Bank robber Juice	3000	Luke Hamilton	The Z Files					
8	For the thirsty gangster inside you	1500	Luke Hamilton	Smocks					

Figure 7.6 This is how your data should display once you've made your edits to Excel.

You can now begin to create your KPIs based on the cells you just added:

Step	Action	Result/Notes
1	Choose Site Actions > More Options.	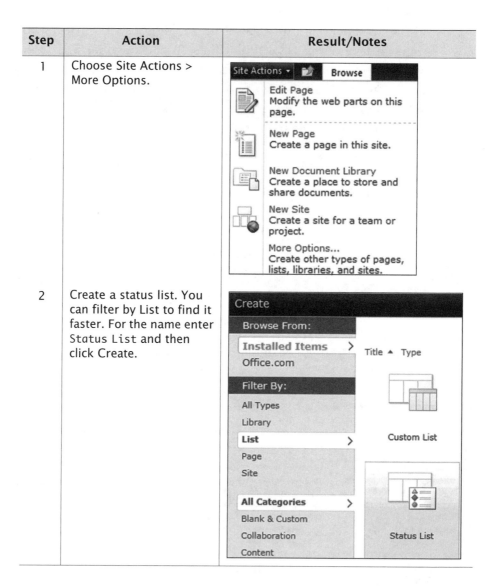
2	Create a status list. You can filter by List to find it faster. For the name enter Status List and then click Create.	

Step	Action	Result/Notes
3	Create a new KPI by choosing New > Excel Based Status Indicator.	New ▾ Actions ▾ Settings ▾ SharePoint List based Status Indicator Create a new Status Indicator using data from SharePoint Lists Excel based Status Indicator Create a new Status Indicator using data from Excel Services
4	Enter the following values: Name: `Overall Sales Performance` Workbook URL: Look up the URL by navigating to the Documents library and selecting Sales-Data.xslx. For the Cell Address enter `'Advertisement Sales'!F2`. For the green circle enter `20,000`. For the yellow triangle enter `10,000`. Click OK to create your KPI.	**Name and Description** Enter the name and description of the indicator. Name: `Overall Sales Performance` * The description explains the purpose or goal of the indicator. Description: **Comments** Comments help explain the current value or status of the indicator. Comments: **Indicator Value** Select the workbook that contains the information for the indicator value. Workbook URL: `http://yvonneharryman/sites/BICenter/Doc` * Select the cell in the workbook that contains the indicator value. Examples: `http://portal/reports/workbook.xlsx` or `/reports/workbook.xlsx` The cell address can be any valid Excel cell address for the selected workbook such as Sheet1!A1 or the name of a cell such as 'Total'. Cell Address for Indicator Value: `'Advertisement Sales'!F2` * Example: Sheet1!A1 or Total

Good job; you should now have your first KPI. Repeat these steps four more times for each sales team member. Label them `<Sales Person Name>` `Performance` and select the Excel cell associated with their total sales. For the green circle enter `5,000` and for the yellow triangle enter `3,000`. Once you've created all your KPIs, your status list should look like figure 7.7.

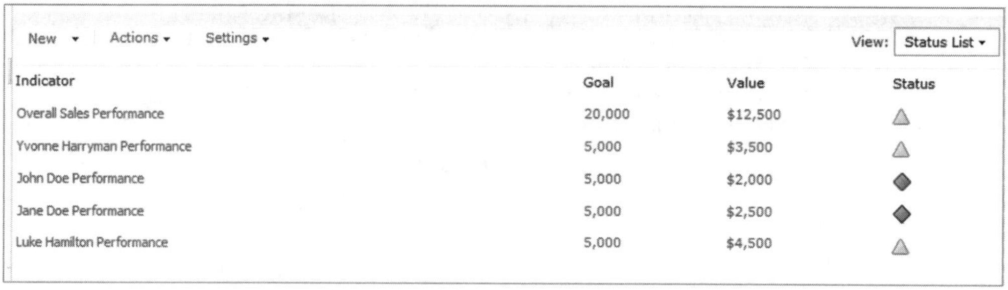

New ▾ | Actions ▾ | Settings ▾ — View: Status List ▾

Indicator	Goal	Value	Status
Overall Sales Performance	20,000	$12,500	△
Yvonne Harryman Performance	5,000	$3,500	△
John Doe Performance	5,000	$2,000	◆
Jane Doe Performance	5,000	$2,500	◆
Luke Hamilton Performance	5,000	$4,500	△

Figure 7.7 KPIs show a status indicator so you can track employee sales and overall sales goals.

Hopefully someone will make it to $5000 in overall sales soon, so you can get a green indicator. Now that you have a list with all your important KPIs and you have the Excel spreadsheet configured so the important information is calculated for you, let's discuss how you can reuse this information in your dashboards.

7.4.3 Adding dashboards

In this exercise you're going to create two dashboards. The first will focus on your top-selling commercials and what clients they're tied to. The second will focus on sales team performance:

Step	Action	Result/Notes
1	Navigate to the Dashboards library in the Documents tab. Select New Document > Web Part Page with Status List.	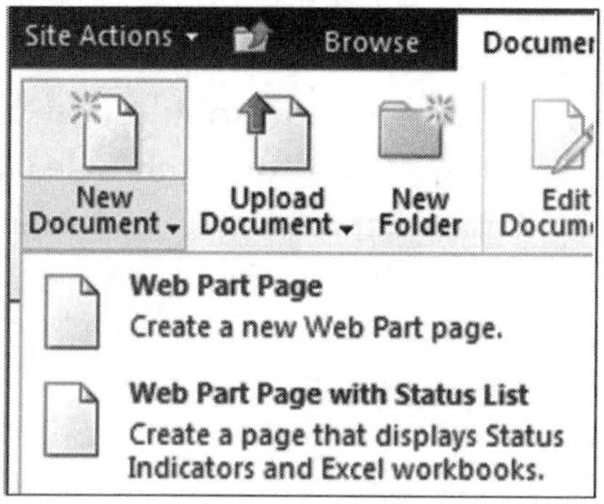

Step	Action	Result/Notes
2	For the Name enter TopClients and for the Page Title enter Top Clients. Select the radio button that says "Do not add a status indicator list to this dashboard." Leave the other fields at their defaults. Click OK.	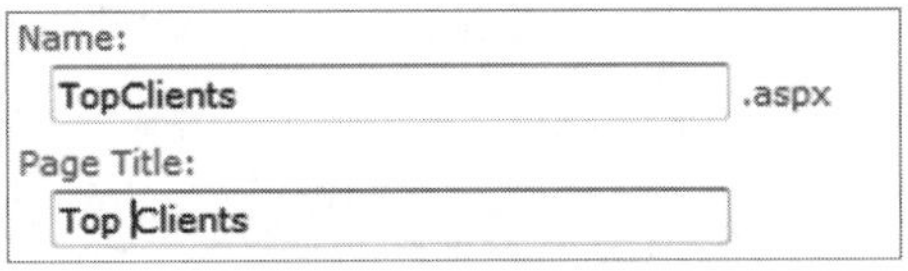 Name: TopClients .aspx Page Title: Top Clients
3	Choose Site Actions > Edit Page.	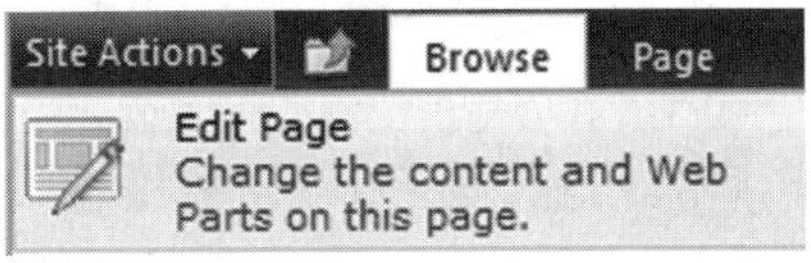 Site Actions ▾ Browse Page Edit Page Change the content and Web Parts on this page.
4	You can delete all the existing web parts with the exception of the Excel Web Access web part in the bottom-right zone.	
5	In the bottom-left zone add a Chart web part.	

You're now ready to configure your web parts. For the Excel Web Access web part you'll most likely need to open and edit your Excel file. You're going to display a named item, as shown in figure 7.8.

To do that you'll need to label the appropriate cells with the name. Navigate to the Commercials worksheet and highlight all the content in the first two columns. In the upper-left corner type Commercials, as shown in figure 7.9. Save your changes back to SharePoint.

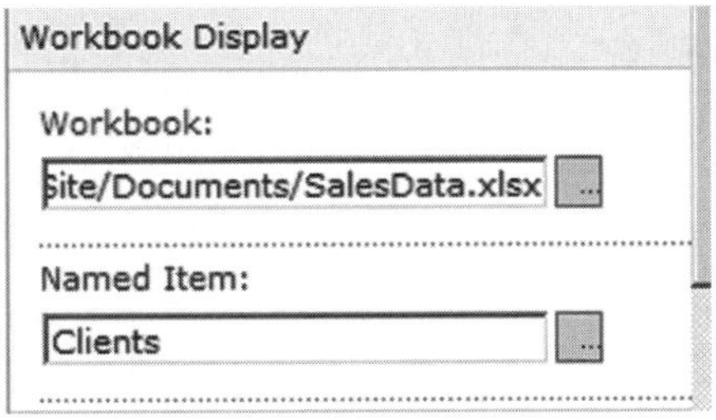

Workbook Display

Workbook:
Site/Documents/SalesData.xlsx

Named Item:
Clients

Figure 7.8 Linking Excel Web Access to a named item

Commercials | Title

	A	B
1	**Title**	**Clients**
2	Bubble Soft	Sjohanson&Sjohanson Inc
3	Morning Dew Moisturizer	Sjohanson&Sjohanson Inc
4	Durante the Right Way for You	Durante Ltd
5	Just run for it	Tike Ltd
6	Get in the Shoe	Tike Ltd
7	Bank Robber Juice	RockNRolla Inc
8	For the thirsty gangster inside you	RockNRolla Inc

Figure 7.9 Creating the Commercials item

You'll need to do the same thing for the sales data shown in the Advertisement Sales worksheet, as shown in figure 7.10. This time label it `SalesData`.

SalesData | Commercial

	A	B	C	D	E	F	G
1	**Commercial**	**Cost**	**Sales Team**	**Show**		**Total**	12500
2	Bubble Soft	1000	Yvonne Harryman	The BaileyShow		Yvonne Harryman	3500
3	Durante the Right Way for You	2000	John Doe	The Z Files		John Doe	2000
4	Morning Dew Moisturizer	2500	Yvonne Harryman	Smocks		Jane Doe	2500
5	Just run for it	1500	Jane Doe	Smocks		Luke Hamilton	4500
6	Get in the Shoe	1000	Jane Doe	The Z Files			
7	Bank robber Juice	3000	Luke Hamilton	The Z Files			
8	For the thirsty gangster inside you	1500	Luke Hamilton	Smocks			

Figure 7.10 Creating the SalesData item

Last, do this for the Totals and label it `Total`, as shown in figure 7.11.

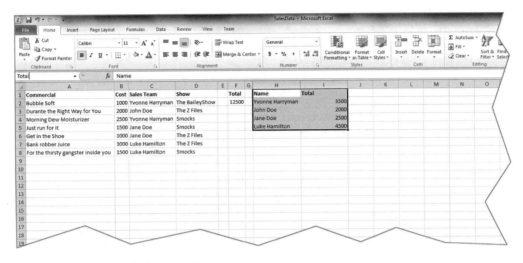

Figure 7.11 Creating the Total item

Save your worksheet back to the site. Now that you've made those changes, I'll walk you through the steps for configuring the Excel Web Access web part:

Step	Action	Result/Notes
1	Under Select a Workbook, choose Click Here to Open the Tool Pane.	**Select a Workbook** To display a workbook in this Web Part, you must first workbook. To select a workbook, open the tool pane, and then ed Workbook property. Click here to open the tool pane.
2	Navigate to your workbook and select it, and for the Named Item enter Clients. Click OK.	**Workbook Display** Workbook: Site/Documents/SalesData.xlsx Named Item: Clients

You should now see the important client and commercial information displayed. For the next series of steps you're going to configure the Chart web part to display the data in graphical format:

Step	Action	Result/Notes
1	Go to the Chart web part and select Connect To Data.	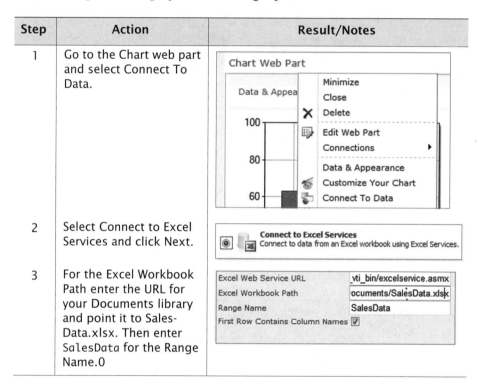
2	Select Connect to Excel Services and click Next.	
3	For the Excel Workbook Path enter the URL for your Documents library and point it to Sales-Data.xlsx. Then enter *SalesData* for the Range Name.0	

Once you complete step 3, you should see your sales data, as shown in figure 7.12.

Figure 7.12 Data retrieved for the Chart web part using Excel Web Services

Click Next, and you'll configure the axis:

Step	Action	Result/Notes
4	For the Y Field select Cost, and for the X Field select Commercial. Then click Finish.	Series Default ▼ + ⊞ Series Properties Y Field — Cost ▼ X Field — Commercial ▼ Group by Field (Optional) — ▼

Good job! You've completed your first dashboard. The page should look like the one shown in figure 7.13.

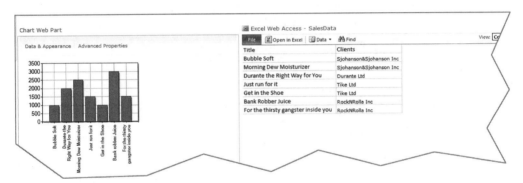

Figure 7.13 Top Clients dashboard displaying commercial sales, and a snapshot of the worksheet information that ties each commercial to a client

As you can see from figure 7.13, RockNRolla Inc has the highest grossing commercial with Bank Robber Juice, although my personal favorite is their commercial For the thirsty gangster inside you. You're going to create a page to display your KPIs:

Step	Action	Result/Notes
1	Navigate to the Dashboards library in the Documents tab, and select New Document > Web Part Page with Status List.	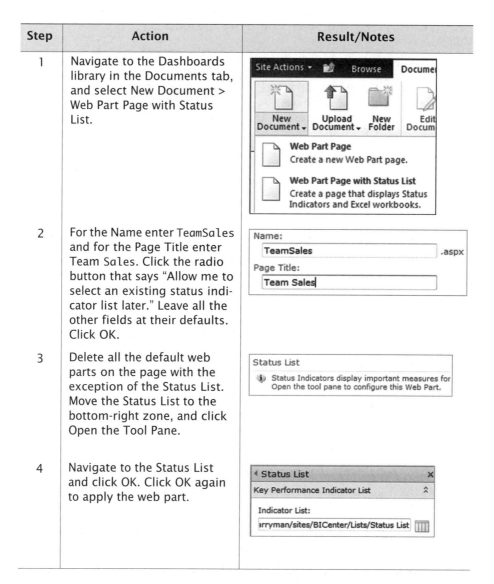
2	For the Name enter TeamSales and for the Page Title enter Team Sales. Click the radio button that says "Allow me to select an existing status indicator list later." Leave all the other fields at their defaults. Click OK.	
3	Delete all the default web parts on the page with the exception of the Status List. Move the Status List to the bottom-right zone, and click Open the Tool Pane.	
4	Navigate to the Status List and click OK. Click OK again to apply the web part.	

You should now see a list of all the KPIs that you created. You'll now need to configure your Chart web part that you'll add to the bottom-right zone:

Step	Action	Result/Notes
1	Add the Chart web part and select Connect To Data.	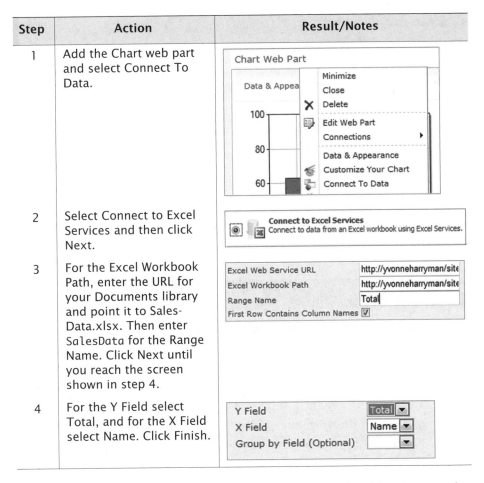
2	Select Connect to Excel Services and then click Next.	
3	For the Excel Workbook Path, enter the URL for your Documents library and point it to Sales-Data.xlsx. Then enter SalesData for the Range Name. Click Next until you reach the screen shown in step 4.	
4	For the Y Field select Total, and for the X Field select Name. Click Finish.	

Good job! That was your last dashboard. You should now see the information displayed on your page as shown in figure 7.14.

You're now on your way to being savvy in BI. If this doesn't impress your boss, I don't know what will. Keep playing around with it and see what other cool dashboards you can create. Let's quickly summarize what you've learned.

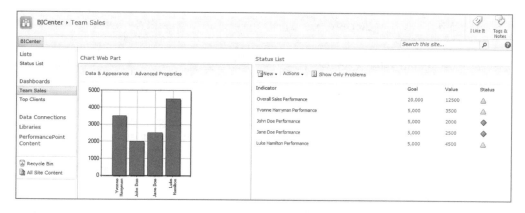

Figure 7.14 Team Sales dashboard, graphically displaying each employee's sales and status against their quota

7.5 Summary

In this scenario we covered the basics of business intelligence functionality. You can take this even further if you use the PerformancePoint options, which are now integrated with SharePoint 2010. I highly suggest that while you're learning the BI pieces of SharePoint you play around with creating different types of data connections and make one of them a PerformancePoint data connection. This will open Dashboard Designer and give you a different experience with working with the data.

Following is a summary to help you understand the functionality that you should now be comfortable with implementing from completing this scenario:

- Viewing the data using Office Web Access
- Connecting to the data using Excel Services
- Configuring KPIs in a status list
- Using the Chart web part to graphically display the data
- Creating dashboards to highlight and group key data elements

Hopefully this chapter has given you some good ideas on how to use SharePoint to knowledge mine your data to create business reports, which you can use to inform your team of sales goals and accomplishments. The same technologies demonstrated here can be used for other types of scenarios when reporting on data. In the next chapter we're going to discuss SharePoint Designer.

Let's test your knowledge. A few of the questions that you should be able to answer are:

- What's the difference between a Business Intelligence Center and other sites?
  Items for configuring dashboards are already enabled and made available, and features are activated to help you work with PerformancePoint.

- What does KPI stand for?
  It stands for key performance indicator.

- What do you create with a Status list?
  You create a status indicator, which is also referred to as a KPI.

8

Creating application sites with SharePoint Designer

This chapter covers

- *Managing and creating lists with SharePoint Designer*
- *Applying conditional formatting with SharePoint Designer*
- *Configuring an out-of-the-box list workflow*
- *Working with survey and status lists*

In the last chapter we discussed functionality that you can use to create business intelligence sites. This chapter begins our section on composite sites and shows how you can build powerful applications using SharePoint Designer. The scenario that you're going to implement, following a step-by-step process, is automating the review process for tracking employees and their certification status. To begin, we'll discuss the scenario you've been given and how you'll create the solution utilizing SharePoint. Throughout this chapter I'll be referencing SharePoint Designer by its commonly used acronym, SPD.

8.1 Gathering certification status

This section focuses on three parts: situation, business priorities, and solution. The first section, situation, gives a detailed explanation of the request that you've received. The next section, business priorities, extracts a list of requirements based on priority to accomplish your goals. The third section provides an overview of the solution that we'll spend the rest of the chapter walking through and building.

8.1.1 Situation

In this scenario you're a functional manager and have asked your employees to complete a series of certifications that you feel will help the business. I've opted to use the Microsoft Certified Technical Specialist exams for this particular scenario, but you could use any series of training/certifications in place of these.

To encourage your employees to complete the certifications, your company provides them with resources to prepare for the exams and recognizes those employees who've passed the exams. You also need to set goals for the team and show them their status as they progress. Let's quickly discuss the business priorities for completing this solution.

Business priorities

I'll now define what the business priorities are so we can put together an appropriate solution:

1 Enable the employees to track their status as they complete the exams.

2 Configure an approval process so their exam results can be verified before displaying them to the organization.

3 Configure notification to the employee's manager upon completion of an exam.

4 Recognize those employees who have passed an exam.

5   Set up a different recognition that includes a picture for those employees who have successfully completed all of the required exams.

6   Create a survey to help the other employees understand how difficult the process is.

7   Set goals for the team to achieve, and let the team track their current status.

The next section highlights the solution you're going to build in this chapter.

I've also provided a process map to help you visualize the system you're going to implement. This is shown in figure 8.1.

You now have a good understanding of what you're going to create based on the requirements and the process. The next section shows the solution you're going to build out in this chapter.

8.1.2   Solution

Once you complete the steps in this chapter, you'll have a site that meets the situation and business priorities specified to you. Your final solution is shown in the images that follow. You'll track the

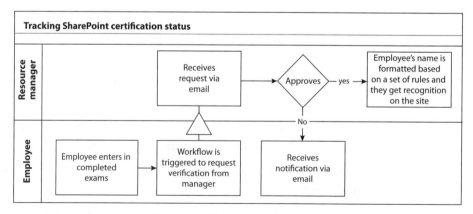

Figure 8.1 Process map for the solution that you're going to build. This explains the roles of the resource manager and employee. It will help you to visualize the requirements and how the users will advance through the system.

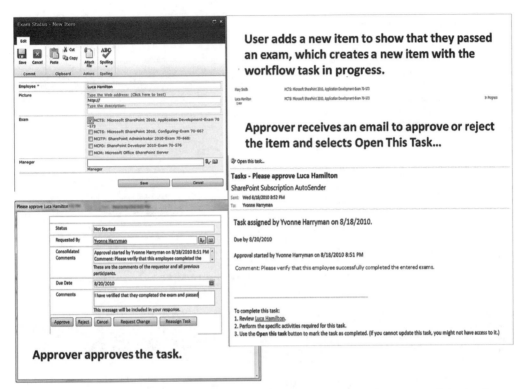

Figure 8.2 Here I'm detailing how the employee will submit the exams that they've successfully completed and the process the task will go through for validation from their manager.

certification status of your end users. Once they enter the information, it will go through an approval process, as explained in figure 8.2.

Once the task is approved, the name of the user will be displayed, with formatting applied based on the status that they've achieved. For example, if the user has become a SharePoint Certified Master, their name and picture will appear on the site. Along with this, you'll set up a survey so the end users can share feedback on study time required, and you'll let management track the overall progress using status indicators against their set goals, as shown in figure 8.3.

Now that you know the solution for the scenario, it's time to start building out the site to implement the solution described.

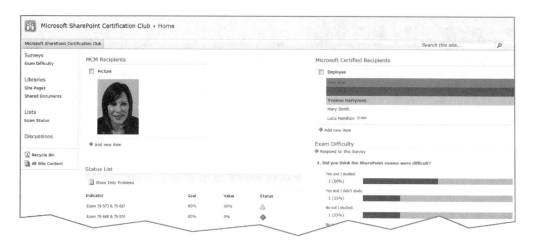

Figure 8.3 Once the exam status for the employee has been validated, their name and picture will display on the site so they can receive recognition.

8.2 Using SharePoint Designer with SharePoint Foundation

In this section we'll cover your approach using SharePoint Foundation and SharePoint Designer. Remember, your goal here is to create a site so you can track your end users' certification status and ensure they get recognition for being experts in the field. You'll start by creating the site and building your list to track the end users' exam status.

8.2.1 Creating your Foundation site

To begin you need to create a site by choosing Site Actions > New Site. Depending on what version of SharePoint you're running, you should select Blank Site or Publishing Site. Remember, if you're running SharePoint Server, you may want to consider a publishing site as an option. Chapter 3 and appendix B cover differences between a blank site and a publishing site. Enter the information from the following table for the title, description, and website address.

Now that you've created your site, you need to set up a custom list to manage the employees and projects.

Property	Value
Title	Microsoft SharePoint Certifications Club
Description	The SharePoint Certifications Club tracks users who have completed any of the Microsoft Certified Technology Specialist exams.
Web Site Address	MSFTSPCertClub

8.2.2 Custom list: creating a data store of current projects

The custom list will help you manage the employees' status on exam certifications. As you learned in the previous scenarios, custom lists are powerful and can be used in almost any site you create. You created custom lists in previous scenarios though the SharePoint user interface. In this scenario you're going to do it using SPD. To get started you'll need to open the site you just created using SPD (as a quick reminder, that's the acronym for SharePoint Designer, which is a free download from Microsoft.com):

Step	Action	Result/Notes
1	Choose Site Actions > Edit in SharePoint Designer.	

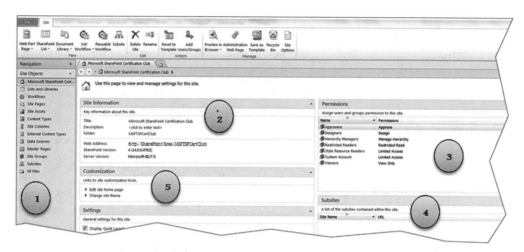

Figure 8.4 SharePoint Designer 2010 has changed a lot since 2007. The numbered callouts correspond to the following explanations of what you can do functionality-wise in each of those sections.

> **NOTE** To launch SharePoint Designer you need the Designer permission level. If you're a site collection owner, you can further specify if the end users with the Designer permission level can use SPD. We'll cover permissions in more detail in chapter 11, which explores governance topics.

Once you've completed step 1, SharePoint Designer will open the site and you'll be able to use the capabilities of SharePoint Designer 2010. The initial page that opens is the site's summary/settings page. Let's discuss the features of this site briefly. A screen shot with callouts is shown in figure 8.4.

In figure 8.4 we've placed callouts for areas of functionality. A description for each callout is listed here:

1 Files and folders are no longer displayed on the left side of the screen as you may be familiar with in SharePoint Designer 2007. This has been replaced with the new Navigation pane. This is part of the initiative to make SharePoint Designer more objects-centric.

2 You can quickly update site information by selecting the text in blue.

3 Here you can edit the permissions for the site.

4 You can create new subsites.

5 You can customize the homepage or change the site's theme.

In the next series of steps you'll create several custom lists. The first list that you'll create will track exam status:

Step	Action	Result/Notes
1	Select Lists and Libraries from the Navigation pane.	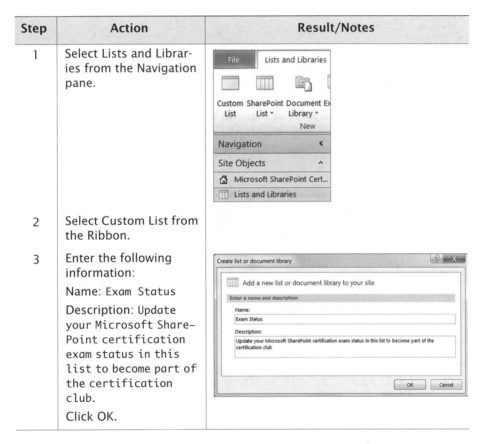
2	Select Custom List from the Ribbon.	
3	Enter the following information: Name: Exam Status Description: Update your Microsoft Share-Point certification exam status in this list to become part of the certification club. Click OK.	

After you create your custom list, you'll return to the list gallery page, which displays all lists for that site. The gallery page for this site is shown in figure 8.5.

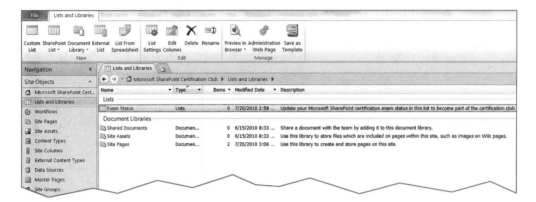

Figure 8.5 This is the list gallery page found in SharePoint Designer 2010. Here you can access all of your lists.

You'll now customize the list so that it will capture the SharePoint certification information. To do this, select Exam Status; that will redirect you to the list summary page, shown in figure 8.6.

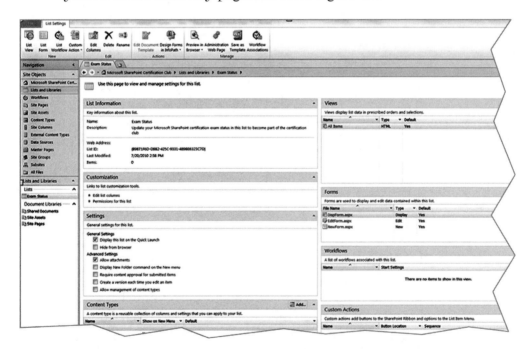

Figure 8.6 The list summary page in SharePoint Designer 2010 lets you manage settings for your list.

The first step is to modify one of the existing fields:

Step	Action	Result/Notes
1	Select Edit List Columns under Customization.	**Customization** Links to list customization tools. ▫ Edit list columns ▫ Permissions for this list
2	Select Title, and change the column name to Employee.	Add New Column / Add Existing Site Column / Add to Default View / Add to All Content Types / Column Settings / Column Type / Column Validation / Delete New · Edit Navigation Site Objects ⌂ Microsoft SharePoint Cert... ▥ Lists and Libraries ✆ Workflows Exam Status ← → · ⌂ Microsoft SharePoint Certification Club Column Name ▾ Type Title · Single line of text

The next series of steps will add some additional columns. This information will feed into the homepage web parts discussed later in this chapter.

Select Add New Column and create the following.

Column Name	Type	Values
Picture	Hyperlink or Picture Go to Column Settings to set the format to Picture.	NA
Exam	Choose Display as Checkboxes.	*MCTS:* Microsoft SharePoint 2010, Application Development Exam 70–573 *MCTS:* Microsoft SharePoint 2010, Configuring Exam 70–667 *MCITP:* SharePoint Administrator 2010 Exam 70–668: *MCPD:* SharePoint Developer 2010 Exam 70–576 *MCM:* Microsoft Office SharePoint Server Set the default value to be blank.

I would encourage your end users to link to the picture on their My Site profile. You can do this by adding text to the description of the column. They can get the URL of their My Site profile picture by right-clicking the picture and selecting Properties. If you want to allow them to use a different picture, you should consider creating a different list where they can upload pictures. While they enter a hyperlink, it will display as a picture, as shown in figure 8.7.

Now that you have the list to capture employee information, you're going to use the SPD XSLT List View web part to display it.

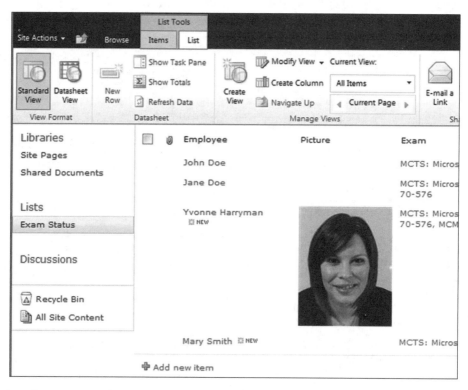

Figure 8.7 If you enter a hyperlink in a column and set it to display as a picture it will appear as shown in this image.

8.2.3 XSLT List View web part (LVWP): displaying Microsoft Certified Technology Specialist

In this section you'll create two list views. The first will display a list of all the users who have successfully completed one of the exams. It will also display those names in bronze if they've completed both of the MCTS exams and in silver if they've completed both MCTS exams and the MCITP and MCPD exams but not the MCM exam. The names of those who have completed all of the exams and have achieved the Microsoft Certified Master (MCM) status will be displayed in gold. The MCM users will also get their picture displayed. To begin, navigate back to the homepage of the SharePoint Certification site and open up SharePoint Designer to create your list view:

Step	Action	Result/Notes
1	In SharePoint Designer select Edit Site Home Page in the customization section. If it opens in split mode, select the option to view it in design mode in the bottom-left corner.	
2	You can delete any web parts that are already on the page, and then you'll need to navigate to the SPD Insert tab. Here you'll find a Data View drop-down list with Exam Status listed as an option. Select Exam Status.	

Step	Action	Result/Notes
3	Click Add/Remove Columns and remove everything except Employee; then click OK.	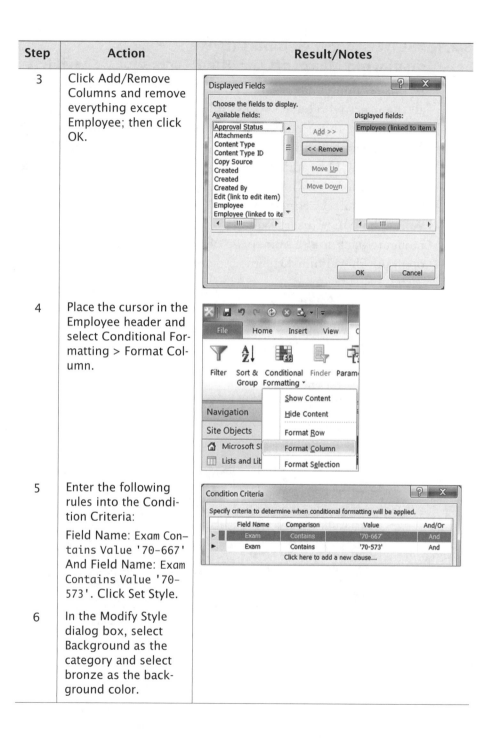
4	Place the cursor in the Employee header and select Conditional Formatting > Format Column.	
5	Enter the following rules into the Condition Criteria: Field Name: Exam Contains Value '70-667' And Field Name: Exam Contains Value '70-573'. Click Set Style.	
6	In the Modify Style dialog box, select Background as the category and select bronze as the background color.	

Step	Action	Result/Notes
7	Select Conditional Formatting > Format Column again, and enter the following rules into the Condition Criteria: Field Name: Exam Contains Value '70-667' And Field Name: Exam Contains Value '70-573'. Click OK and enter Field Name: Exam Contains Value '70-668' And Field Name: Exam Contains Value '70-576'. Click Set Style.	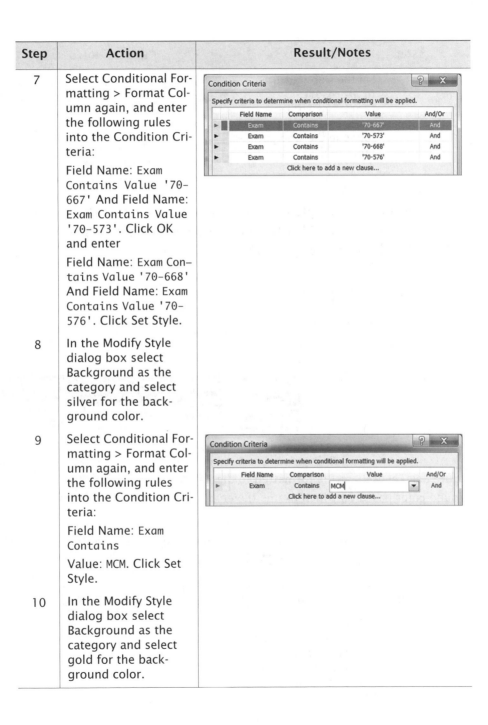
8	In the Modify Style dialog box select Background as the category and select silver for the background color.	
9	Select Conditional Formatting > Format Column again, and enter the following rules into the Condition Criteria: Field Name: Exam Contains Value: MCM. Click Set Style.	
10	In the Modify Style dialog box select Background as the category and select gold for the background color.	

Step	Action	Result/Notes
11	Set the web part title to Microsoft Certified Recipients. This can be found in the web part properties.	

Once you've completed these steps, you can select Preview in Browser to see it in action. With data entered, you should get results similar to those displayed in figure 8.8.

Figure 8.8 The web part is formatted to display the name with a different background color based on which exams the employee has successfully completed.

In the next series of steps you'll add another view to the left, which displays pictures of the MCM recipients:

Step	Action	Result/Notes
1	In SharePoint Designer select your current List View web part, and click the left arrow to put your cursor in front of the LVWP.	

Step	Action	Result/Notes
2	You'll then be able to select the Data View dropdown list with Exam Status listed as an option. Select Exam Status. This is found under the Insert tab. **Note:** If the current data view is placed below the new one, you can drag and drop it to the right side.	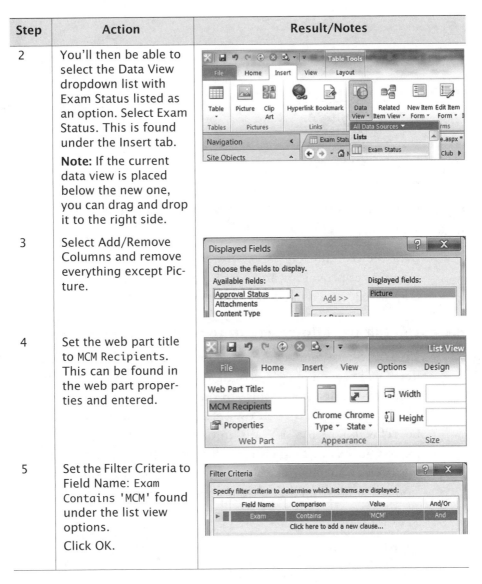
3	Select Add/Remove Columns and remove everything except Picture.	
4	Set the web part title to *MCM Recipients*. This can be found in the web part properties and entered.	
5	Set the Filter Criteria to Field Name: *Exam* Contains 'MCM' found under the list view options. Click OK.	

Your page should now look like the image in figure 8.9, assuming you've entered some data into the Exam Status list.

Now that you've configured your LVWP to display and format your end users based on their certifications, you'll want to verify that the

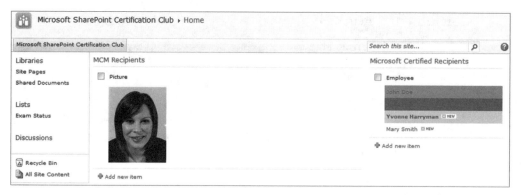

Figure 8.9 Microsoft SharePoint Certification Club site with the two List View web parts added

data they're entering is accurate. To do this you're going to request manager approval for any certifications that the employees say they've completed. You'll use SharePoint workflows to do this.

8.2.4   Default workflows: creating an approval process

Lists in SharePoint can have content approval turned on so that list items will remain in a draft state until they're approved. There are multiple reasons for doing this. In our scenarios we're going to allow the employees to update their own status, but we don't want the changes to be reflected in the LVWP until someone has verified that they've passed the exam. To do this we'll need to turn on approval and versioning. Versioning will enable users to see the previously approved version when they're editing their current status. To turn this on you need to complete the following steps:

Step	Action	Result/Notes
1	Select Exam Status from the Quick Launch navigation bar.	

Step	Action	Result/Notes
2	Select the List option in the Ribbon and choose List Settings.	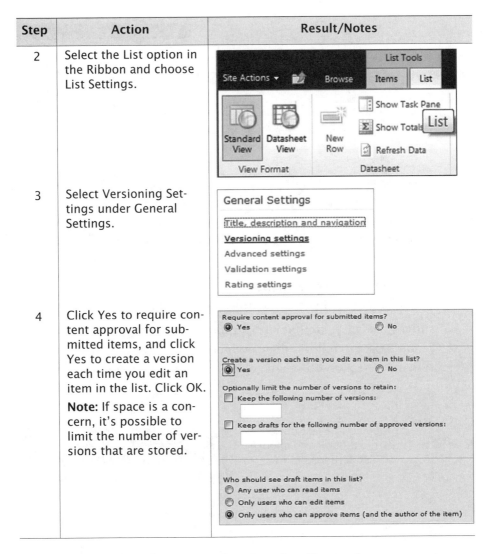
3	Select Versioning Settings under General Settings.	
4	Click Yes to require content approval for submitted items, and click Yes to create a version each time you edit an item in the list. Click OK. **Note:** If space is a concern, it's possible to limit the number of versions that are stored.	

When an approver logs onto the site, they'll now have an option to approve any changes, as demonstrated in figure 8.10. An Approval Status field will also be added to your list to capture the current status.

Now that you've turned on the approval capability for the Exam Status list, you also need to enable the item-level permissions to control which items users can edit.

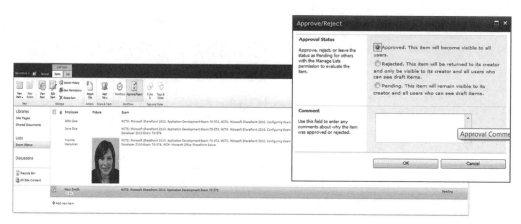

Figure 8.10 Process for approving an item in a list with content approval enabled

8.2.5 Item-level permissions: configuring the items users can manage

Item-level permissions are important to configure when you want to limit a user to editing their own entries, such as in our Exam Status list. From the List Settings page, you need to complete the following steps:

Step	Action	Result/Notes
1	Select the List option in the Ribbon and choose List Settings.	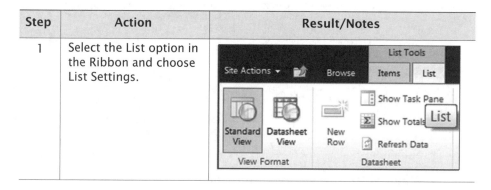

Step	Action	Result/Notes
2	Select Advanced Settings under General Settings.	**General Settings** Title, description and navigation Versioning settings **Advanced settings** Validation settings Rating settings
3	Select Create Items and Edit Items That Were Created by the User. Click OK.	**Read access:** Specify which items users are allowed to read ● Read all items ○ Read items that were created by the user **Create and Edit access:** Specify which items users are allowed to create and edit ○ Create and edit all items ● Create items and edit items that were created by the user ○ None

Configuring this will prevent employees from changing someone else's exam status. The next section covers the out-of-the-box survey technology. Because you have end users going here to let you know they've completed an exam, you might as well capture some information from them so they can help their peers. To do this you're going to ask them some questions that will help other employees understand how much they need to study.

8.2.6 Survey: getting input from your end users

Now that you're capturing the information for what exams your employees have passed, you may want to gather some additional information from them to help other employees. In this section you'll add a survey and some additional lists to capture important information for the use of other employees preparing for the exam. To create your survey you'll need to complete the following steps:

Step	Action	Result/Notes
1	Choose Site Actions > More Options.	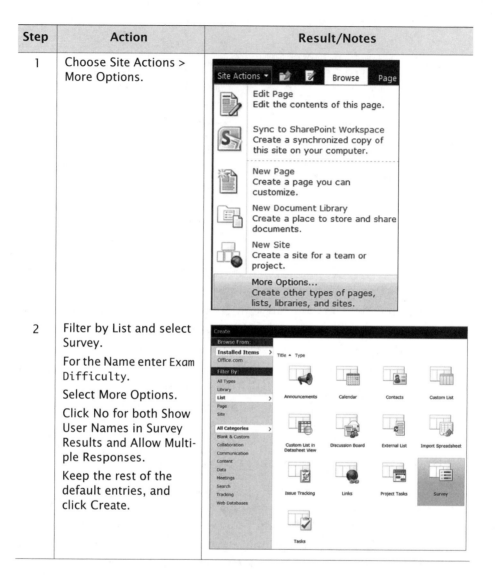
2	Filter by List and select Survey. For the Name enter Exam Difficulty. Select More Options. Click No for both Show User Names in Survey Results and Allow Multiple Responses. Keep the rest of the default entries, and click Create.	

This will keep the survey anonymous so other users won't see their answers and will prevent users from entering multiple responses and swaying the results. This will bring you to a new question page, where you can enter the questions you'd like the users to complete:

Step	Action	Result/Notes
3	Enter Did you think the SharePoint exams were difficult? for your Question. Click Choice (Menu to Choose From). Click Yes to require a response. Type the following choices, each on a new line: – Yes and I studied. – Yes and I didn't study. – No but I studied. – No and I didn't study. Leave the rest of the options at their default selection, and click Finish.	Question: Did you think the SharePoint exams were difficult? The type of answer to this question is: ○ Single line of text ○ Multiple lines of text ◉ Choice (menu to choose from) ○ Rating Scale (a matrix of choices or a Likert scale) ○ Number (1, 1.0, 100) ○ Currency ($, ¥, €) ○ Date and Time ○ Lookup (information already on this site) ○ Yes/No (check box) ○ Person or Group ○ Page Separator (inserts a page break into your survey) ○ External Data ○ Managed Metadata Require a response to this question: ◉ Yes ○ No Enforce unique values: ○ Yes ◉ No Type each choice on a separate line: Yes and I studied. Yes and I didn't study. No but I studied. No and I didn't study.

Adding branching

For this scenario you're creating a very simple survey. Some may call it a poll rather than a survey although it uses the same underlying technology as a survey. If you wanted to create a more extensive survey instead of clicking Finish here, you could select Next Question and continue to elaborate on your survey questions. At this point you wouldn't be able to add branching because not all the questions have been entered.

(continued)

What is branching? Branching is the ability to jump to specific questions based on the answer to the current question. To add branching, you'll need to access the Survey Settings and select Question under Questions at the bottom of the Edit Question screen. You'll now see the branching logic enabled for you to complete.

The next series of steps will add a graphical view of the survey to your homepage. To do this you need to complete the following steps:

Step	Action	Result/Notes
1	Choose Site Actions > Edit Page.	
2	In the Ribbon select the Insert tab under Editing Tools.	
3	Select Existing List.	Doing this will present you with a list of available lists that you can add, as shown in figure 8.11.
4	Place your cursor below the List View web part that you added.	

Figure 8.11 To add a web part that's based on an existing list, you'll need to select it from the Ribbon, which appears once you select Existing List from the Insert tab.

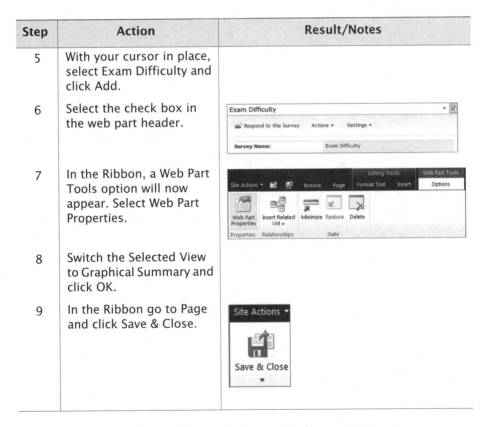

Step	Action	Result/Notes
5	With your cursor in place, select Exam Difficulty and click Add.	
6	Select the check box in the web part header.	
7	In the Ribbon, a Web Part Tools option will now appear. Select Web Part Properties.	
8	Switch the Selected View to Graphical Summary and click OK.	
9	In the Ribbon go to Page and click Save & Close.	

Your survey will now look like the image in figure 8.12.

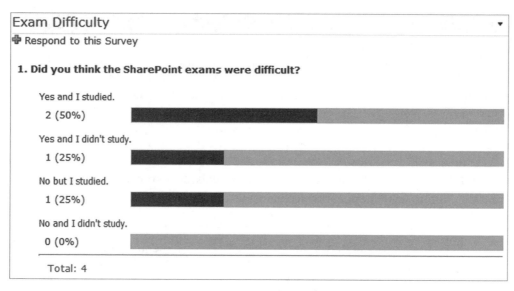

Figure 8.12 Exam Difficulty Survey web part with information entered

> **Survey quirks**
>
> Quirk 1: Although the underlying structure of a survey is a list, you won't find all of the same options. For instance, you can't modify the views of a survey.
>
> Quirk 2: If you add branching or a page separator, an option to save and close is added to each page with questions. This can confuse end users, and instead of clicking Next they may click Save & Close and not finish, thinking that they've completed the survey.

Congratulations! You've just completed configuring and adding the SharePoint Foundation functionality to your blank site. Some additional items that you may want to configure would be a discussion board for your users, a document library for study materials, and a calendar to track upcoming courses and exams. The next section is going to walk you through key performance indicators (KPIs) and an additional approval workflow. These will use functionality associated with SharePoint Server.

8.3 Leveraging SharePoint Server to take it further

In the previous section you built out your site using functionality in SharePoint Foundation. This section takes it a step further by integrating two pieces of powerful SharePoint Server functionality. The first one we'll discuss is the Approval Workflow and the second is Status Indicators. We'll start off by discussing the out-of-the-box workflows that come with SharePoint. You'll find that unlike the approval process that you can configure for a list, as shown in the previous section, this has many more configuration options. The following section, which covers Status Indicators, will help you to track and indicate if you are meeting the company's goals for certifications. So let's get started.

8.3.1 Approval workflow: adding actions to your workflows

In the first section we used SharePoint Foundation approval for a list. In this section we'll discuss advantages of using the approval workflow that comes with SharePoint Server. The only predefined workflow that comes with SharePoint Foundation is the Three-state workflow. Later in this book we'll dive into more detail on creating your own workflows using SharePoint Designer, but before we do that let's get started by discussing how to use the predefined workflows. To access your workflow options you'll want to complete the following steps:

Step	Action	Result/Notes
1	Navigate to the Exam Status list.	
2	Choose the Lists tab > Workflow Settings > Add a Workflow.	

This will take you to the Add a Workflow page. In the next series of steps you'll add an approval workflow:

Step	Action	Result/Notes
3	Select Approval for your workflow template.	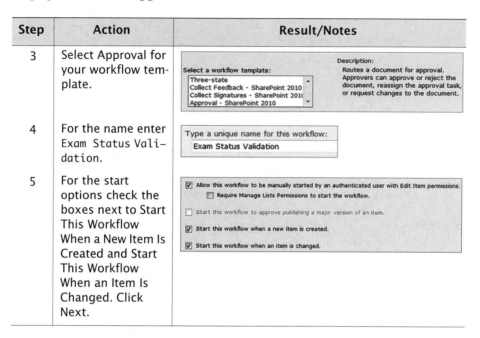
4	For the name enter Exam Status Validation.	
5	For the start options check the boxes next to Start This Workflow When a New Item Is Created and Start This Workflow When an Item Is Changed. Click Next.	

This will automatically start the Exam Status Validation workflow as soon as a change is made or a new entry is added. The next series of steps will walk you through the configuration of your workflow. Using the SharePoint Server Approval workflow, you have the ability to assign multiple approvers. You can set up the approval process to be serial or in any order. You can also provide them with the option to assign another approver or request a change:

Step	Action	Result/Notes
6	Enter the names of the users you want to validate the exam status and approve it for viewing.	

Step	Action	Result/Notes
7	Enter the following message to be sent to the approvers in the Request section: Please verify that this employee completed the entered exams.	Request — Please verify that this employee completed the entered exams. This message will be sent to the people assigned tasks.
8	Enter 2 Days for the duration period for approving each item.	Duration Per Task — 2. The amount of time until a task is due. Choose the units by using the Duration Units. Duration Units — Day(s). Define the units of time used by the Duration Per Task.

You also have the option to CC other users about the approval request. You could use this option to CC someone in your company who would be responsible for any test reimbursement for the employees:

Step	Action	Result/Notes
9	Select the check box End on First Rejection.	End on First Rejection — Automatically reject the document if it is rejected by any participant.
10	Select the check box Enable Content Approval and click Save.	Enable Content Approval — Update the approval status after the workflow is completed (use this workflow to control content approval). Save Cancel

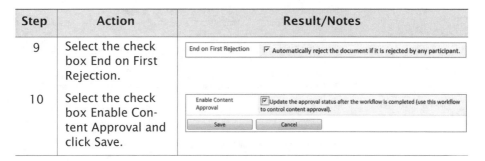

Figure 8.13 shows more configuration options when configuring the approval workflow.

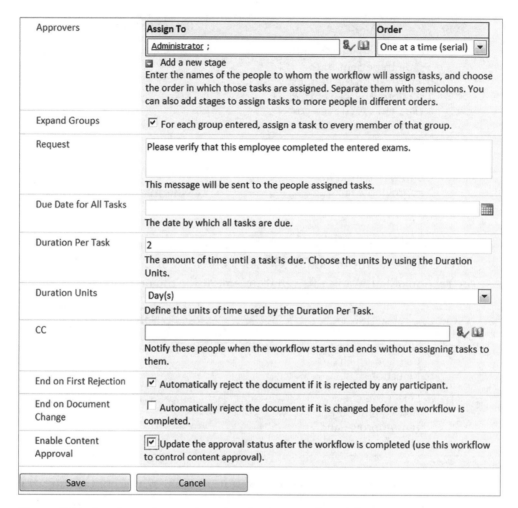

Approvers	Assign To		Order
	Administrator ;	&✓ 📖	One at a time (serial) ▼
	▣ Add a new stage Enter the names of the people to whom the workflow will assign tasks, and choose the order in which those tasks are assigned. Separate them with semicolons. You can also add stages to assign tasks to more people in different orders.		
Expand Groups	☑ For each group entered, assign a task to every member of that group.		
Request	Please verify that this employee completed the entered exams. This message will be sent to the people assigned tasks.		
Due Date for All Tasks	[ ] 📅 The date by which all tasks are due.		
Duration Per Task	2 The amount of time until a task is due. Choose the units by using the Duration Units.		
Duration Units	Day(s) ▼ Define the units of time used by the Duration Per Task.		
CC	[ ] &✓ 📖 Notify these people when the workflow starts and ends without assigning tasks to them.		
End on First Rejection	☑ Automatically reject the document if it is rejected by any participant.		
End on Document Change	☐ Automatically reject the document if it is changed before the workflow is completed.		
Enable Content Approval	☑ Update the approval status after the workflow is completed (use this workflow to control content approval).		
Save	Cancel		

Figure 8.13 Configuration options for the Approval workflow

Once you complete the configuration, you'll be on a landing page for the workflow setting. This is where you can go to manage or modify your workflow in the future. You've set that up so that the next time a user goes to edit or enter an item, the workflow will automatically initiate. Figure 8.14 shows what it looks like in action.

Additional workflow options can be used if you use SharePoint Designer, or Visio 2010 can be used to create a visual diagram of the

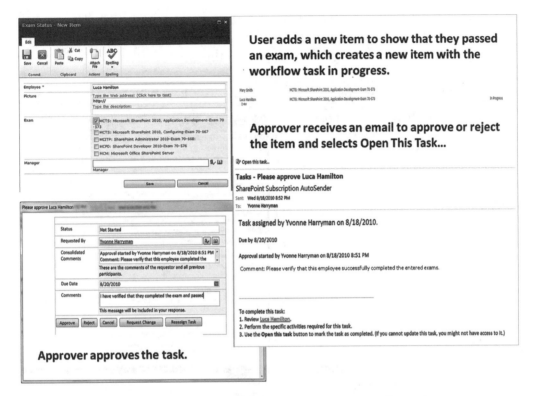

Figure 8.14 SharePoint Approval workflow in action once configured

workflow at a high level. The workflow designer can then export the Visio model to SharePoint Designer 2010 to fill in the details. We'll detail this further in chapter 10.

Now that we've discussed the different options for configuring approval on the exam status, let's talk about a way to leverage SharePoint Server functionality to indicate the overall status of the team for reaching their certification goals.

8.3.2 Status indicators: tracking the certification goals

Status indicators can provide your users an easy-to-understand graphical image of their current status on meeting defined goals. In this scenario you want to set goals for users for achieving their SharePoint certification exams. There are multiple steps for displaying indicators on your website. To begin you'll need to create a status list. The second step is to add a web part to display the indicators set up in the status list. Let's walk through the steps to do this:

Step	Action	Result/Notes
1	Choose Site Actions > More Options.	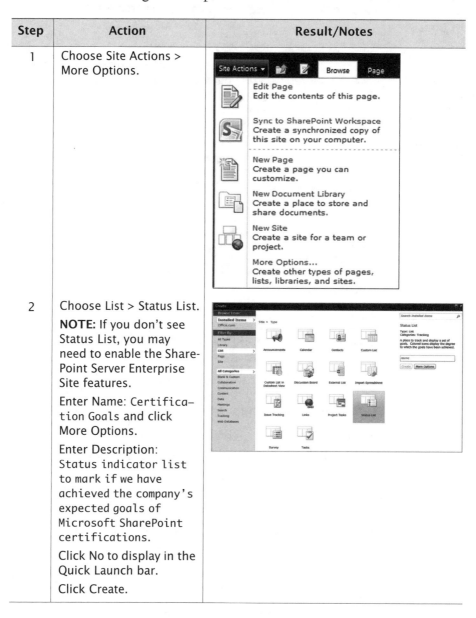
2	Choose List > Status List. **NOTE:** If you don't see Status List, you may need to enable the Share-Point Server Enterprise Site features. Enter Name: Certification Goals and click More Options. Enter Description: Status indicator list to mark if we have achieved the company's expected goals of Microsoft SharePoint certifications. Click No to display in the Quick Launch bar. Click Create.	

The next few steps will walk you through the configuration of your KPIs. There are two that you need to create. The first will track your goal for end users who have completed both MCTS exams 70–573 and 70–667, and the second will track your goal for end users who have completed exams 70–576 and 70–668. Note that in order for this to work effectively; you'll need to enter the names of all the end users you're tracking, even if they haven't completed an exam:

Step	Action	Result/Notes
3	Choose New > SharePoint List Based Status Indicator.	**New** ▾ Actions ▾ Settings ▾ **SharePoint List based Status Indicator** **Create a new Status Indicator using data from SharePoint Lists** Excel based Status Indicator Create a new Status Indicator using data from Excel Services SQL Server Analysis Services based Status Indicator Create a new Status Indicator using data from SQL Server Analysis Services Fixed Value based Status Indicator Create a new Status Indicator using manually entered information

Step	Action	Result/Notes
4	To create the first status indicator, enter or set the following values: Name: Exam 70-573 & 70-667 Select Exam Status as your List URL. Set Value Calculation to Percentage of List Items in the View Where Exam Contains 70-573 And Exam Contains 70-667. Set the status icon to the green circle if 80 and the yellow triangle if 40. Click OK.	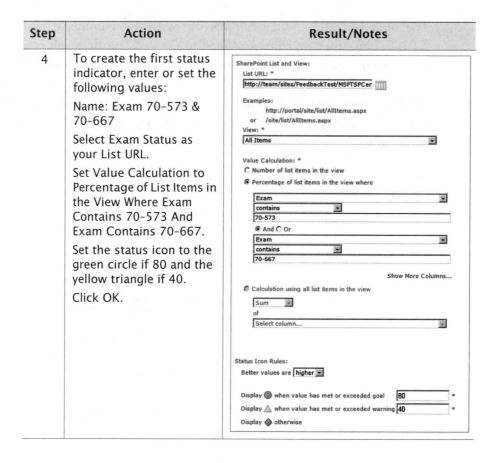

Step	Action	Result/Notes
5	To create the second status indicator, enter or set the following values: Name: Exam 70–668 & 70–576 Select Exam Status as your List URL. Set Value Calculation to Percentage of List Items in the View Where Exam Contains 70–576 And Exam Contains70–668. Set the status icon to the green circle if 80 and the yellow triangle if 40. Click OK.	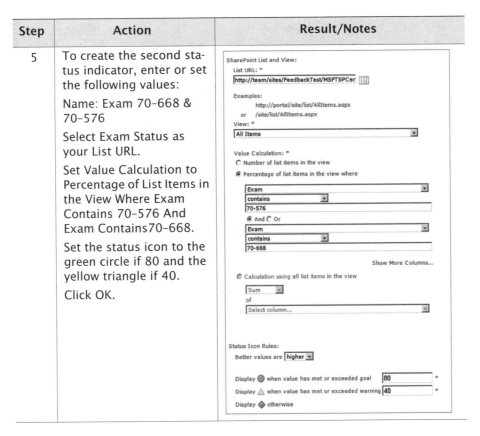

Now that you've configured your indicators, the next steps will be to configure the web part to display it on the homepage of the certification site. To do this you need to complete the following steps:

Step	Action	Result/Notes
1	Navigate back to the Microsoft SharePoint Server Certifications Club homepage.	
2	Choose Site Actions > Edit Page.	Site Actions ▾ Browse Page Edit Page Edit the contents of this page.

Step	Action	Result/Notes
3	Put your cursor below the MCM Recipients web part and select Insert > Web Part under Editing Tools. Under the category Business Data you'll find the Status List that you'll add.	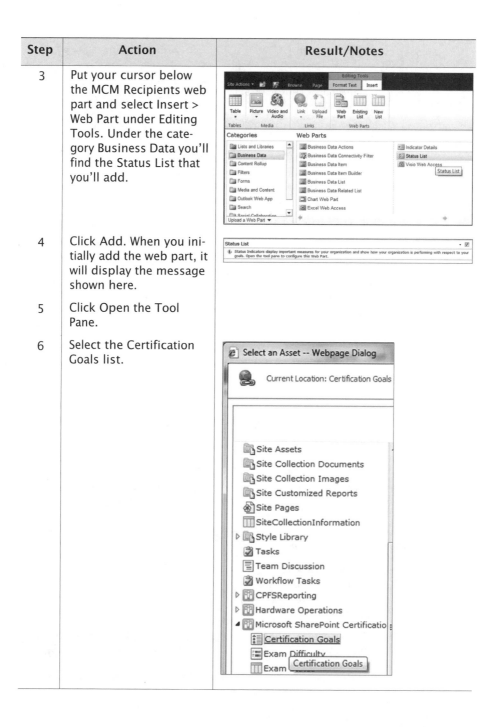
4	Click Add. When you initially add the web part, it will display the message shown here.	
5	Click Open the Tool Pane.	
6	Select the Certification Goals list.	

Step	Action	Result/Notes
7	Click OK.	
8	In the Ribbon go to Page and select Save & Close or Stop Editing.	Site Actions ▾ Save & Close ▾

Your site should now look like the image in figure 8.15.

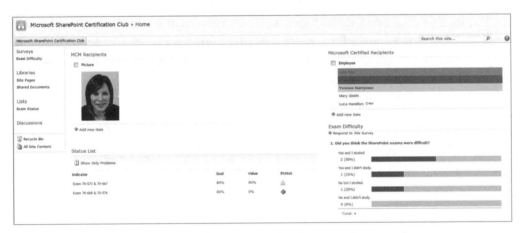

Figure 8.15 SharePoint Server solution once implemented

You've completed both our SharePoint Foundation and SharePoint Server scenarios. Let's summarize what you've learned.

8.4 Summary

Following is a summary to help you understand the functionality that you should now be comfortable with implementing from completing this scenario:

⦿ Working with SharePoint Designer to customize your SharePoint Foundation and SharePoint sites

- Creating and customizing a List View web part
- Adding conditional formatting to a List View web part
- Creating Approval workflows for both SharePoint Foundation and SharePoint Server
- Setting item-level permissions for a list to manage what users can view or edit at the individual item level
- Creating surveys and displaying the results graphically
- Setting status indicators and knowing how to leverage them to visually display progress toward set goals

In this chapter I introduced you to some of the capabilities of SharePoint Designer. The next chapter will walk you through some advanced functionality for developing workflows by using the workflow tools in SharePoint Designer and the new visual diagraming capabilities provided with Visio 2010.

Let's test your knowledge. One question that you should be able to answer is this:

- Out of the functionality listed here, what's the one item that you can't use SharePoint Designer for?
    1. Create list
    2. Add web parts to your site
    3. Manage permissions
    4. Develop a sandboxed solution
    5. Develop workflows
    6. Create subsites
    7. Create themes

The answer is 4. Sandboxed solutions are customizations developed using .NET leveraging Visual Studio. Because that's a core development feature, we won't be going into detail on that in this book, but it's important to understand what development capabilities you have without having to write .NET code. As you can see from the list, SharePoint Designer can be very powerful.

9

Collecting and managing data by integrating with InfoPath

This chapter covers

- Forms libraries
- InfoPath forms
- Forms services

In the last chapter we began our discussion of composite sites and how to build powerful applications using SharePoint Designer. We'll continue our discussion of composite sites in this chapter. The tool we'll focus on is InfoPath. The scenario that you're going to implement, following a step-by-step process, is for automating the review process of employees at the end of a project. To begin, we'll discuss the scenario you've been given and how you'll attain the solution utilizing SharePoint.

9.1 Gathering employee feedback

This section consists of three parts: situation, business priorities, and solution. The first part, situation, provides a detailed explanation of the request that you've received. The next part, business priorities, extracts a list of requirements based on priority to accomplish your goals. The third part gives you an overview of the solution that we'll spend the rest of the chapter walking through and building.

9.1.1 Situation

You're a manager of a group of employees. One of your responsibilities is to gather feedback from various clients and peers that they've worked with. Each employee can work on many different projects that are run by different managers. Employee reviews are approaching, and you want to gather the necessary feedback with an organized and consistent solution. Now that you understand the situation, let's discuss the business priorities.

Business priorities

I'll now define what the business priorities are so you can put together an appropriate solution:

1 Keep an up-to-date store of the projects and managers that each of your employees is assigned to.

2 Develop a consistent form to gather feedback after a project is complete.

3 Track which feedback forms have been sent out for input.

4 Create a central repository with an easy way to find the information by employee for completed feedback forms.

I've also provided a process map to help you visualize the system you're going to implement. This is shown in figure 9.1.

The next section highlights the solution you're going to build in this chapter.

9.1.2 Solution

Once you complete the steps in this chapter, you'll have a site that meets the situation and business priorities specified to you. Your final

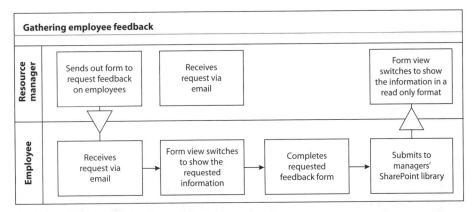

Figure 9.1 Process map for the solution that you're going to build. This explains the roles of the resource manager and the project manager. It will help you to visualize what the requirements are and how the users will advance through the system.

solution is shown in figure 9.2. To initiate the form, you'll use a Forms Library web part view.

Once a manager has initiated the form, they'll be prompted to select the information for the project and employee that they'd like to gather feedback on. This request will go out as an email submission, as shown in figure 9.3.

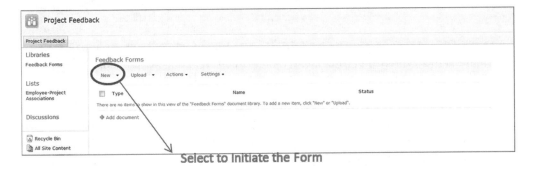

Figure 9.2 Click the New button in the web part to initiate your form. This is what your solution will look like if you choose to initiate the form without Forms Services, which is described in section 9.3.

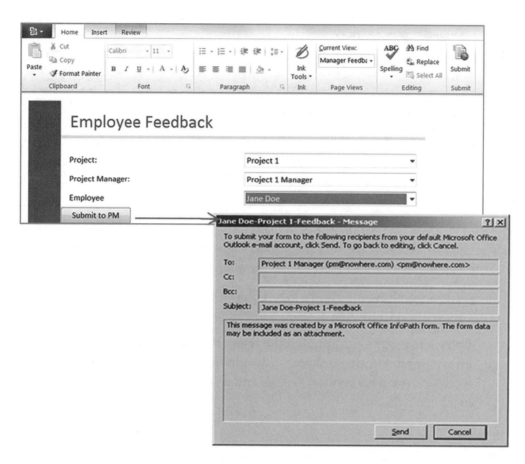

Figure 9.3 Once a resource manager initiates a request for feedback, an email is generated and sent to the project manager. The project manager will get this request and be able to open the form to fill it out.

The form will also be submitted to SharePoint, and the status will be updated as submitted. The reason you'll do this is to track the status of the form as submitted and/or completed. Figure 9.4 shows you an example of the feedback request that just went out.

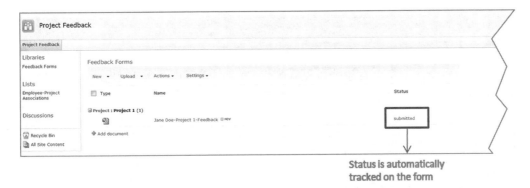

Status is automatically
tracked on the form

Figure 9.4 The form will also be submitted to a SharePoint library so the resource manager can track how many requests they've sent and their status. As you can see, the status for your recent request is submitted because it hasn't been completed.

Once the user receives the form, they can open it via an attachment, or if they have Outlook 2010, they should see the form as displayed in figure 9.5 and will have the ability to complete it via Outlook.

When the project manager opens the form, it will open InfoPath, unless the site is configured to use Forms Services, which will open it in a web browser. If the user has Outlook 2007 or above it will open as shown in figure 9.6.

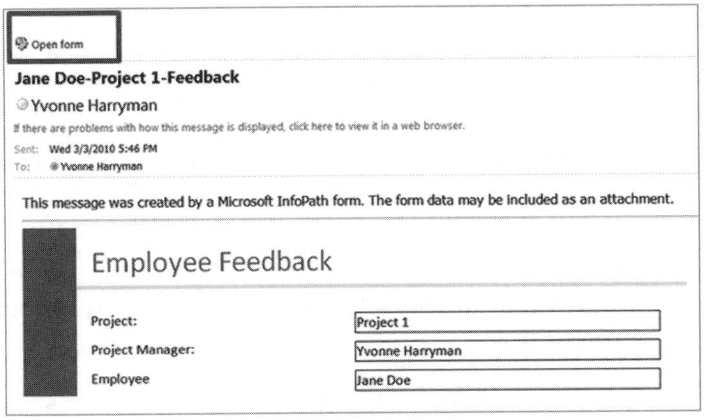

Figure 9.5 This is what the project manager will receive when they get a request for feedback. Note here that the Open Form option will enable users to open the form from Outlook.

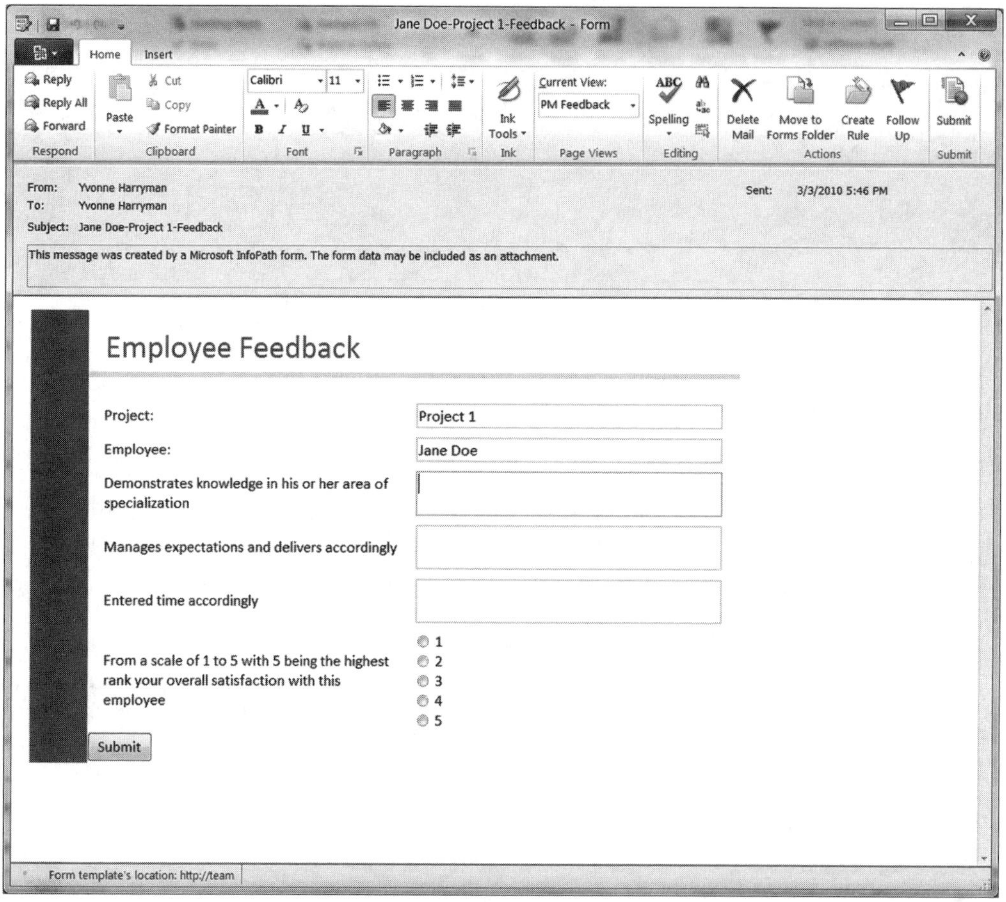

Figure 9.6 If the user is using Outlook 2007 or above when they open the email, it will appear as shown here, and the user will have the ability to complete and submit it without leaving Outlook.

Once the project manager has completed the request, the form will be submitted to a SharePoint library. An example of what this could look like is shown in figure 9.7.

Now that you know the solution for your scenario you can start building out the site to reach the solution described previously.

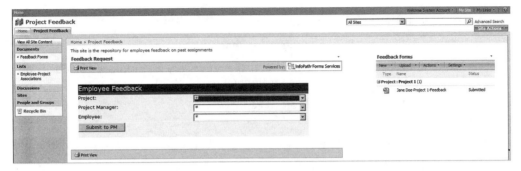

Figure 9.7 This example shows the scenario built out with Forms Services. To the right is the form library that you'll create, which will display the forms that have been sent out for feedback and returned.

9.2 Using InfoPath with SharePoint Foundation

This section covers your approach to using SharePoint Foundation and InfoPath. You'll start by developing several lists in SharePoint to store the data. You'll then design a form using InfoPath. Topics that you'll learn pertain to designing the form, leveraging controls, connecting to data sources, and implementing different views. Finally, you'll publish your form to SharePoint so others can access it. The first section focuses on your approach with InfoPath. Your second approach, covered in section 9.3, uses Forms Services. This is part of SharePoint Server and is important if your end users don't have InfoPath installed on their PC.

9.2.1 Creating your site

To begin, make sure your site is created using a Publishing or Blank Site template. Enter the following for Title, Description, and Web Site Address:

Property	Value
Title	Project Feedback
Description	This site is the repository for employee feedback on past assignments.
Web Site Address	ProjectFeedback

Now that you've created your site, you'll set up a custom list to manage the employees and projects.

9.2.2 Custom list: creating a data store of current projects

To begin, you'll create a list to manage your employees and the projects they work on. To do this, create a custom list:

Step	Action	Result/Notes
1	Choose Site Actions > More Options, filter by Blank & Custom, and select Custom List.	
	For the name enter Employee–Project Associations.	
	Select More Options, and for the description enter The following list stores information about current projects and the employees assigned to them.	
	Click Yes for displaying this list in the Quick Launch bar.	
2	Click Create.	This will redirect you to the main page of your newly created list.

You should now be looking at the main page for the Employee-Project Associations list. A series of menu options in the Ribbon have been provided to help you manage these items, as shown in figure 9.8. You'll focus on the List Settings option, which is found in the Settings section in the far-right side of the Ribbon, to customize the list's metadata.

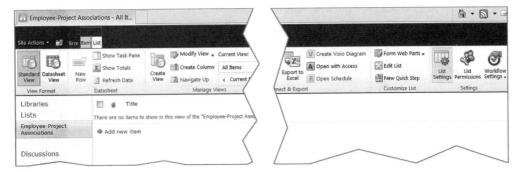

Figure 9.8 Menu options for a list in SharePoint. The List Settings option is selected on the right side of the Ribbon.

Now that you have a list, it's time to get creative and begin to customize the list settings.

List Settings: disabling attachments

By default when you create this list, a paper clip icon will display any attachments associated with an item. For our scenario, there's no need for a user to upload an attachment, so you're going to disable the feature:

Step	Action	Result/Notes
1	Choose List Settings.	
2	Select Advanced Settings	This is located under the General Settings grouping.
3	Click the radio button to disable attachments to list items.	This will remove the paper clip icon shown in figure 9.8 next to Title.
4	Click OK.	

Your users will no longer have the ability to add an attachment. Next we'll discuss how to customize the rest of the columns in the list. What you've done so far may seem a bit boring, so let's have some fun and customize the rest of the columns in the list to match our scenario.

List columns: customizing the data captured

This section deals with modifying the columns associated with the Employee-Project Associations list under List Settings. You want to track Project Manager, Employee, and Project. First, modify the existing Title column:

Step	Action	Result/Notes
1	Choose List Settings.	You're probably already there if you just completed the previous section. You'll know this if you see the following image at the top of the page. Project Feedback › Employee-Project Associations › List Settings
2	Select Title, which is displayed in the Columns section.	**Columns** A column stores informa Column (click to edit) Title
3	In the Column Name field enter Project and click OK.	Title by default is a required field requiring that you enter information in it. Because you renamed Title to Project, you now have a required field for Project. Next you'll create the Employee and Project Manager columns.
4	In the Columns section select Create Column. For Column Name enter Employee. Choose Single Line of Text. Click Yes under Require That This Column Contains Information. Click OK.	

Step	Action	Result/Notes
5	Repeat step 4, but enter Project Manager for the column name.	You now have a list that will enable you to track your employees and their projects.
6	Complete these steps again, but enter Project Manager for the column name in step 3.	

Yay! You're now able to track your employees and their projects and have a consistent approach for the data that needs to be entered. Now that you've completed this, let's get started with the creation of a Forms library so you'll have a consistent form to gather feedback at the end of a project. You'll need some data in the list you just created to complete the next section, so add a few items to the Employee-Project Associations list.

9.2.3 Forms library: creating a library to manage the feedback form

To create the Forms library to manage the form, complete the following steps:

Step	Action	Result/Notes
1	Choose Site Actions > More Options, filter by Library, and select Forms Library. For Name and Description enter Feedback Forms. For the Description enter The following library is set up to manage the feedback forms.	
2	Click Create.	This will redirect you to the main page of your newly created list.

Your Forms library is in place, so next you'll open up InfoPath to create a form.

9.2.4 InfoPath: creating your feedback form

Microsoft Office InfoPath is part of Office Professional Plus. It helps users to create rich dynamic forms without having to write a line of code. For the SharePoint Foundation section of this chapter, you're going to use the client version of InfoPath. The SharePoint Server section, 9.3, will cover Forms Services, which will allow users to access the form without InfoPath. For this example you're going to generate a feedback form using InfoPath. To start, you'll need to open InfoPath by doing the following:

Step	Action	Result/Notes
1	Choose Library Settings for the Forms library.	You're probably already there if you just completed the previous section.
2	Select Advanced Settings under the General Settings section.	**General Settings** Title, description and navigation Versioning settings **Advanced settings**
3	Select Edit Template (under the Template URL field) to open a blank InfoPath template.	Template URL: **Feedback Forms/Forms/template.xml** (Edit Template)
		You'll now see a blank form that has been opened in InfoPath Designer.

NOTE   If you have an existing template that you'd like to publish, you can open InfoPath in design mode and click the Office button. Here you'll see a series of options; the one you're interested in is called Share. There you can publish to a SharePoint Server.

You'll now see a blank form that you can design. We're now going to walk through the powerful features of InfoPath so you can learn to create powerful forms. The designer enables you to quickly add controls, style, and logic to your forms.

Design task: designing your form

You now have a blank form open that you can begin to design. The Ribbon has a menu of actions that you'll use to design your form, along with a column to the right to manage your fields, as shown in figure 9.9.

Figure 9.9 Ribbon is used often when designing your form. In this image it's displayed at the top of the page.

To begin you'll create the layout of your form:

Step	Action	Result/Notes
1	Click the Insert tab in the Ribbon.	
2	In the Page Layouts section select the fourth table, described as Title with Vertical Emphasis Bar.	You'll now see an empty layout table displayed, as shown in figure 9.10.
3	Click the section with the text Add Section Layouts.	
4	In the Section Layouts section of the Insert tab of the Ribbon, select the fourth section layout, described as Two-Column with Label Left-Aligned and No Heading.	
5	Select the text Click to Add Title and enter Employee Feedback.	You'll now see the updated layout table displayed; see figure 9.11.

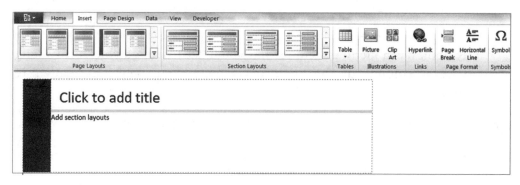

Figure 9.10 InfoPath form with a layout table added. This will help you to quickly format the content and get started on your form.

These simple steps will enable you to quickly get started with setting a design and format for your forms.

Now that you've designed your form, we'll discuss how to input or display data through the use of controls. A pretty form can take you only so far without the use of controls to capture the data. So let's get started discussing how to add value to this form.

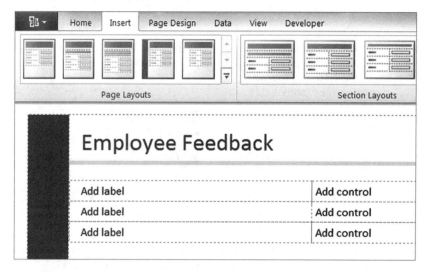

Figure 9.11 InfoPath form with a layout table and section layout added. This will help you to quickly format the content and get started on your form.

Controls: enabling users to input data

In this section you're going to add a series of controls and a data connection to populate them with data from a SharePoint list. First, you'll add the controls to your form:

Step	Action	Result/Notes
1	Click the top row on the right containing the text Add Control.	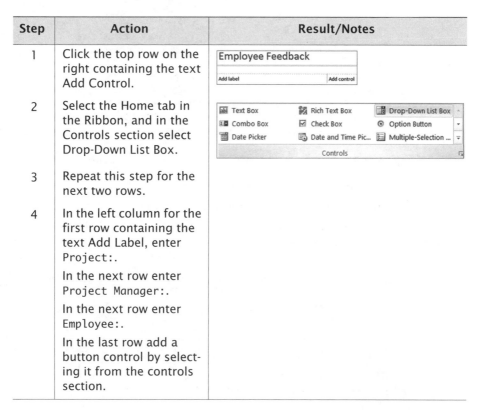
2	Select the Home tab in the Ribbon, and in the Controls section select Drop-Down List Box.	
3	Repeat this step for the next two rows.	
4	In the left column for the first row containing the text Add Label, enter Project:. In the next row enter Project Manager:. In the next row enter Employee:. In the last row add a button control by selecting it from the controls section.	

Before moving on to dealing with the forms data source, let's update the color scheme:

Step	Action	Result/Notes
1	Select the Page Design tab in the Ribbon.	

Step	Action	Result/Notes
2	In the Colors drop-down list select Civic.	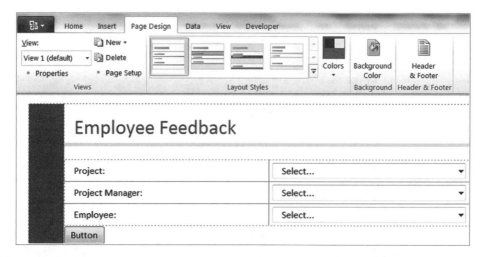

Once you've finished your form should look like the one in figure 9.12.

Congratulations! You've now created and designed your own form. But what can you do with the data? It's great to have a form, but you need something to put in it. Aren't you excited? That's what you're going to do next!

Figure 9.12 Color schemes are a quick and easy way to modify the look and feel of an InfoPath form. Here you've applied the Civic color scheme.

Data source: managing the data

A forms data source is important because it structures the data. One common mistake that new users of InfoPath make is that they don't ever go back and give meaningful names to the data they capture. It's important for you to understand the data in the form when you're creating your views. Your data can be viewed in the column marked Fields displayed on the right side of the page.

Here you'll notice that there are three fields under myFields named field1, field2, and field3. Each of these fields corresponds with one of the drop-down list box controls. You need to rename each field to a meaningful value. You'll do this by right-clicking each drop-down list box control and selecting Drop-Down List Box Properties to display the properties associated with it. Figure 9.11 shows the properties for your drop-down list box.

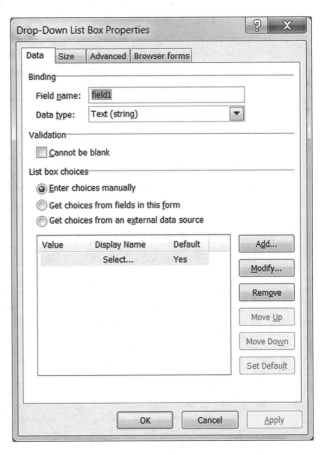

Figure 9.13 This is the dialog box that will appear for each of the field properties associated with the drop-down list boxes. This will help you provide additional power and logic to your controls.

Updating the properties associated with your controls will help you provide additional functionality to how users enter the information. The following steps walk you through the needed changes to the properties:

Step	Action	Result/Notes
1	Right-click the first drop-down list box control and select Drop-Down List Box Properties. Enter Project for the Field Name. Select Cannot Be Blank under Validation. Select Get Choices from an External Data Source under List Box Choices.	

You now want to configure this to look up values from an external data source. The source that you're interested in accessing is the Employee-Project Associations list you created earlier in this chapter in section 9.2.1. To do this you must create a data connection.

Click Add, and the Data Connection Wizard will appear. Figure 9.14 shows the Data Connection Wizard.

Now you'll configure your data connection:

Step	Action	Result/Notes
1	Click Create a New Connection To and choose Receive Data. Then click Next to go to the next step.	
2	For the location where you would like to receive your data, select SharePoint Library or List, and click Next to go to the next step.	By pulling the data from a SharePoint list, you can modify the values without having to republish the form.
3	Enter in the URL to the site where the Employee-Project Associations list is located, and go to the next step.	

Step	Action	Result/Notes
4	Under Select a List or Library select Employee-Project Associations and go to the next step.	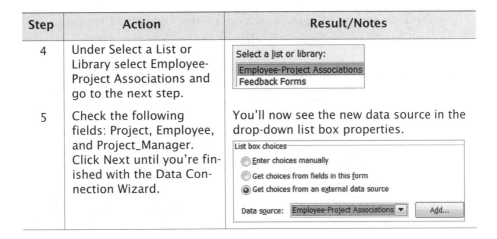
5	Check the following fields: Project, Employee, and Project_Manager. Click Next until you're finished with the Data Connection Wizard.	You'll now see the new data source in the drop-down list box properties.

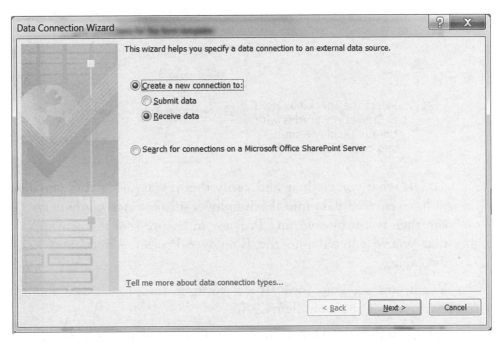

Figure 9.14 To retrieve data from a SharePoint site you have to create a connection to receive data by configuring the Data Connection Wizard. This will enable you to populate your drop-down list boxes from lists that exist in SharePoint.

You should now be in the Drop-Down List Box Properties dialog box and ready to configure the details for pulling the data:

Step	Action	Result/Notes
1	Click the XPath icon next to Entries. Expand dataFields. Expand the SharePoint List Item grouping. Select Project.	
2	Click OK.	Your configured entries should look like the following:
3	Select the check box next to Show Only Entries with Unique Display Names, and click OK.	☑ Show only entries with unique display names

To test what you've done and verify that it was successful, you'll need to have entered data into the Employee-Project Associations list. You can then test it by selecting Preview to ensure that the project values that you've entered into the Employee-Project Associations list are displaying.

You'll now see your form. If it's working, the project data should be displayed, as shown in figure 9.15.

When you've finished testing your form, you can exit the preview mode by selecting Close Preview, as shown in the ribbon in figure 9.15.

You'll need to perform these steps again for the drop-down list box for Project Manager and Employee with a few minor exceptions:

⊚ For Field Name enter ProjectManager or Employee.

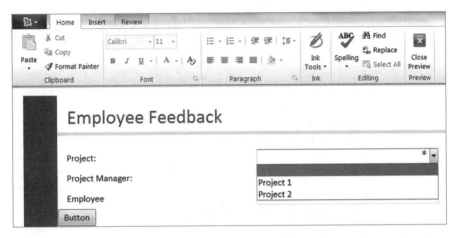

Figure 9.15 The drop-down list displayed is dynamically pulling information from a list on your SharePoint site. If you were to add new values to the SharePoint list, they'd automatically appear in the drop-down list.

- You won't have to add another data source.
- For the XPath entries select Project Manager or Employee.
- On the XPath entries you'll need to define a filter by completing the following steps:

Step	Action	Result/Notes
1	Click the Filter Data button on the Select a Field or Group dialog box.	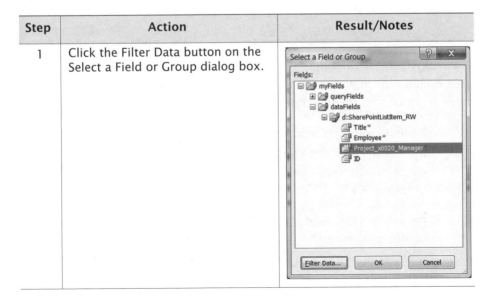

Step	Action	Result/Notes
2	Click Add. For the Project Manager field, select Project Is Equal To Project from the main data source. For the Employee field, create two rules, one that matches the Project Manager rule and a second that sets Project Manager equal to ProjectManager from the main data source. It should look like figure 9.16. To get to the main data source, choose Main from the drop-down list at the top of the dialog box labeled Fields, as shown in figure 9.17.	

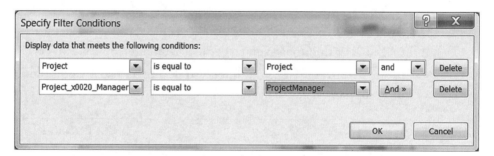

Figure 9.16 This is what the filter conditions for the Employee field should look like. This will add the logic to your drop-down controls to show only the values that are valid based on the previous selection.

You've now applied a filter to your drop-down lists so they'll show only the values that are valid based on the previous selection. To make sure we're on the same page, verify that your data source looks like the one in figure 9.17.

In this next section we're going to cover views. This will enable you to create a flow to the form so that different users will see only the data that pertains to them. So far you have a powerful form, but you'll want the resource manager to see different information than the project

Figure 9.17 Your data source so far should appear like this. Naming your fields with recognizable terms is important when you start to build out forms that have many fields.

manager. This will make the information that the form is requesting easy to identify. Remember that once you've finished with this, you'll have an automated way to gather feedback on employees and to track it. You'll be able to quickly send out many requests within minutes and keep the data organized.

InfoPath views: changing the way the form is displayed

This section walks you through the process of creating views. The default view that you just created is for the resource manager to complete before sending out a feedback request. The next view will be for the project manager to complete in order to give feedback on an employee:

Step	Action	Result/Notes
1	Navigate to the Page Design tab in the Ribbon of InfoPath.	
2	Select Properties, and for the View Name enter Manager Feedback Request.	
3	Locate the New drop-down list box next to the views and select New View.	

Step	Action	Result/Notes
4	The Add View dialog box will appear and prompt you to enter a view name. Enter PM Feed–back.	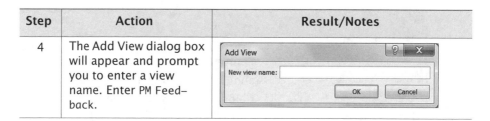

You'll now begin to design your new view. This view is for the project managers to give feedback on the employees assigned to their projects. You'll design a similar layout to that completed in the *Design task: designing your form* section. You'll complete the same steps; the one new step is to add three new rows to the section layout. Once that's complete, you'll lay out the controls:

Step	Action	Result/Notes
1	In the Fields section select Project and drag it to the upper-left cell of your layout.	If you drag it into the right column, it won't autoformat the label and control across the two columns.
2	In the Fields section select Employee and drag it to the upper-left cell.	**Fields:** Main ☐ 📂 **myFields** 📄 Project * 📄 ProjectManager 📄 Employee
3	For each control you just added, right-click the text box and select Text Box Properties. Navigate to the Display tab and check the text box to make the control read-only.	Text Box Properties Data | Display | Size | Advanced | Browser forms Options Placeholder: ____ Example: "Click here and type." ☑ Read-only
4	Click OK.	

Step	Action	Result/Notes
5	For the next few rows, enter the following questions and choose a control for each based on the next table.	

Questions	Controls
Demonstrates knowledge in his or her area of specialization	Rich text box
Manages expectations and delivers accordingly	Rich text box
Enters time accordingly	Rich text box
From a scale of 1 to 5 with 5 being the highest, rank your overall satisfaction with this employee	Option button set for 5

For the final control, add a button to the bottom of the page. Now that you've added the controls, you'll need to customize them.

For the rich text boxes complete the following:

- Enter Question 1, Question 2, or Question 3 for the field name:
- For the option button complete the following:
- For the field name enter Employee_Ranking.
- Modify the text to be labeled 1-5.

Once you've completed these steps, your form will look like the one in figure 9.18.

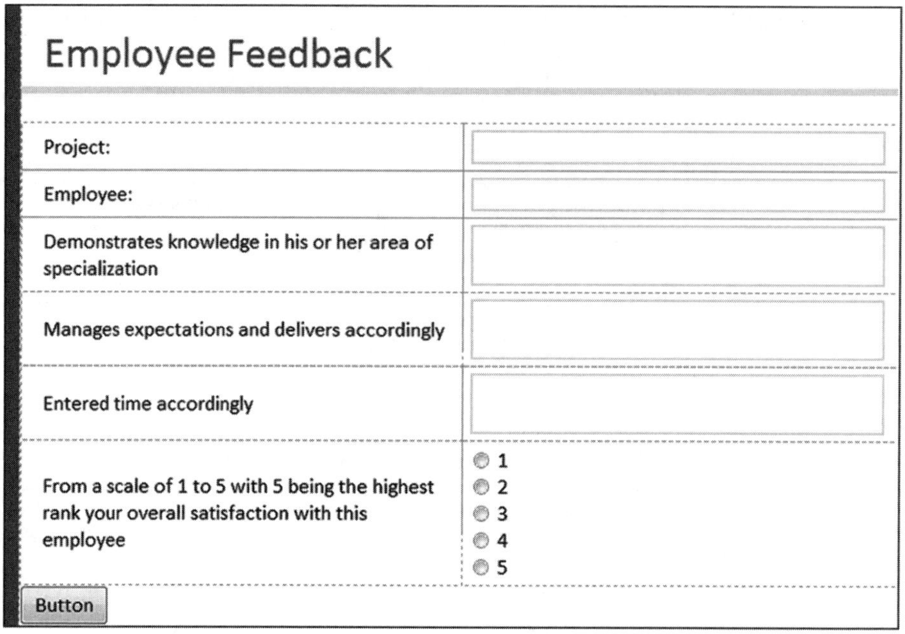

Employee Feedback

Project:	
Employee:	
Demonstrates knowledge in his or her area of specialization	
Manages expectations and delivers accordingly	
Entered time accordingly	
From a scale of 1 to 5 with 5 being the highest rank your overall satisfaction with this employee	⊙ 1 ⊙ 2 ⊙ 3 ⊙ 4 ⊙ 5

Button

Figure 9.18 Your form will look like this once the controls have been added to the page. Exciting to see it in action! Was it really that hard? No, I didn't think so.

You'll now create a third view that will be identical to the previous view except all the controls will be read-only. This view will be the one that displays when forms are submitted to SharePoint:

Step	Action	Result/Notes
1	Select everything in the PM Feedback view by pressing Ctrl-A, and then press Ctrl-C to copy.	
2	Locate the New drop-down list box next to the views and select New.	A dialog box will appear and prompt you to enter a view name. Enter Submitted Feedback.
3	Click OK.	
4	Right-click the new view and select Paste.	

You should now be looking at a version of the form that matches figure 9.18. There are just a few modifications that you'll need to make to this form:

Step	Action	Result/Notes
1	Delete the buttons.	Delete both the option and classic buttons at the bottom of the page.
2	Change the properties for all the controls to read-only.	Remember that this is under the Display tab.
3	Go to Fields, and select and drag Employee_Ranking over to the section where the options buttons had been.	

Once you've finished your form for the Submitted Feedback view should like figure 9.19.

Congratulations! You've now completed your form, and you should be proud of yourself. The information that you'll capture will now be consistently entered and managed. Your end users have a nice way to view the data and see it in a format that applies to them. To finish this off, you'll want to configure your data connections so you can send the form to SharePoint and also send it via an email to request the recipient to enter feedback. You'll also want to ensure that this form and its information are published to SharePoint so managers can quickly access it and send out a request and track the responses that they receive. To begin, you'll configure your data connections.

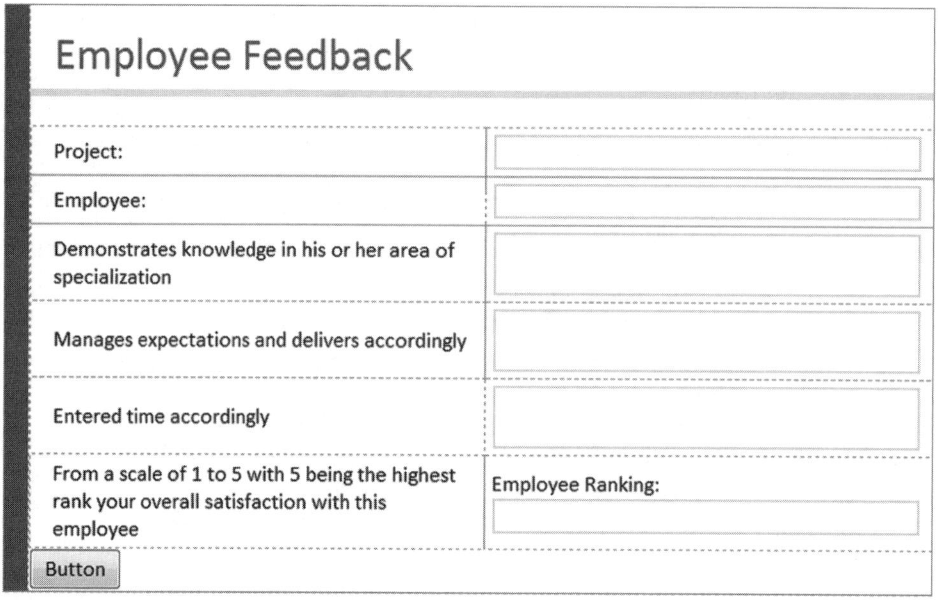

Figure 9.19 Once you've added and configured the data source, verify that your form appears like this one. Also, once you run the form, the controls that are marked Required will now have either a red dotted line or an asterisk to denote that they're required.

9.2.5 InfoPath workflow: configuring how users see the data

InfoPath doesn't necessarily have workflow, but it does have the ability to dynamically switch views as end users go through the different stages of completing the form. In this section you're going to define data connections to share the data with SharePoint and the end users through Outlook. You'll also configure submission behaviors and form behaviors to dynamically switch the views. To begin, you'll define the data connections.

Data connections: sending the data to SharePoint and Outlook

The next series of steps walks you through configuring the data connections. The first step is to configure a field to track the different phases of the form submission. To begin, you'll create a new field in the data source to track the status of the form:

Step	Action	Result/Notes
1	Click the drop-down arrow for myFields in the Data Source section of the Fields bar displayed to the right of your InfoPath form.	**Fields:** Main ⊟ 📁 **myFields** 📄 Project * myFields (Group)
2	Click Add. For Name enter Status.	
3	Click OK.	You'll now have a new data field to store the status of the form so the web can track what stage of the submission process you're in.

The next section walks you through the steps to create a data connection:

Step	Action	Result/Notes
1	Select Manage Data Connections under Actions in the Data Source section of the Fields bar displayed to the right of your InfoPath form.	**Actions** Add Field Manage Data Connections...
2	Click Add.	**Data Connections** Data connections for the form template: Employee-Project Associations Add... Submit to SharePoint
3	Select Create a New Connection To and select Submit Data. Click Next to go to the next step.	◉ Create a new connection to: ◉ Submit data ○ Receive data
4	Select As an Email Message, and go to the next step.	This will generate an email that will notify the project manager when the resource manager would like feedback on an employee.

Step	Action	Result/Notes
5	For the To line, select the option Insert a Formula, and from there choose Insert Field or Group. Select ProjectManager and click OK.	Formula: ProjectManager Insert Field or Group... Insert Function... Verify Formula

NOTE Sending an email using the name of the project manager works only if Outlook can resolve the names that are entered into the Employee-Project Associations list. If this doesn't work for you, then you may want to add an Email column to your list and use that field instead.

Step	Action	Result/Notes
6	For the Manage Data Connections Subject line, select the option Insert a Formula, and from there choose Insert Field or Group. Add both Employee and Project. Add concat(before the two fields. Separate the fields with , "-", and add ,"-Feed-back") at the end. Click OK.	Formula: concat(Employee, "-", Project, "-Feedback") Insert Field or Group... Insert Function... Verify Formula
7	Click Next twice and leave the defaults.	
8	In the next screen enter the following name for the data connection: PM Submit.	Enter a name for this data connection: PM Submit
9	Click Finish.	

Good job! Now that you have your data connections completed for sending an email, you'll also want to configure the data connection for submitting the data to SharePoint. Don't worry—this will be just as easy as the last set of steps:

Step	Action	Result/Notes
1	Select ... in the Data Source section of the Fields bar displayed to the right of your InfoPath form.	You should already have the Manage Data Connections dialog box open if you're continuing from the previous steps.
2	Click Add.	Data connections for the form template: Employee-Project Associations Submit to SharePoint Add...
3	Select Create a New Connection and then click Submit Data. Click Next to go to the next step.	Create a new connection to: Submit data Receive data
4	Select the destination To a Document Library on a SharePoint Site, and go to the next step.	Select a destination for submitting your data. How do you want to submit your data? To a Web service To a document library on a SharePoint site
5	For the Document Library field, enter the URL for the Forms library.	Document library: <Enter URL> Example: http://www.example.com/yourlibrary/

Step	Action	Result/Notes
6	For the File Name line, select the option Insert a Formula, and from there choose Insert Field or Group. Add both Employee and Project. Add `concat(` before the two fields; separate the fields with , "-", and add ,"-Feed-back") at the end. Click OK.	Formula: `concat(Employee, "-", Project, "-Feedback")` [Insert Field or Group...] [Insert Function...] [Verify Formula]
7	Select the check box next to Allow Overwrite if File Exists, and go to the next step.	☐ Allow overwrite if file exists
8	In the next screen enter the following name for the data connection: `Submit to SharePoint`.	Enter a name for this data connection: `Submit to SharePoint`
9	Click Finish.	

Now that you've configured your data connections, you need to configure how to link these connections to the different submission phases. The next section covers the configuration of form submissions.

Submissions: setting rules to customize the behavior of form submissions

The next series of steps is to configure the submissions. In this section you're going to submit forms using a series of rules so multiple actions can take place. To begin you'll work with the Manager Feedback Request view:

Step	Action	Result/Notes
1	Select the button control.	The Ribbon will automatically default to the Control Properties tab when the button is selected.
2	For the label enter Submit to PM.	
3	Select Rules.	The rules manager will open on the right side of the page.
4	Select New > Action.	
5	In the section marked Details For, enter Submit to PM.	
6	Select Add > Set a Fields Value. For the field select Status, and for the value enter Submitted and click OK.	**Note:** InfoPath is case sensitive.
7	Select Add > Submit Data. In the Data Connection drop-down list, select Submit to SharePoint and click OK.	

Step	Action	Result/Notes
8	Select Add > Submit Data.	In the Data Connection drop-down list, select PM Submit and click OK.
9	Select Add > Close the Form.	If the option to prompt the user to save is selected, then deselect it and select OK.

You'll complete the same series of steps for the button control on the PM Feedback view with the following exceptions:

- For step 5 enter Completed Feedback for the Details For section.
- Change the label to Submit.
- For step 6 enter the value as Completed.
- Skip step 9.

In this section you added the actions behind the user submit and updated the Status field. You'll now work on customizing the form behavior based on the Status field.

Page options: customizing the form behavior when opened

You have several options for dynamically switching the view. One common way is to do it when setting the rules. Another way is to do it through the Page Options settings. For this section you're going to set up the dynamic behavior of the form based on the Form Load rules, which can be found in the Data section:

Step	Action	Result/Notes
1	Navigate to the Data tab in the Ribbon.	
2	Select Form Load.	The rules manager for form load will display on the right side of your form.

Step	Action	Result/Notes
3	Select New > Action.	New ▼ ⬚ Validation ⬚ Formatting ⬚ Action Condition: None Rule type: Validation
4	In the section marked Details For, enter Open PM Feedback View.	
5	Click the hyperlink under Condition to set a condition. Set it to Status Is Equal to (Type a Text) Submitted, and click OK.	Condition: None - Rule runs when form is ... Rule type: Action Run these actions:* Add ▼ None ☐ Don't run remaining rules if the condition of this rule is met
6	Select Add > Switch Views.	Select PM Feedback from the View drop-down list and click OK.
7	Select New > Action.	New ▼ ⬚ Validation ⬚ Formatting ⬚ Action Condition: None Rule type: Validation
8	In the section marked Details For enter Final Submission View.	

Step	Action	Result/Notes
9	Click the hyperlink under Condition to set a condition. Set it to Status Is Equal to (Type a Text) Completed, and click OK.	Condition: None - Rule runs when form is ... Rule type: Action Run these actions:* [Add ▼] None
10	Select Add > Switch Views.	Select Submitted Feedback from the View drop-down list, and click OK.

The rules you created should look like those in figure 9.20 once they're completed.

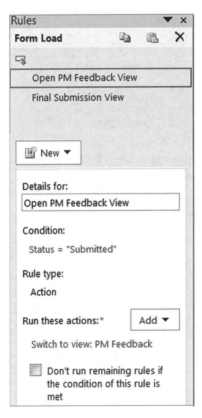

Figure 9.20 The rules you set up for your form load should look like these once you've completed them. In SharePoint 2010 the rules manager makes it easy to see all your rules in one place.

Congratulations! You've finished creating your form. Now all that's left is to publish it. This is important because it impacts how the users will access it. Publishing your form to a Forms library ensures that all your end users open the same form, and any updates that you make go to one central location, so you can ensure all of the end users are using the same template.

9.2.6 Publishing: publishing the form to SharePoint

Now that you've created your library, we will go through the steps to update the form associated with that library. If you ever need to make changes, you can complete the following steps to republish the updates you make:

Step	Action	Result/Notes
1	To get to the full publishing capabilities, click the Office button, navigate to Share, and select Publish.	Here you should see the Quick Publish bar for the current location along with other capabilities, such as publishing to a SharePoint library, email, or network location.
2	Select SharePoint Server.	This will open a dialog box that will enable you to configure various publishing options. By default, the location should already be entered for the first step of the dialog box. If it isn't, enter the URL for the site that has your Forms library and click Next.
3	Leave the default setting for Document Library and click Next.	
4	Select Update the Form Template in an Existing Library. Select Feedback Forms and go to the next step.	

Step	Action	Result/Notes
5	Click Add.	This step is important because it allows you to select columns from the form so they'll be available in SharePoint. This is useful when working with views in a SharePoint list because it will allow the users to view and access the data in different ways.
6	Add all the columns and click Next.	The fields listed below will be available as columns in SharePoint folders. Column Name — Add... / Remove / Modify... Project Project Manager Employee Employee Ranking Status
7	Click Publish.	

Good job! The form is now published and your users have access to it. Let's now discuss how to share the data with SharePoint.

9.2.7 Form library views: displaying the forms

Now that the form is created and uploaded, you'll need to reconfigure the site to display the data. To begin, you'll add a web part view of the Feedback Forms library:

Step	Action	Result/Notes
1	Choose Site Actions > Edit Page.	
2	Select Add a Web Part in the Left Zone.	
3	Select Feedback Forms in the Web Parts section of the Ribbon, and click Add.	Web Parts Employee-Project Associations Feedback Forms

Step	Action	Result/Notes
4	On the web part that you just added, select Edit Web Part.	If you're having trouble finding the Edit Web Part option, make sure you hover your mouse over the title of the web part. On the right side a drop-down arrow will display with the option to edit the web part.
5	Select Edit the Current View. Deselect Modified, Modified By, and Checked Out To. Select Status. Expand Group By, and select First Group by the column Project. Click OK.	
6	You've not finished editing your web part, so go back to Edit Web Part.	
7	For Toolbar Type select Show Toolbar, and then click OK.	

In the web part you just created you'll now have an option to click the New button to initiate a form, as shown in figure 9.21.

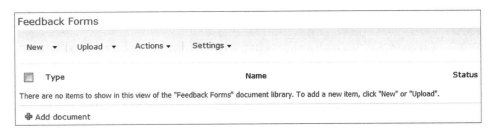

Figure 9.21 You now have the ability to click the New button in the web part to initiate your form. This step won't be necessary in the next section using Forms Services. Instead, you'll display the form in the browser.

You've finished configuring your feedback form for the SharePoint Foundation portion of this scenario. The one catch is that it requires your users to have InfoPath in order to complete the form. There's a browser-based option called InfoPath Forms Services, which is part of SharePoint Server, that we'll discuss in the following section. This will allow you to use the same scenario we walked through, but it won't require your end users to have InfoPath installed on their machine. One key area where this would be of significant use is public-facing sites on the internet. You have no control over the software that users have installed on their machines. This feature will be key to ensuring they can complete the forms.

9.3 Leveraging Forms Services with SharePoint Server

SharePoint Server provides some new options to InfoPath 2007 and above through the addition of Forms Services. In the 2003 release, users were required to have InfoPath in order to complete the forms, but this was resolved when InfoPath Forms Services was released, which enabled users to access the forms though a browser. This continues to be a strong feature with SharePoint Server 2009. This scenario leverages the steps from section 9.2, where you created your form, but instead it walks you through the publishing steps to make it a web-based form that doesn't require your end users to have InfoPath installed on their PC.

9.3.1 Forms Services: accessing the form without InfoPath

You'll start by enabling Forms Services on the Document library and on the form so that the behavior will change to open the forms via the web browser when a user clicks New:

Step	Action	Result/Notes
1	Select file and choose Form Options.	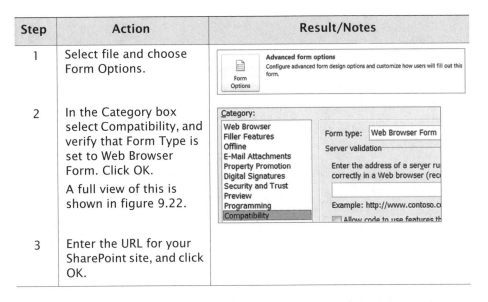
2	In the Category box select Compatibility, and verify that Form Type is set to Web Browser Form. Click OK. A full view of this is shown in figure 9.22.	
3	Enter the URL for your SharePoint site, and click OK.	

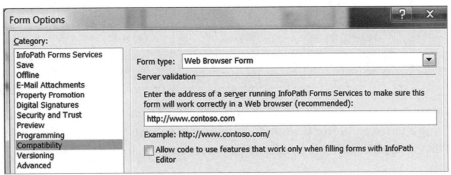

Figure 9.22 Enable browser compatibility from InfoPath to verify your design. This will ensure that you have Forms Services. Although you may have SharePoint Server, the site that you're implementing it on might have that feature turned off.

When you go to publish the form, you'll need to check the check box to enable this form to be filled out using a browser, as shown in figure 9.23.

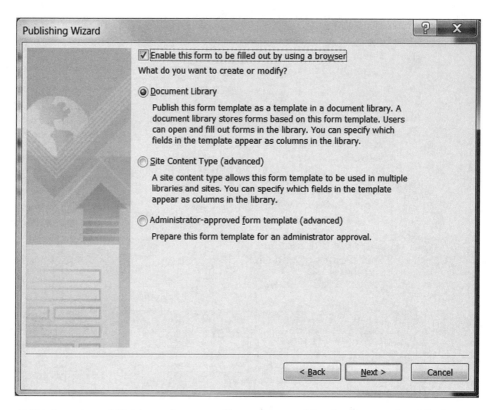

Figure 9.23 Step in publishing where you'll need to enable the form to be filled out using a browser. Notice the option here to also publish a form as a site content type. This can be useful if you need to push your template to multiple libraries.

The next time you go to view the form, it will display in the browser, as shown in figure 9.24.

You're finished with that section, so now it's cleanup time. Your focus will be on the toolbar to remove some of the functionality from the users; this will prevent them from doing something that you don't want them to do. An example would be switching around the views and not following that nice logic that you put into your form for showing the end user the appropriate view.

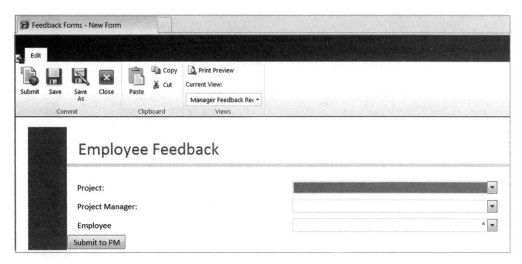

Figure 9.24 The view of the feedback form for the resource manager to request feedback from the project manager is displayed using InfoPath Forms Services. This enables the form to be filled out without having the client version of InfoPath installed.

Browser properties: modifying the toolbar

When you view a form using Forms Services, two toolbars will be displayed above and below the form. You can modify both toolbars or remove them altogether. Because it displays specific items that you won't want your users seeing, you're going to remove some of those features:

Step	Action	Result/Notes
1	Click the File button and choose Form Options.	

Step	Action	Result/Notes
2	Uncheck Save, Save As, Close, and Views,	The following options apply when the form is opened in a Web browser. User Interface Options ☑ Show InfoPath commands in Ribbon or toolbar When the Ribbon is unavailable ○ Show toolbar at the top of the form ○ Show toolbar at the bottom of the form ◉ Show toolbars at the top and bottom of the form Show the following commands: ☑ Submit ☐ Save ☐ Save As ☐ Close ☐ Views ☑ Print Preview ☐ Update
3	Republish the form.	

Now that you've designed your form and published it to the site, let's discuss an alternative approach for displaying your browser-based form.

9.3.2 Page Viewer web part: displaying your form

The Page Viewer web part used with Forms Services can provide a fantastic option for enabling users to have quick access to a form once they go to a page. To add the form to your SharePoint site without having your users click New, you can do the following:

Step	Action	Result/Notes
1	Navigate to the homepage of the Project Feedback site.	
2	Select Site Actions > Edit Page.	Site Actions ▾ Bro Pag Edit Page Modify the web parts on this page.

Step	Action	Result/Notes
3	Select Add a Web Part in the Left zone.	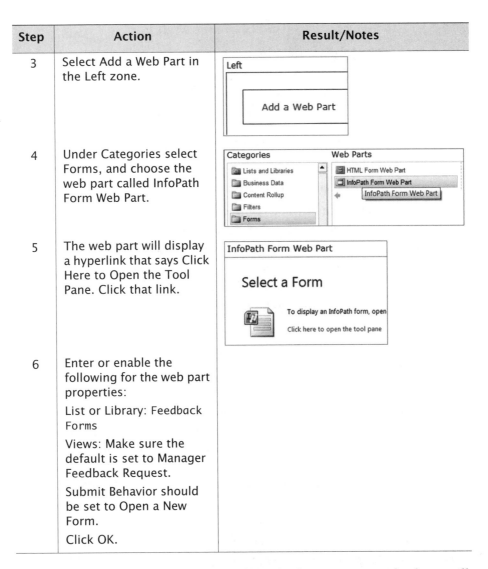
4	Under Categories select Forms, and choose the web part called InfoPath Form Web Part.	
5	The web part will display a hyperlink that says Click Here to Open the Tool Pane. Click that link.	
6	Enter or enable the following for the web part properties: List or Library: Feedback Forms Views: Make sure the default is set to Manager Feedback Request. Submit Behavior should be set to Open a New Form. Click OK.	

Next, you'll clean up the way the page is laid out. Because the form will need more space, you may want to play around with where items are located. To remove the scroll bars from around your form, you'll need to complete the following:

1   Select Edit > Modify Shared Web Part.

2   Expand Appearance.

3   Modify the height and width so the entire form can be viewed in the Page Viewer web part.

4   Keep modifying and clicking Apply until you have it correct.

5   Before exiting, update the title to Feedback Request.

6   Click OK.

7   Your page should look like figure 9.25 if formatted correctly.

The current email data connections will now be sent from the server computer. If an error appears on the submission, then it's likely this hasn't been configured. You'll need to contact your administrator and request that they configure email on the server or consider granting users permissions to the feedback forms sites so they can enter the data in the forms without the use of the email connections.

Good job! You can now develop web-enabled forms with advanced capabilities such as filtering data, print views, enhanced data submission options, and much, much more. You can see the power of Forms Services in this example, but imagine it on a public-facing site. That didn't take too long to create, did it? This can be used as an enterprise solution on public-facing sites to gather information from users everywhere on the internet. Now doesn't that sound appealing?

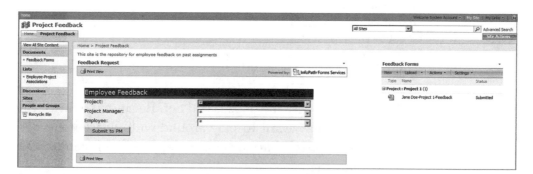

Figure 9.25 Feedback site with the form displayed on the homepage using the Info-Path Form web part. This way you don't have to open the form on a different page. It's automatically displayed for you when you come to the site.

9.4 Summary

Following is a summary to help you understand the functionality that you should now be comfortable with implementing from completing this scenario:

- Creating a custom list and modifying the columns
- Publishing to and creating Forms libraries
- Designing a form in InfoPath
- Adding controls to capture data for your InfoPath form
- Working with data sources to retrieve and submit data via Share-Point and email
- Creating views and dynamically changing them based on the status of the form
- Displaying your form via a web browser using Forms Services

Up to this point, you've designed your sites in silos. They all function perfectly without leveraging any of the data or functionality from other sites. The next chapter will walk you through some features for integrating these sites and provide some management tips without having to maintain each site individually.

Let's test your knowledge. A few of the questions that you should be able to answer are these:

- What's the difference between InfoPath and InfoPath Forms Services?
  InfoPath requires that your users have a license for Microsoft Office InfoPath to complete the form. InfoPath Forms Services doesn't require a license because it displays the forms via the web.

- Why would you use a filter when populating a drop-down list box when retrieving your values?
  This enables you to create dynamic drop-down lists where the values in the drop-down lists that follow will show different values that are specific to the entry in a previous drop-down list.

⊚ What are some of the benefits of using views?
   You can dynamically switch between different views, based on a value in your form, so it shows the information in a relevant format.

The same data can be displayed in edit mode or read-only mode while using the same data source.

10

Reporting and web applications using Access

This chapter covers

- *Access features and how they can be used with SharePoint*
- *Linked and local tables*
- *Queries*
- *Reports*
- *Forms*
- *Access Services*

In this chapter you're going to complete a scenario where you'll capture equipment/hardware requests by clients. I chose this scenario because it's a common process that you'll find in IT teams. Even more often I've seen hosting providers capture such requests to keep track of their servers. But this process can be used in any other scenario where you need to create a reservation-type system to prevent communal resources from being double booked and to keep individual users from checking out more items than they should. Another example where this could be used, apart from the IT-related scenario we have here, is for reserving a book from a communal library. Keep using your imagination; the techniques you'll learn here can be used for many other scenarios.

In this chapter we're going to walk through two options for capturing the information and reporting on it. The first approach, implemented with SharePoint Foundation, will work as long as your users have SharePoint Foundation and Access. The second approach will require SharePoint Server, and because you're going to use Access Services, the advantage is that it doesn't require your end users to have Access. Let's start by talking about the scenario you've been given and how you'll attain the solution utilizing SharePoint.

10.1 Managing hardware reservations

This section consists of three parts: situation, business priorities, and solution. The first part, situation, provides a detailed explanation of the request that you've received. The next part, business priorities, will extract a list of requirements based on priority to accomplish your goals. The third section will give you an overview of the solution that we'll spend the rest of the chapter walking through and building. By completing this you'll learn how to build dynamic reports and web-based systems hosted on SharePoint, using Access. Many of you are probably already familiar with Access and will be excited to learn that SharePoint 2010, unlike SharePoint 2007, directly integrates with Access and allows you to host the database on a SharePoint site. We'll dive into that technology and ensure that not only will you learn some of the basics of Access, but you'll also know how to use the integration capabilities with SharePoint.

10.1.1 Situation

In this scenario you're part of an IT team that manages hardware that different clients can use. For example, you have rental laptops, projectors, and even servers. You need to find a way for the IT team members to capture approved requests and to report on what items are reserved. Reporting back on that data is important. Gathering data is great, but you really can't benefit from the data until you slice and dice it using reports to extract and visually display the valuable information that was gathered. Now that you understand the situation, let's discuss the business priorities.

Business priorities

I'll now define the business priorities so you can put together an appropriate solution:

1   Enable the IT team to manage information in relation to their hardware and clients.

2   Track approved requests with the hardware and client information.

3   Make this information dynamically available so the IT team can quickly track current reservations by hardware type and client.

4   Advanced requests: Publish this same information dynamically for the clients who don't have Access.

I've also provided a process map to help you understand the system you're going to implement. This is shown in figure 10.1.

The next section discusses the solution we're going to build in this chapter.

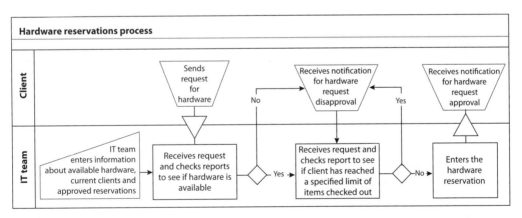

Figure 10.1 Process map for the solution that you're going to build. This explains the roles of the IT team and the client. It will help you to visualize what the requirements are and how the users will flow through the system.

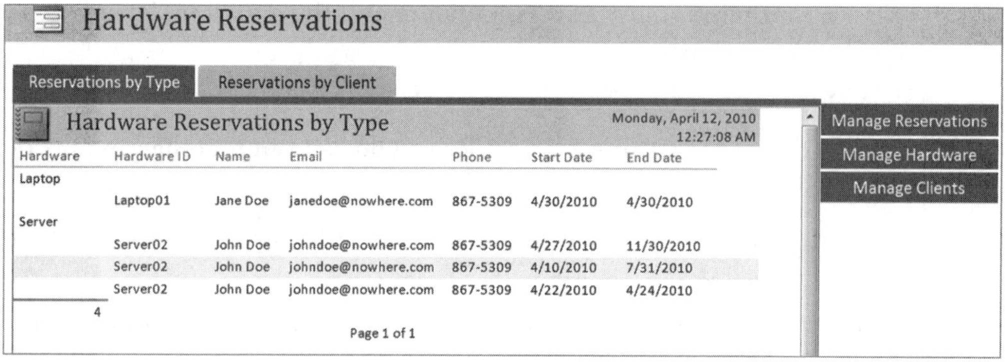

Figure 10.2 Navigation form that displays the different reports at the top of the form. Links to manage the input of the data are displayed on the right side of the form.

10.1.2 Solution

Once you complete the steps in this chapter, you'll have a site that meets the situation and business priorities specified to you. For this solution you'll create a navigational form view that contains the reports shown in the tabs at the top of the form. To manage the input of the information, you'll use the links on the right side of the form. The solution is displayed in figure 10.2.

A separate page will track the information the IT team enters, including the hardware, clients, and reservations. An example of managing reservations is shown in figure 10.3.

Building out this solution should take less than an hour. You'll be impressed to find how easy it is to now dynamically generate reports on information stored in SharePoint or to allow your end users to work with data in Access though a web application published to your Share-Point site. Now that you understand the solution and its benefits, let's get started building it out.

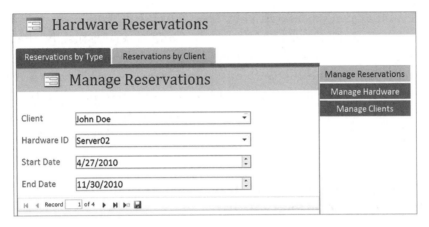

Figure 10.3 This reservation form captures the start and end dates for hardware reservations that are approved for the clients.

10.2 Leveraging Access with SharePoint Foundation

This section covers our approach for implementing this scenario using SharePoint Foundation and Access. You'll start by creating a blank site in this scenario and potentially a publishing site if you have SharePoint Server. We'll then cover some of the core components of Access such as tables, queries, and reports. The data that you'll be using is pulled from a SharePoint list and managed through a SharePoint site, but the reports will be generated using Access. I'm excited, so let's get started.

10.2.1 Creating your Foundation site

To begin you'll want to make sure you create a site using a Blank or Publishing Site template. Enter the following for Title, Description, and Web Site Address:

Property	Value
Title	Hardware Reservations
Description	This site enables IT to manage hardware reservations.
Web Site Address	HardwareReservations

Now that you've created your foundation site, you'll set up a custom list to manage the clients, hardware, and reservations. In the Share-Point Foundation section of this chapter, you'll do this utilizing Share-Point lists. In the SharePoint Server scenario, you'll take a different approach, which uses Access tables and publishes them via Access Services to a SharePoint site. This will allow you to meet your advanced requirement, which enables end users without Access to dynamically work with the data.

10.2.2 Custom list: creating a data store to manage clients, hardware, and reservations

You want to create a SharePoint list to manage your clients. You need this list so you can track important information about them such as how to contact them in case you need to follow up with them on their hardware reservation. Luckily, SharePoint has an out-of-the-box list that has already been configured to help you maintain your contacts. You can reuse this list to manage your clients by following the two easy steps listed here:

Step	Action	Result/Notes
1	Choose Site Actions > More Options, choose Filter By: List, and select Contacts List. For the Name enter Clients. Select More Options, and for the Description enter The following list stores information about our current clients. Click Yes for displaying this list in the Quick Launch bar.	
2	Click Create.	This will redirect you to the main page of your newly created list.

Now that you've created this list, you need to create a custom list that will store the information pertaining to the hardware that can be reserved. If there isn't an out-of-the-box list like Contacts, it's easiest to start with a custom list, which has only one column, Title. Essentially you're starting out with a blank list, and you can easily add in your own custom columns to track information. In this scenario you want to track information about the type of hardware you're renting out and the ID for that hardware:

Step	Action	Result/Notes
1	Choose Site Actions > More Options, choose Filter By: Blank & Custom, and select Custom List. For the name enter Hardware. Select More Options, and for the Description enter The following list stores information about our current hardware available for reservations. Click Yes for displaying this list in the Quick Launch bar.	
2	Click Create.	This will redirect you to the main page of your newly created list.

Because this is a custom list, you need to update the columns in this list to capture the appropriate information regarding your hardware, such as an ID and the type of hardware. For simplicity, you're going to implement a basic list that captures just those two items. If you want to capture additional information, I recommend that you read the short sidebar so you can get additional ideas to further enhance this list:

Implementing with content types

If you want to make the list more robust, you could create content types associated with each hardware type. This would allow you to have unique columns associated with that hardware type. For instance, if you're entering a server, you may want to capture information about it such as processing power and/or RAM, and this may not be valid information to capture for a projector. Creating content types is covered in more detail in chapter 5.

Step	Action	Result/Notes
1	Choose List Settings.	
2	Select Advanced Settings.	This is located under the General Settings grouping.
3	Click the radio button to disable attachments to list items.	This will remove the paper clip icon.
4	Click OK.	
5	Select Title, which is displayed in the Columns section.	**Columns** A column stores inform Column (click to edit) Title
6	In the Column Name field enter Hardware ID and click OK. Check Enforce Unique Values.	You'll now have a required field for the project. Next you'll create the Hardware Type column.
7	In the Columns section select Create Column. For Column Name enter Hardware Type. Choose Choice. For each choice enter the following options: Server, Printer, Projector, Phone, and Laptop. Click OK.	

Finally, you'll create a list that manages the reservations and the associated client information and hardware information from the lists you've already created. When entering data regarding a reservation, you'll want to track the contact info for the client and the hardware info for the reservation. You won't want to track this information in multiple places, so you'll create a lookup field that can link the reservation to the client and hardware ID. Later on when you generate your reports, you'll combine the information from these three tables to provide the full details about the reservation in one place:

Step	Action	Result/Notes
1	Choose Site Actions > More Options, choose Filter By: Blank & Custom, and select Custom List. For the name enter Reservations. Select More Options. Click Yes for displaying this list in the Quick Launch bar.	
2	Click Create.	This will redirect you to the main page of your newly created list.

Similar to the previously created custom list, you need to update the columns in this list to capture the appropriate information regarding your reservations, such as client and hardware lookups and a start date and end date for the reservation:

Step	Action	Result/Notes
1	Choose List Settings.	
2	Select Advanced Settings.	This is located under the General Settings grouping.
3	Click the radio button to disable attachments to list items.	This will remove the paper clip icon.
4	Click OK.	
5	Select Title, which is displayed in the Columns section.	Columns A column stores inform Column (click to edit) Title
6	In the Column Name field enter Description and click OK.	You'll now have a required field to describe the reservation. Next you'll create the Lookup columns.

Step	Action	Result/Notes
7	In the Columns section select Create Column. For Column Name enter Client. Choose Lookup. Make it a required field. For the Get Information From drop-down list select Client. For the In This Column drop-down select Full Name. Click OK.	
8	In the Columns section select Create Column. For Column Name enter Hardware. Choose Lookup. Make it a required field. For the Get Information From drop-down select Hardware. For the In This Column drop-down select Title. Click OK.	
9	For Column Name enter Start Date. Choose Date and Time. Make it a required field. For Date and Time Format select Date Only. Click OK.	
10	In the Columns section select Create Column. For Column Name enter End Date. Choose Date and Time. Make it a required field. For Date and Time Format select Date Only. Click OK.	

Good job! Your end users now have a way to track all the vital information to get this application going. Now that you've built that out, we'll jump from SharePoint to Access to show how you can pull in this data and dynamically report on the content, getting up-to-date reports as multiple end users update the tables you just created.

10.2.3 Linked tables: pulling the data into Access

In the previous section you created several tables that you can work with in SharePoint to manage your information. You now want to pull that data into Access so you can generate your reports. To do this you'll use linked tables. There are two types of tables in Access that we cover in this chapter: local and linked. To learn more about the local tables, read the following note or skip to the implementation with SharePoint Server.

> **NOTE**   In the next section, associated with SharePoint Server, we'll cover a different approach to this architecture. For the implementation with SharePoint Server you'll use local tables instead of linked tables and maintain the information using web forms. This can also be done with SharePoint Foundation. Linked tables have many advantages over local tables, but they can't be used with the SharePoint Server's Access Services.

A linked table can dynamically share data between Access and SharePoint. This allows you to pull in the data from SharePoint so you can generate real-time reports. Let's walk through the steps to create your linked table. These steps will need to be completed in Access 2010, not SharePoint. So go ahead and open Access, but make sure you have a connection to your SharePoint environment:

Step	Action	Result/Notes
1	Open Access 2010.	
2	Select the External Data tab.	

Step	Action	Result/Notes
3	Select More in the Import & Link section.	This is next to the ODBC Database option.
4	Select SharePoint List.	A dialog box will appear asking you to specify how you want to store the data in the current database. Make sure the radio button Link to the Data Source by Creating a Linked Table is selected and the URL for your hardware reservations site is entered.
5	Click Next.	You may be prompted for credentials.
6	Click the check boxes for the Clients, Hardware, and Reservations lists and click OK.	Select the lists you want available in the database: | Link	Type	Name
✓		Clients
✓		Hardware
✓		Reservations
		UserInfo	

You now have the data in a format that Access understands, and you didn't have to re-create the tables in Access. You just had to follow some simple steps to pull in the data. This is useful if you need to start reporting on data that's already been stored in various SharePoint sites. A common example of this would be user information stored in a Contacts list across projects. If you need to consolidate that information, one easy approach would be to pull in the information using this method and create a query, which creates a union between the tables. This would prevent you from having to maintain the data in multiple places but still pull it into a central location to report on. In the next section you're going to create a query so you can pull together the data from the different tables and use it to report useful information to the end users.

10.2.4 Client query: integrating the data in the different tables

You now have access to the data using your database, but you need to query across the tables so you can later generate a report containing information about the client, hardware, and reservation that was made.

For the first report you want to show the hardware that's reserved grouped by type. The fields that you want to display are Hardware Type, Hardware ID, Client Name, Email, Phone, Reservation Start Date, and End Date. To do this you'll need to pull information across all three tables:

Step	Action	Result/Notes
1	In Access 2010 select the Create tab.	
2	Select Query Wizard in the Client Queries drop-down list.	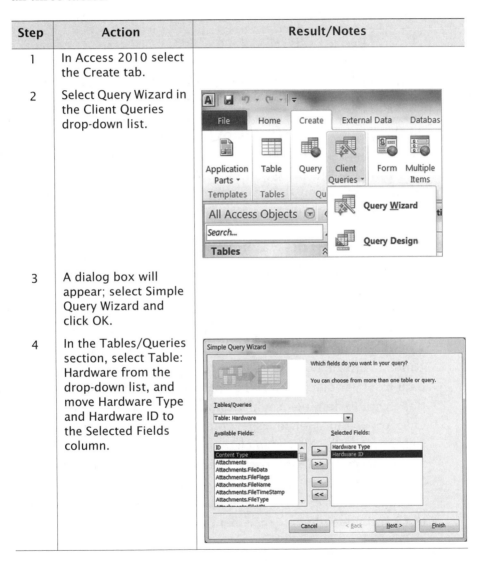
3	A dialog box will appear; select Simple Query Wizard and click OK.	
4	In the Tables/Queries section, select Table: Hardware from the drop-down list, and move Hardware Type and Hardware ID to the Selected Fields column.	

Step	Action	Result/Notes
5	Move Full Name, Email Address, and Business Phone to the Selected Fields column.	
6	Move Start Date and End Date to the Selected Fields column.	
7	Click Next twice.	For the Title enter Hardware Reservations by Type and click Finish.

In this section you created a SQL query using the wizard to pull the information together across the three tables. This will make it easy for you to generate your reports because you now have the logic in place for the information that you want to pull together. Let's see just how easy it is by diving into the next section, where you'll create the report.

10.2.5 Client reports: displaying the data

Reporting is crucial to mining data and getting together valuable information that your end users can understand. If you were to show your clients or manager the raw information in those three tables, it would be cumbersome to look up. If you were to store it all in one table, it would be frustrating and error prone to have to enter the same client contact information for each reservation. Reports help you take the data from various tables and display it dynamically. Some of this can be done with lookup fields and views in SharePoint, which was covered in chapter 3, but I encourage you to play around with these Access reports as well. You'll quickly find that they can provide additional functionality to pull information across sites and site collections as well as enhanced reporting options to create appealing reports and to share the data. In this example you'll create a simple report using the wizard, but I recommend you experiment more once you finish this exercise to continue learning about the power of Access 2010:

Step	Action	Result/Notes
1	In Access 2010 select the Create tab.	
2	Select Report.	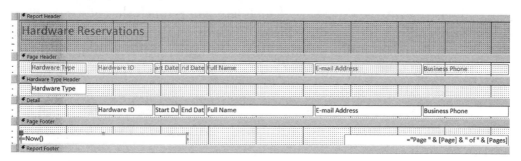
3	Select Query Hardware Reservations and add all available fields by clicking >>.	
4	Select to view your data by Hardware Type and click Next.	
5	Click Next twice more and select Landscape for the orientation.	
6	Click Next again, enter Hardware Reservations by Type, and click Finish.	

At this point you'll need to do some formatting to get your report to fit the page. I'm not going to walk you through this step by step; play around with the boxes in the layout view, shown in figure 10.4. You can select the boxes and resize them until you get your report in a format that you want.

Figure 10.4 Hardware Reservations report by type in layout view. Using this view you can select boxes and move them around and/or resize them until you get the design that you're aiming for.

Hardware Reservations by Type						Monday, April 12, 2010 12:27:08 AM	
Hardware	Hardware ID	Name	Email	Phone	Start Date	End Date	
Laptop							
	Laptop01	Jane Doe	janedoe@nowhere.com	867-5309	4/30/2010	4/30/2010	
Server							
	Server02	John Doe	johndoe@nowhere.com	867-5309	4/27/2010	11/30/2010	
	Server02	John Doe	johndoe@nowhere.com	867-5309	4/10/2010	7/31/2010	
	Server02	John Doe	johndoe@nowhere.com	867-5309	4/22/2010	4/24/2010	
4							

Page 1 of 1

Figure 10.5 The Hardware Reservations by Type report can dynamically pull data from the three SharePoint lists and display it as shown.

With six simple steps you should now have a report that looks similar to figure 10.5.

See how easy it is to create reports? I suggest that you run though the Report Wizard again and see what other reports you can create by doing some brainstorming and playing around with the additional features. Once you save the report you generated, you can open this Access database at any time to rerun the report on the information that's been entered into your SharePoint list.

Now that you understand how to create linked tables, queries, and reports, we'll discuss how you can take this further using Access Services in conjunction with SharePoint Server. Many of the features other than Access Services, which lets you publish the information to SharePoint, are still available to the end users as long as they have Access 2010. So I encourage you to continue reading even if you have SharePoint Foundation, so you can get a better understanding of Access 2010 functionality.

10.3 Using Access Services with SharePoint Server

We've discussed how to create this scenario with SharePoint Foundation and Access Client, and you can continue to use this approach even if you have SharePoint Server. An alternate approach would be to manage the data using local tables instead of a SharePoint list. You might be wondering why that would provide you an advantage and how you could provide an easy way for your end users to enter the data. The advantage of using a local table is that you can then use the web reports to publish the information to SharePoint and allow your end users to dynamically access this information without having to own Access 2010. This can be extremely helpful when you need to provide Access functionality to end users but you aren't certain what software they have installed. If they don't have Office or a version with Access installed, they won't be able to run the reports. You could also use web forms, which can be published to SharePoint so your end users can enter data into the local tables. Let's begin by creating your local tables to manage hardware, clients, and reservations.

10.3.1 Local tables: managing the data in Access

You want to create a table to manage your clients. To do this you create a local table in Access. Then you create the web forms that will allow your end users to easily maintain the data in these tables, without having to open Access:

Step	Action	Result/Notes
1	In Access 2010, choose File > New > Blank Web Database. Click Save, and for the table name enter Clients.	

Step	Action	Result/Notes
2	On the Click to Add drop-down list, select Text, and Access will add a text column that by default will be labeled Field1.	Field1 ▾ / Click to Add ▾ AB Text 12 Number 🖳 Currency 📆 Date & Time ☑ Yes/No 🏛 Lookup & Relationship AB Memo 📎 Attachment 🌐 Hyperlink Calculated Field Paste as Fields
3	Double-click Field1 to select it and enter FullName for the label.	Field1 Click to Add ▾
4	Repeat steps 2 and 3 twice, but name the two new columns Email and Phone.	

Now that you've created this list, let's create another local table that will store the information pertaining to the hardware that can be reserved:

Step	Action	Result/Notes
1	In Access 2010 choose Create > Table. Click Save, and for the table name enter Hardware.	

Step	Action	Result/Notes
2	On the Click to Add drop-down list, select Text, and Access will add a text column that by default will be labeled Field1.	Field1 · Click to Add · AB Text 12 Number Currency Date & Time Yes/No Lookup & Relationship AB Memo Attachment Hyperlink Calculated Field Paste as Fields
3	Double-click Field1 to select it, and enter Hardware Type for the label.	Field1 Click to Add ·
4	Repeat steps 2 and 3 one more time, but name the new column Hardware ID.	

You'll now create your last local table. This one manages the reservations and the associated client and hardware information from the list you've already created:

Step	Action	Result/Notes
1	In Access 2010 choose Create > Table. Click Save, and for the table name enter Reservations.	

Step	Action	Result/Notes
2	On the Click to Add drop-down list, select Lookup & Relationship, and a dialog box will appear. Leave the first page at its default settings, and click Next.	
3	Select the Clients table, and go to the next step.	
4	Select Name, and go to the next step. Leave the defaults, and click Next twice more until you're on the final screen.	
5	For the label enter Client.	
6	Repeat steps 2–5, but name the new column Hardware ID, and connect to the Hardware table and select Hardware ID.	
7	For the last two fields select Click to Add and select Date & Time.	This will add a Date & Time column, which by default will be labeled Field1.
8	Double-click Field1 to select it, and enter Start Date for the label.	Do this one more time to create the End Date column.

You've now created local tables in Access similar to those you created in the previous section as lists when you were implementing SharePoint

Foundation. The benefit of using SharePoint is that it provides a nice web interface for your end users to work with the information. A local table in Access won't do that without some additional configuration. In the next section we'll walk through how to do this by creating web forms. It's an additional step, but don't worry; it doesn't take much effort.

10.3.2 Web forms: entering data using a web form

Because we don't want our end users opening the database to work with the data, we'll provide a friendlier way of managing the information using web forms. We'll begin by creating a web form that's linked to each of the tables that we've created. Later we'll publish these forms to our SharePoint site, so end users can quickly get to them to enter the client, hardware, and reservation information. Let's get started with creating your first web form:

Step	Action	Result/Notes
1	In Access 2010 choose Create > Blank Form.	
2	Click Show All Tables to get a list of tables that can be added to the form on the right side of your screen.	
3	Expand Clients and double-click Name, Email, and Phone.	This will add these fields to your form. Once your web form is published to the web, additional controls will be available so you can manage the data.
4	Save the form as Manage Clients.	

Figure 10.6 Record Management options in Access 2010 when publishing your tables using web forms

Once you've finished creating the form, it won't show the management features to let you flip though the records and add a new record. Later when you publish the form and save using Access Services, these features will appear for the end user, as shown in figure 10.6.

Now that you've created your form to manage the client information, you need to do something similar for hardware and reservations. You'll create the Manage Hardware form next:

Step	Action	Result/Notes
1	In Access 2010 choose Create > Blank Form.	
2	Available tables that can be added to the form will display in the Field List shown on the right side of your screen.	Field List ☒ Show only fields in the current record source Fields available in other tables: ⊞ Clients Edit Table
3	Expand Hardware and double-click Hardware Type and Hardware ID.	This will add these fields to your form. Once this form is published to the web, additional controls will be available so you can manage the data.
4	Save the form as Manage Hardware.	

The final form that you need to create is the form to maintain the hardware reservations. This is important so you can capture the information from the hardware and client tables and associate it with start and end dates for the requested reservation:

Step	Action	Result/Notes
1	In Access 2010 choose Create > Blank Form.	
2	Available tables that can be added to the form will display in the Field List shown on the right side of your screen.	
3	Expand Reservations, and double-click Client, Hardware ID, Start Date, and End Date.	This will add these fields to your form. Once the form is published to the web, additional controls will be available so you can manage the data.
4	Save the form as Manage Reservations.	

That extra step wasn't too bad, was it? Now that you've done that, you'll be able to use these web forms in your Access web application to publish to a SharePoint site. This will allow your end users to leverage the power of Access without having Access. You now want to prep the data from these tables for your reports. To do this, you'll need to create a SQL query that pulls the information together so you can then view it in a report.

10.3.3 Web query: generating a web query

This section guides you through some simple steps for creating a web query. A query provides the capability to pull together the data from the three local tables that you created. This will be used for your report in the next section, so you can easily report on the reservation and pull in important client information and hardware information:

Step	Action	Result/Notes
1	In Access 2010 choose Create > Query.	
2	A dialog box will pop up and list the tables that you can select. Make sure you add Clients, Hardware, and Reservations.	
3	Save the query and name it *Hardware Operations Query*.	
4	In the Hardware table double-click Hardware Type and Hardware ID.	
5	In the Clients table double-click Name, Email, and Phone.	
6	In the Reservations table double-click Start Date and End Date.	Save your query.

You now have the tables, the web forms to manage the tables, and the query to pull all the information together. This is a good time to start creating your reports. In this next section you'll create two web reports so you can see your reservations by type and client.

10.3.4 Web reports: generating reports to see reservations by type and client

The first report you'll create will be grouped by hardware type. This will help you to quickly look at how many servers have reservations, for example. The other type of report that you'll create will be grouped by client. This will allow you to quickly see how many reservations a client has made:

Step	Action	Result/Notes
1	From the design view of the Hardware Operations Query select Run.	
2	Select Create > Report.	
3	Select Group & Sort from the Ribbon under the Design tab.	
4	Select Add a Group.	This option will display at the bottom of the screen.
5.	Select Hardware Type for the field to group on.	
6	Resize the fields so they fit nicely on the page.	
7	Click Save, and enter *Hardware Reservations by Type* for the name.	

Now that you've created a report by hardware type, we'll focus on doing something similar but group it instead by client. To do this follow the previous steps, but select Client for step 5, and for step 7 save it as Hardware Reservations by Client. You now have all the individual components for your Access web application. You just need to tie it all together, and you'll do this in the next section using a navigation web form.

10.3.5 Navigation web form: tying your reports and forms together

The navigation web form that you'll create will have tabs on the top and on the right side of the screen. This will allow you to display your reports and web forms to manage the information using two menus. It will consolidate the information so your end users need to remember only one URL, which defaults to the navigation web form. From there they can navigate to the individual components:

Step	Action	Result/Notes
1	Select Create > Navigation > Horizontal Tabs and Vertical Tabs, Right.	
2	Locate Hardware Reservations by Type in the Reports section, and drag and drop it onto the first horizontal tab, labeled [Add New].	
3	Repeat step 2 for the report Hardware Reservations by Client.	

Step	Action	Result/Notes
4	Locate the Manage Reservations form, and drag and drop it onto the first vertical tab, labeled [Add New].	
5	Repeat step 4 for the Manage Hardware and Manage Clients forms.	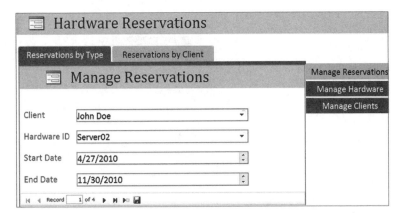
6	Double-click Navigation Form and enter the title *Hardware Reservations*.	
7	Save the form as *Hardware Reservations*.	

Now that you've created your navigation web form, your finished form should look like the one in figure 10.7.

Figure 10.7 The Navigation web form will provide horizontal and vertical menu navigation to allow your end users to navigate between the reports and web forms that you created.

You're almost finished. Although you have everything in place, you still need to publish this to SharePoint so your end users don't have to own Access 2010 to start working with the data. It's also a good idea to not give them direct access to the database so they can't start mucking around. To do this, you're going to use Access Services. Let's get started.

10.3.6 Access Services: publishing your data to SharePoint

Access Services will allow you to publish the web application that you create in Access 2010 so your end users can work with the reports and dynamically manage the information within the tables. This doesn't require them to own Access 2010 and can be very useful when you don't have control over what software your end users have. To publish you need to complete the following four simple steps:

Step	Action	Result/Notes
1	In Access 2010 choose File > Options.	

Step	Action	Result/Notes
2	Select Current Database. For Web Display Form select Hardware Reservations.	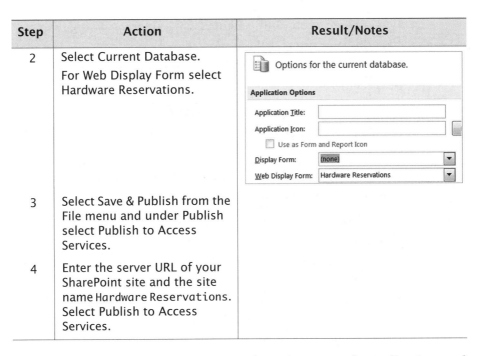
3	Select Save & Publish from the File menu and under Publish select Publish to Access Services.	
4	Enter the server URL of your SharePoint site and the site name *Hardware Reservations*. Select Publish to Access Services.	

Congratulations! You've just created an Access web application and published it to SharePoint so any of your end users will have the ability to get to these reports to dynamically work with the data. Now that you're finished with this, let's discuss what you've learned.

10.4 Summary

Following is a summary to help you understand the functionality that you should now be comfortable with implementing from completing this scenario:

- Creating a custom list and working with the contact list in Share-Point
- Pulling the data into Access from SharePoint using a linked table
- Creating local tables in Access
- Creating web forms in Access to manage the data in the local tables

- Generating web and client SQL queries using Access 2010's friendly user interface
- Providing web and client reports on the data stored in the local and/or web tables
- Leveraging a navigational web form
- Publishing your Access web application to SharePoint using Access Services

Let's test your knowledge. A couple of questions that you should be able to answer are these:

- What are some of the advantages and disadvantages of using a linked table over a local table to SharePoint?

  Advantage: A table linked to a SharePoint list allows you to connect to data that already exists.

  Advantage: A linked table enables you to take advantage of the SharePoint user interface to work with the data.

  Disadvantage: A linked table can't be used in a web report or query, but a local table can.

- What are some of the advantages and disadvantages of implementing with Access versus Access Services?

  Advantage: If you're running the client, you'll have more capabilities in creating client reports and queries than if you're using a web report or query.

  Disadvantage: To leverage the client features, your end users must have a valid install of Access to use the system.

This chapter along with the information you learned in chapter 4 regarding the use of document libraries and views will empower you with the tools to report on the information that's being stored. In the next chapter we'll cover search, My Sites, cross-site configuration, and site-collection capabilities.

Pulling it all together with search, My Sites, and cross-site functionality

This chapter covers

- *Search options, web parts, centers*
- *My Sites*
- *Site collections versus subsites*
- *Content Query web part*
- *RSS*
- *Site Aggregator*
- *Permissions*
- *Reporting*

This chapter is a bit unique, in the sense that we're going to focus on technologies that span sites and site collections and we're going to discuss site collection administrator features. The core focus of this book is on site owners, and the scenarios are based on building out a singular site. This chapter introduces you to concepts for functionality that will span sites and can be configured if you're a site collection administrator. The first section focuses on

Search. The second focuses on cross-site functionality, which is something you can do as a site owner of many sites. The third part focuses on site collection administrator capabilities. We'll finish it off by discussing My Site functionality. You won't build out full scenarios for all of these items, but we will use the scenarios that you've already built to help you get an idea of how each of these new features you're learning could be used to enhance those sites.

11.1   Search

One of the core features that you need to understand when working with SharePoint is search. Search is a critical mechanism that's used for finding information. Depending on which edition of SharePoint you have, search comes with many different options.

Site Search is the only feature available in SharePoint Foundation; it lets you search the current site or list. It has been improved from previous versions, allowing you to refine your search results. New or improved features that are available with SharePoint Server Standard are as follows:

- *Search scopes*—This allows you to define a subset of information to search. For example, you may want to set up a scope to search blog sites but nothing else. An example of a scope is shown in figure 11.1.

- *Social behavior–based relevance*—This increases the rank that a document has based on the number of user clicks on the item.

- *Social tags*—These let you quickly add metadata to improve search results. Tagging options are shown in figure 11.2.

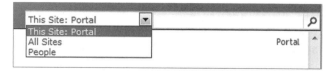

Figure 11.1 Example of search scope for searching the current site, all sites, or people

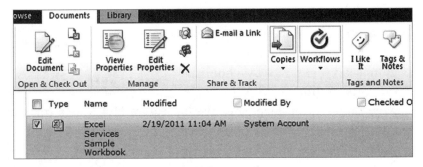

Figure 11.2 Example of a user selecting a document and having tagging options displayed

- *Taxonomy tag integration*—This is the ability to refine results based on tags.
- *View in browser*—This enables you to view the document in the browser without having to open up the Office client application.

In the Enterprise version of SharePoint, the new features include all these features plus the following:

- *Similar results*—This is the ability to view additional results based on items that are similar to what you searched for.
- *Sorting on custom properties*—This lets you define custom properties to sort your data on.
- *Thumbnails and previews*—The search results will show a thumbnail preview of the item, as shown in figure 11.3.
- *Visual best bets*—This is the ability to associate an image with a search keyword.

Along with the default search that's available when you create a SharePoint site, you also have the ability to create a Search Center, which we'll discuss in the next section.

Figure 11.3 Example of a visual thumbnail preview

11.1.1 Search Center

As a site collection administrator, you have the ability to modify your search settings by choosing the Site Actions > Site Settings page on your top-level site. We'll dive into the different options in greater detail in section 11.1.2, but for now I want to discuss how you find out what your current search settings are, to determine if you want to create a Search Center. Once you're on the Site Settings page, under the Site Collection Administration section, you'll see the following search configurations: Search Settings, Search Scopes, and Search Keywords. This is shown in figure 11.4.

Site Collection Administration
Search settings
Search scopes
Search keywords

Figure 11.4 Search configurations

To configure your search settings to span site collections, you'll need to create a Search Center. One may already exist by default, or you can create a new one and configure it. To do this you would select one of the Search Center templates shown in figure 11.5: Basic Search Center, Enterprise Search Center, or FAST Search Center.

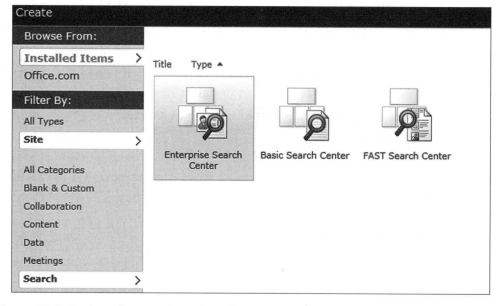

Figure 11.5 Options for creating a Search Center

The FAST Search Center is part of the Enterprise license (purchase of FAST Search Server 2010 for SharePoint is needed), and the Basic and Enterprise Search Centers are both part of the Standard license. The key difference between the Basic and Enterprise Search Centers is that in Enterprise, the people search page is part of the search results, shown as a tab on the Search Center homepage. Now that you're aware of how to create a Search Center, let's discuss the search web parts.

11.1.2 Search web parts

In addition to creating a Search Center, you can add and configure search web parts on your site's page. Often people will do this to customize their Search Center experience, but you can also do it for a regular SharePoint site. For example, you could have added a search box to the business proposal site that you built in chapter 4. I'll walk you through the steps for doing this. If you have your site built out for chapter 4 and available, feel free to follow along.

In the scenario in chapter 4 you created a Proposal Reviews site. Figure 11.6 should jog your memory.

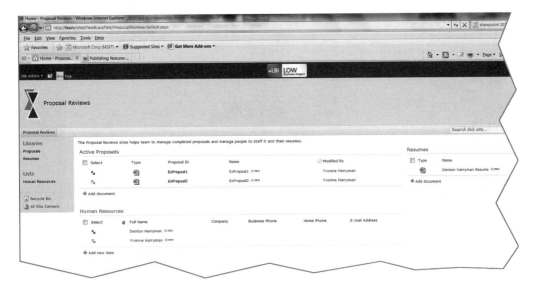

Figure 11.6 Proposal Reviews site created in chapter 4

Figure 11.7 New Scope option in the Search Scopes settings

In the next series of steps you're going to create two new scopes and add a search box at the top of the homepage, so you can quickly search those two scopes to find certain documents. The scopes you'll be creating are for the proposals and resumes. To do this, choose Site Actions > Site Settings and select Search Scopes from the Site Collection Administration group. At the top of the page you'll see an option to create a New Scope, as shown in figure 11.7.

The first one you'll create is the Proposals scope, as shown in figure 11.8. Enter a descriptive name and a description for your scope. Select the Search Dropdown check box and use the default Search Results Page. Click OK.

Next, you'll need to configure your scope. Click the Add Rules link to the right of the scope that you just created. You're going to tie it to a new scope rule where you enter a web address that points to the URL for the proposal's Document library. This is shown in figure 11.9.

Title and Description	Title: *
Type a unique title and description for your scope. The title is displayed in the search dropdown, search results pages, advanced search, and elsewhere.	Proposals Description: Search for proposals Last modified by: SPDEV\Administrator
Display Groups Select scope groups in which you would like to include this scope. Select as many scope groups as you want.	☑ Search Dropdown ☐ Advanced Search
Target Results Page Specify a specific search results page to send users to for results when they search in this scope, or choose to use the default.	⦿ Use the default Search Results Page ○ Specify a different page for searching this scope Target results page: *
	OK Cancel

Figure 11.8 Creating the Proposals scope

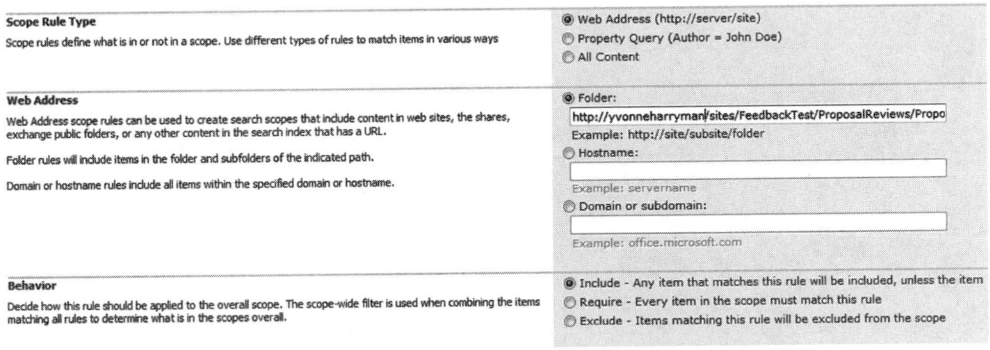

Figure 11.9 Configuration settings for the Proposals scope

You now need to duplicate the steps that you took to create the Proposals scope and create a Resumes scope. Once you've done that, you can create a new display group. Select Display Groups, which is the option next to the New Scope option in the Search Scopes settings; then select New Display Group. The display group will be configured as shown in figure 11.10, with the Proposals search scope being the first one displayed in the drop-down list. In this example I called the display group Proposals.

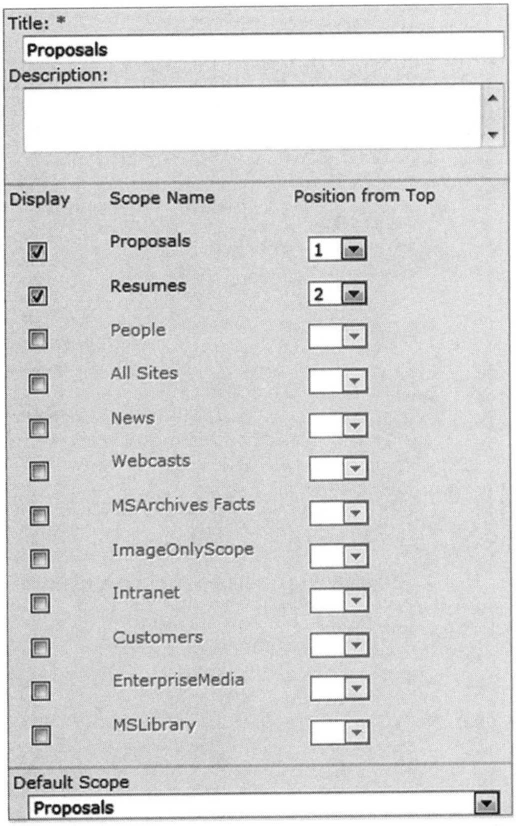

Next, you'll modify the homepage of the proposal reviews scenario by editing the page and adding an Advanced Search box at the

Figure 11.10 Settings for the display group

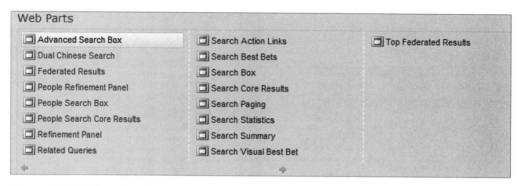

Figure 11.11 Search web parts

top. In figure 11.11 you can see all the different search web parts available to you.

Figure 11.12 shows the Search Box web part added to the page. To see and configure the Scope drop-down list, you'll need to edit the web part as shown in figure 11.12.

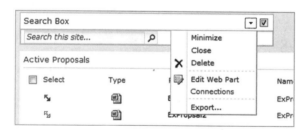

Figure 11.12 Advanced Search Box web part

Once in you're in edit mode, you can select Dropdown Mode, which displays the search scopes, expand the Miscellaneous section, and set Scope Display Group to your newly created display group, as shown in figure 11.13.

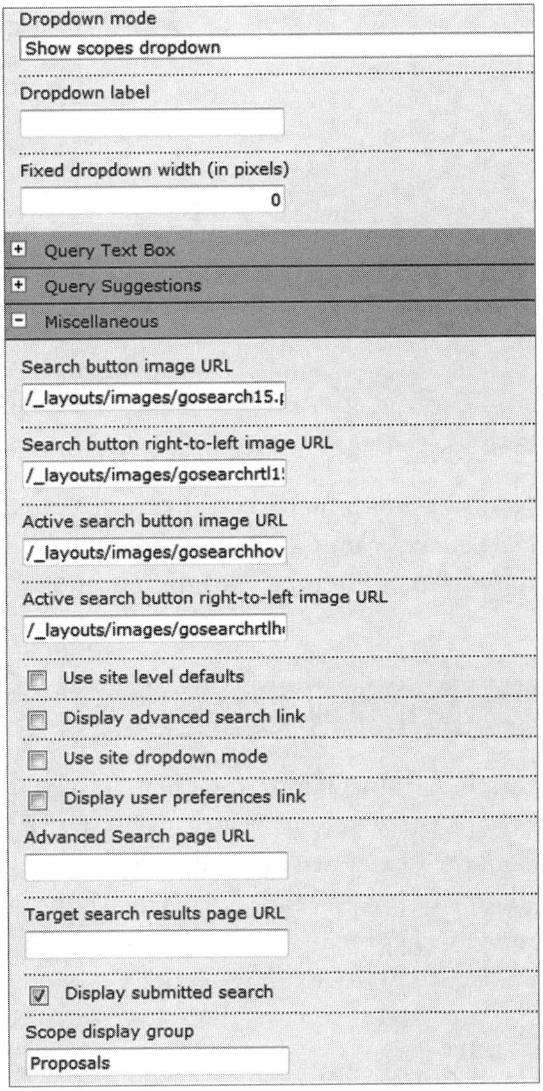

Figure 11.13 Advanced Search Box web part properties

Now that you've completed the steps, the scenario in Chapter 4 for proposal reviews should show a search box at the top of the page, as shown in figure 11.14, which will help your end users quickly search for proposals or reviews. This may be very handy for you depending on the number of proposals or resumes you're planning to upload.

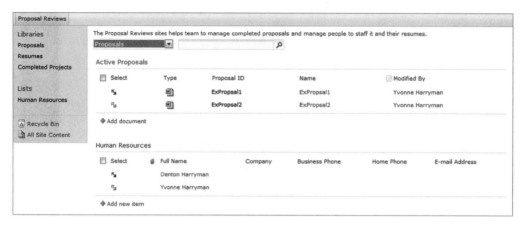

Figure 11.14 Proposal Reviews homepage with the advanced search box added

This should give you a good idea of how you can use search to enhance your websites and find sites across sites and site collections. Next, let's talk about some commonly used, additional site configurations that can span sites.

11.2 Cross-site configurations

There are options for pulling information together across sites; the three that we'll focus on are the Content Query web part, RSS, and Site Aggregator. The Content Query web part can span sites within a site collection to pull data. The RSS and Site Aggregator can pull across many site collections to aggregate data. We'll show an example of each and how you can use it in the next few sections.

11.2.1 Content Query web part

The Content Query web part enables you to pull data based on list and content type. We'll walk through a brief example where you could use this web part for your fictional company, Durante Inc. They're a consulting firm, and for this scenario you're going to pretend they have three divisions that specialize in IT consulting. Those three are Share-Point, .NET, and Java. Each consulting division would like to have its own subsite under the main portal. One unique item that headquarters would like each division to share is the latest projects they're working on. We'll walk through an implementation of this, using the Content Query web part.

To start, you'll need to create an announcements list for each division's subsite. Before we dive into that, I want to mention Site Features. Site Features can be found on the Site Settings page under Site Actions. You can configure this as a site owner or site administrator. For example, if you had created a publishing site, you'd see a subset of the web parts, because the team collaboration list won't be enabled by default. To turn this on, view your site features and activate Team Collaboration Lists, as shown in figure 11.15.

Hopefully you didn't have to do that step, but if you did, you should now see the Announcements option when you go to create a list. For each site, .NET, Java, and SharePoint, you'll create an announcements list and call it Latest Projects, as shown in figure 11.16.

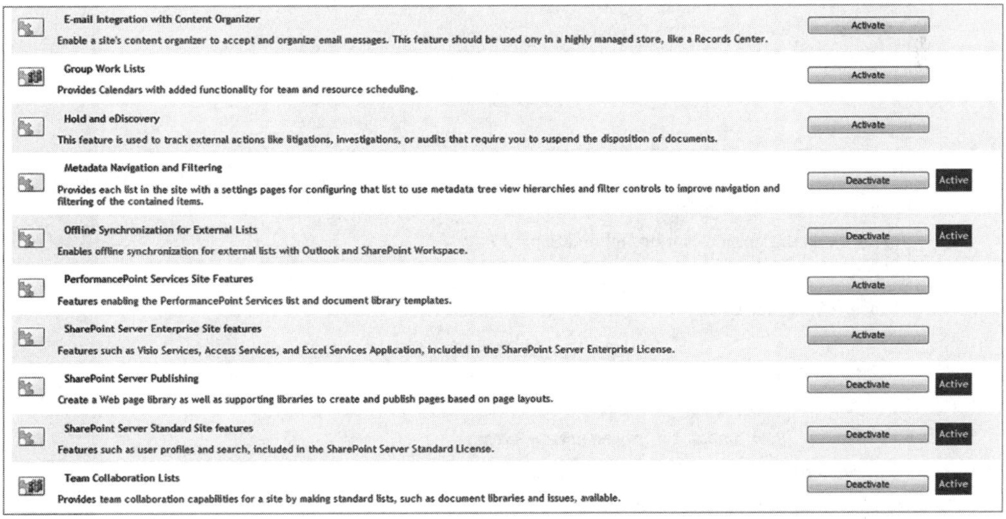

Figure 11.15 Activating Team Collaboration Lists, so additional options are available on the site

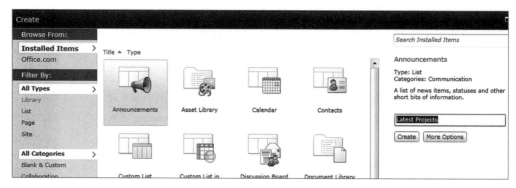

Figure 11.16 Creating an announcements list

One item that I changed so the content will be pulled into a format that the content query understands is the setting for the Body column (List tab > List Settings > Body). I changed the default to plain text, as shown in figure 11.17.

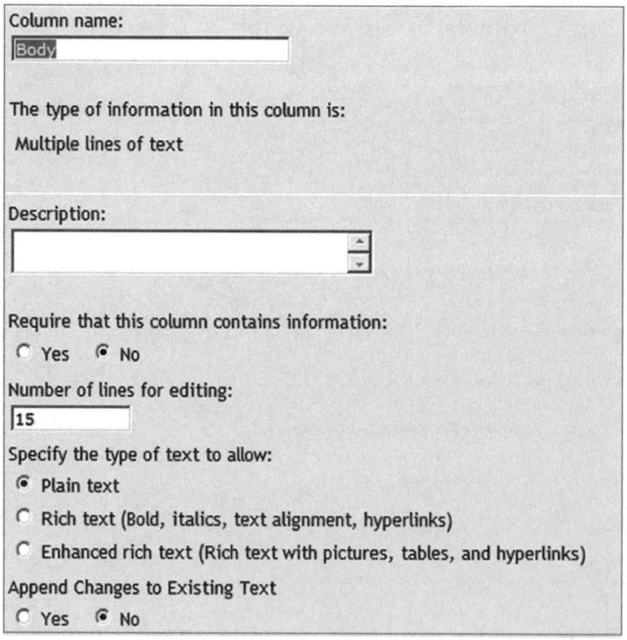

Column name:

Body

The type of information in this column is:

Multiple lines of text

Description:

Require that this column contains information:

○ Yes   ● No

Number of lines for editing:

15

Specify the type of text to allow:

● Plain text

○ Rich text (Bold, italics, text alignment, hyperlinks)

○ Enhanced rich text (Rich text with pictures, tables, and hyperlinks)

Append Changes to Existing Text

○ Yes   ● No

Figure 11.17 Modifying the default properties for the announcements list

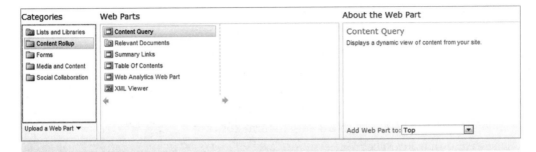

Figure 11.18 Content Rollup web parts

Once you've completed this for all three subsites, you can move on to the next series of steps, which will involve configuring the content query. You can find this under the Content Rollup category for creating a web part, as shown in figure 11.18. You'll want to configure this in the top site of the subsites that were created for the .NET, Java, and SharePoint sites. Once you've added the web part to the page, you'll then configure it.

The configuration settings are shown in figures 11.19 and 11.20. You're going to configure the web part to show all items from the

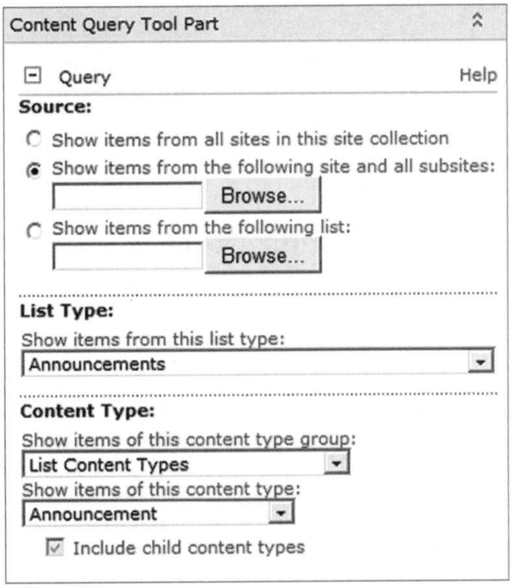

Figure 11.19 Content Rollup web part properties

top-level site and subsites. You'll set List
Type to Announcements and configure the
Content Type to Announcement. This scenario works well for you because you're not
creating additional announcements lists. If
that wasn't the case for you, you could configure this to pull from a custom content
type that you created.

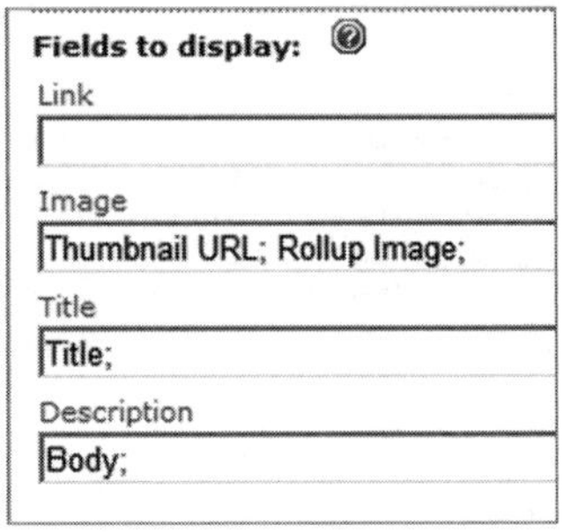

Fields to display: ⓘ
Link

Image
Thumbnail URL; Rollup Image;

Title
Title;

Description
Body;

Figure 11.20 Setting the content query fields

In addition to the configuration changes,
you may also need to modify the fields that
you'd like to display. I changed the
Description field in the Presentation section to pull in Body, as shown
in figure 11.20.

Once you've completed these actions, your content query should display, assuming you've entered some announcements, as shown in figure 11.21.

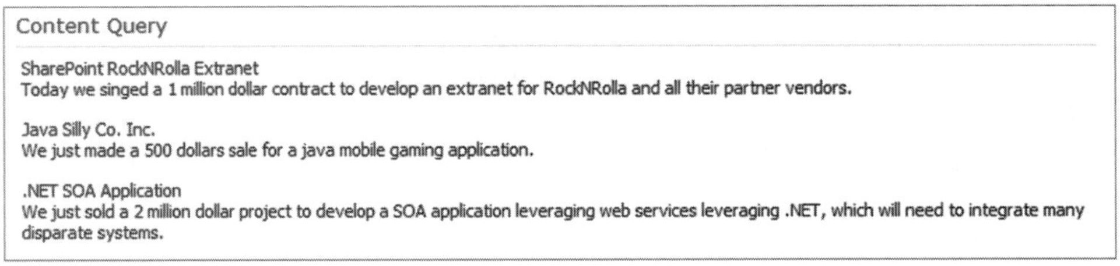

Content Query

SharePoint RockNRolla Extranet
Today we singed a 1 million dollar contract to develop an extranet for RockNRolla and all their partner vendors.

Java Silly Co. Inc.
We just made a 500 dollars sale for a java mobile gaming application.

.NET SOA Application
We just sold a 2 million dollar project to develop a SOA application leveraging web services leveraging .NET, which will need to integrate many
disparate systems.

Figure 11.21 Content query in action

Good job! You now have the basics of the Content Query web part.
Let's discuss another content roll-up option called RSS.

11.2.2 RSS

RSS not only enables you to pull in data from other lists, but it also
allows you to pull it in from other websites if your SharePoint site is
exposed to the internet. In this example, shown in figure 11.22, you'll

add the RSS view to the Microsoft Share-Point Certification Club that you created in chapter 8. You'll do this by adding an RSS web part and configuring it to pull from the Microsoft SharePoint team blog.

Once you've added and configured the RSS web part, the scenario you created in chapter 8 should look similar to figure 11.23.

That was easy enough! The last example that we'll discuss for content aggregation is the Site Aggregator.

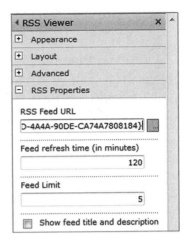

Figure 11.22 RSS web part settings

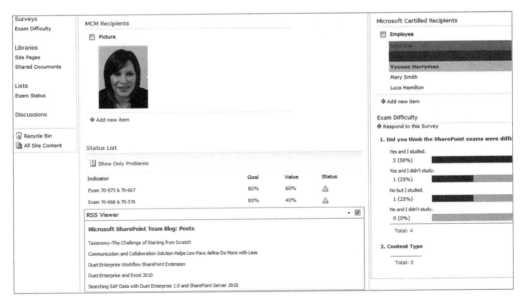

Figure 11.23 Microsoft SharePoint Certification Club example

11.2.3 Site Aggregator

This popular tool was widely used in SharePoint 2007. At the time of my writing this, there was a known problem: it didn't display the Add New Tab icon. If you have the latest cumulative update installed this should be fixed for you. In the event that you don't, here's a work-around I found when adding the Site Aggregator to my My Site > My Content page. I opened it in SharePoint Designer and in the code view modified the ShowMemberships property to be equal to True. I could then see the Add New Tab option, as shown in figure 11.24.

Figure 11.24 Site Aggregator

You can now add your sites using the Add New Tab button. Once you click Add New Tab, you'll see two ways to add a site. In this example I'm adding links to the other sites that we created in this book, as shown in figure 11.25.

Site Aggregator

My Site

Create a new site tab

○ Select site from Memberships list

● Type SharePoint site URL and name

Site URL

http://yvonneharryman/sites/BICenter/Pages/Default.aspx

Site Name

Chapter 7

| Create | Cancel |

Figure 11.25 Example for adding a SharePoint site using the Site Aggregator

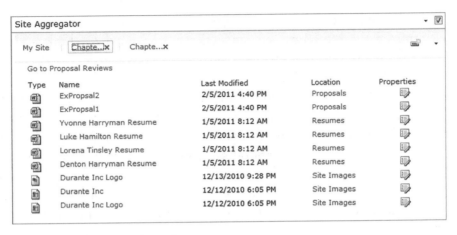

Figure 11.26 Site Aggregator in action

Once you add a site, the content will be pulled in, as shown in figure 11.26. This allows you to quickly see the content associated with this site.

Now that you have a good understanding of how to view data across sites and site collections, let's discuss some other aspects that are handy to know as a site collection administrator.

11.3 Site collection administrator capabilities

This section discusses some broader topics such as information architecture and its relation to site collections and sites. We'll also cover reporting, access requests, and permissions.

11.3.1 Information architecture

A key question that often comes up is the difference between a site collection and subsites. A site collection is a container of data with shared resources, such as navigation, permissions, site templates, reports, and branding. If you're never going to span beyond 100 GB (depending on usage scenarios this could go up some) of data, you could keep all of your data within one site collection, and from an administrative perspective you could share the majority of your resources. But to scale you need to break out your sites into many site collections. Once you start to create many site collections, you need to think about your information architecture and start to break out sites based on shared elements. For example, you may want all division portals to stay within your portal site collections and all team sites to stay in a team site collection. This is the most common scenario you'll find. You can break this down even further by creating a site collection for project sites or other variants of collaboration sites. I typically don't recommend breaking out site collections by your organization, although that's commonly done. Eventually your organization will change, and you'll need to move sites around. Often your site templates and branding elements will be the same regardless of organization, because they're geared more toward the function.

It's important when starting out with SharePoint that you spend some time up front strategizing on the different options and weighing the pros and cons of the various approaches. In the next section, we'll discuss the Web Analytics reporting capabilities.

11.3.2 Web Analytics reports

In SharePoint 2010 Web Analytics was introduced for reporting purposes. You now have access to more powerful reports and also the ability to create custom reports. To get to them navigate to your Site Settings page, and under Site Actions you'll see two options to view Web Analytics reports, as shown in figure 11.27.

Figure 11.27
Site Actions reporting options

If you were to select the Site Web Analytics Reports option for a site, you'd be presented with the Summary report shown in figure 11.28; additional reports that are available are shown on the left side of the page.

Site Web Analytics Reports - Summary

This report shows all of the available Web Analytics metrics for the date range specified, as well as the change trend from the preceding date range.

Date Range 2/9/2011 - 3/10/2011 (UTC-08:00) Pacific Time (US and Canada) Change Settings

Summary
Traffic
Number of Page Views
Number of Daily Unique Visitors
Number of Referrers
Top Pages
Top Visitors
Top Referrers
Top Destinations
Top Browsers

Inventory
Number of Sites
Top Site Product Versions
Top Site Languages

Data Last Updated: 3/10/2011 2:00:19 AM

Category	Metrics	Value (Current)	Value (Previous)	Trend
Traffic				
	Total Number of Page Views	15	0	-
	Average Number of Page Views per Day	0	0	-
	Total Number of Daily Unique Visitors	5	0	-
	Average Number of Unique Visitors per Day	0	0	-
	Total Number of Referrers	1	0	-
	Average Number of Referrers per Day	0	0	-
Inventory				
	Total Number of Sites	-	-	-

Figure 11.28 Site Web Analytics Reports

If you were to select the Site Collection Web Analytics Reports option for a site, you'd be presented with the Summary report shown in figure 11.29; additional reports are shown in the left column.

You now understand reporting and the core management differences between site collections and subsites, so let's get into the nitty-gritty of permissions.

Site Collection Web Analytics Reports - Summary

This report shows all of the available Web Analytics metrics for the date range specified, as well as the change trend from the preceding date range.

Date Range 2/9/2011 - 3/10/2011 (UTC-08:00) Pacific Time (US and Canada) Change Settings

Summary
Traffic
Number of Page Views
Number of Daily Unique Visitors
Number of Referrers
Top Pages
Top Visitors
Top Referrers
Top Destinations
Top Browsers

Search
Number of Queries
Top Queries
Failed Queries
Best Bet Usage
Best Bet Suggestions
Best Bet Suggestions Action History
Search keywords

Inventory
Storage Usage

Data Last Updated: 3/10/2011 2:00:19 AM

Category	Metrics	Value (Current)	Value (Previous)	Trend
Traffic				
	Total Number of Page Views	15	0	-
	Average Number of Page Views per Day	0	0	-
	Total Number of Daily Unique Visitors	5	0	-
	Average Number of Unique Visitors per Day	0	0	-
	Total Number of Referrers	1	0	-
	Average Number of Referrers per Day	0	0	-
Search				
	Total Number of Search Queries	0	0	-
	Average Number of Search Queries per Day	0	0	-
Inventory				
	Total Number of Sites	-	-	-
	Total Storage Used (MB)	-	-	-

Figure 11.29 Site Collection Web Analytics Reports

11.3.3 Managing access requests

Assuming email has been configured for the form you're using, you'll see an option for managing access requests on the site permissions page. You can configure this at the site collection level or at the subsite level. This will allow your end users to request access to your site if they try to go to the site and are denied access. An example of configuring this is shown in figure 11.30 and figure 11.31.

Figure 11.30 Configuring access requests

When you select the option Manage Access Request, you can set it to a specific email address. If you have a distribution list, you should tie it to that versus a specific user. This is good practice in case the site owner leaves the company or switches roles.

You're now ready to grant the user access, so let's discuss how you should manage the permissions that will be tied to that user.

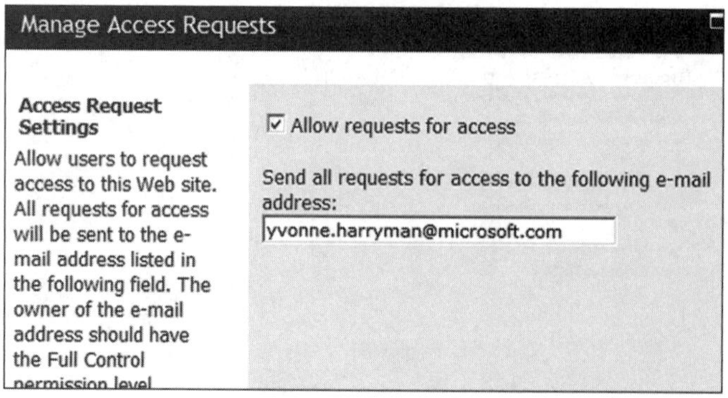

Manage Access Requests

Access Request Settings

Allow users to request access to this Web site. All requests for access will be sent to the e-mail address listed in the following field. The owner of the e-mail address should have the Full Control permission level

☑ Allow requests for access

Send all requests for access to the following e-mail address:

yvonne.harryman@microsoft.com

Figure 11.31 Linking access requests to an email address

11.3.4 Custom permissions

In the Site Actions bar for your site, you can select the option to manage permissions. This can also be found on your Site Settings page. When you create a site and view the permissions, you'll find the default groups created for you and tied to a default permission level, as shown in figure 11.32.

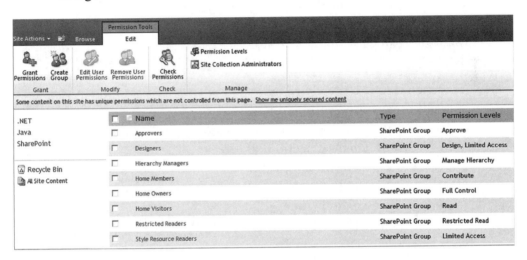

Figure 11.32 Default SharePoint groups and their permission levels

If you select the Permission Levels option, as shown in the Ribbon of figure 11.32, you'll see all the default permission levels. Notice that you can select one of the permission levels, with the exception of Full Control, and modify it, or you can add a new permission level. This is shown in figure 11.33.

	Permission Level	Description
☐	Full Control	Has full control.
☐	Design	Can view, add, update, delete, approve, and customize.
☐	Contribute	Can view, add, update, and delete list items and documents.
☐	Read	Can view pages and list items and download documents.
☐	Limited Access	Can view specific lists, document libraries, list items, folders, or documents when given permissions.
☐	Approve	Can edit and approve pages, list items, and documents.
☐	Manage Hierarchy	Can create sites and edit pages, list items, and documents.
☐	Restricted Read	Can view pages and documents, but cannot view historical versions or user permissions.

Figure 11.33 Default SharePoint permission levels

If you were to add a permission level or modify one, you'd be presented with a series of granular permission options. A subset of these is shown in figure 11.34. One option that I commonly see people add is a contributor with no delete permissions. This way the user can add data but not delete it.

You should now be ready to manage and create your sites and site collections. But what about using your My Site? This last section of the book is going to dive into the My Site functionality, which is something that you and other individual users may have access to in your SharePoint environment.

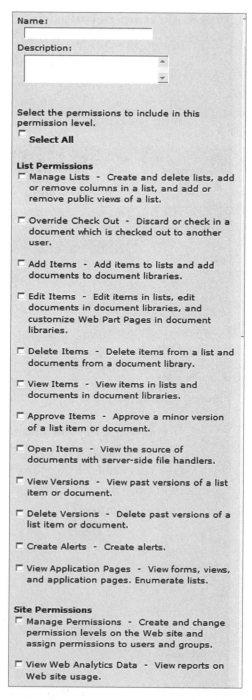

Figure 11.34 Permissions that can be used for the permission levels

11.4 My Site

My Site is a site collection for an individual user. It has many purposes, which we'll cover in the next few sections. We'll discuss the creation of a My Site and the options you have for working with My Site. To get started, let's discuss creation.

11.4.1 Creating your My Site

When you log into a SharePoint site, your name is displayed in the upper-right corner of the site. If you click the drop-down list next to your name, you'll find options associated with your user profile, which will integrate with your My Site, but having a My Site is not required in order to have a user profile. To see if you have the rights to create a My Site, select the option My Site, as shown in figure 11.35. If this is your first time doing this, you'll need to wait a bit while the My Site is being created.

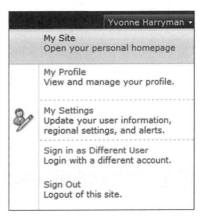

Figure 11.35 User profile and My Site options

Once you've created a My Site, you'll be presented with a series of options for configuring it. First, we'll discuss working with your colleagues.

11.4.2 Working with your colleagues

Figure 11.36 shows a brand-new My Site. You have several options to immediately get started. To begin, add your colleagues. This will populate your activities feeds, so you can see their latest activities.

You have several options when adding colleagues, as shown in figure 11.37. You can manage what profile elements they see based on whether you add them as team members and keep them organized by

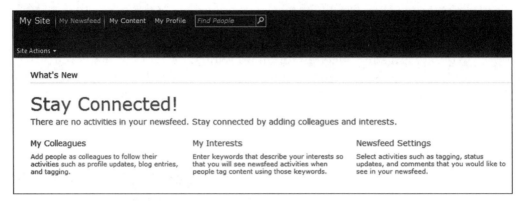

Figure 11.36 Homepage of a My Site when first created

creating groups. You can also decide who can see the information about your colleagues.

Now that you've identified the people you work with, let's update your profile.

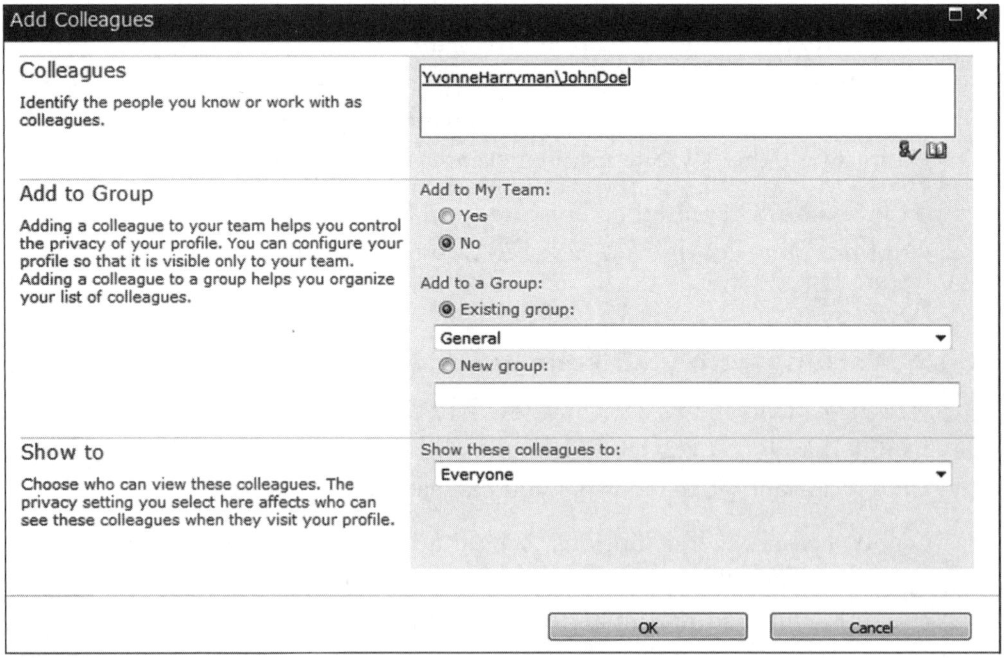

Figure 11.37 Adding a colleague

11.4.3 Setting your interests

Your interests are tied to your profile, so when you select the My Interests option, not only will you have the ability to add interests, but you can also add other information about yourself in your profile. This information will help enhance the people search as well as notify you when content is tagged with one of your topics of interest, as shown in figure 11.38.

Figure 11.38 Setting your interests

Lower down on this page you'll see the newsfeed settings. We'll discuss these next.

11.4.4 Working with newsfeeds

As you can see in figure 11.39, there are many activities that you can track, but you're not required to track them all. For example, you may have no interest in using your My Site for non-work-related social purposes, such as tracking someone's birthday.

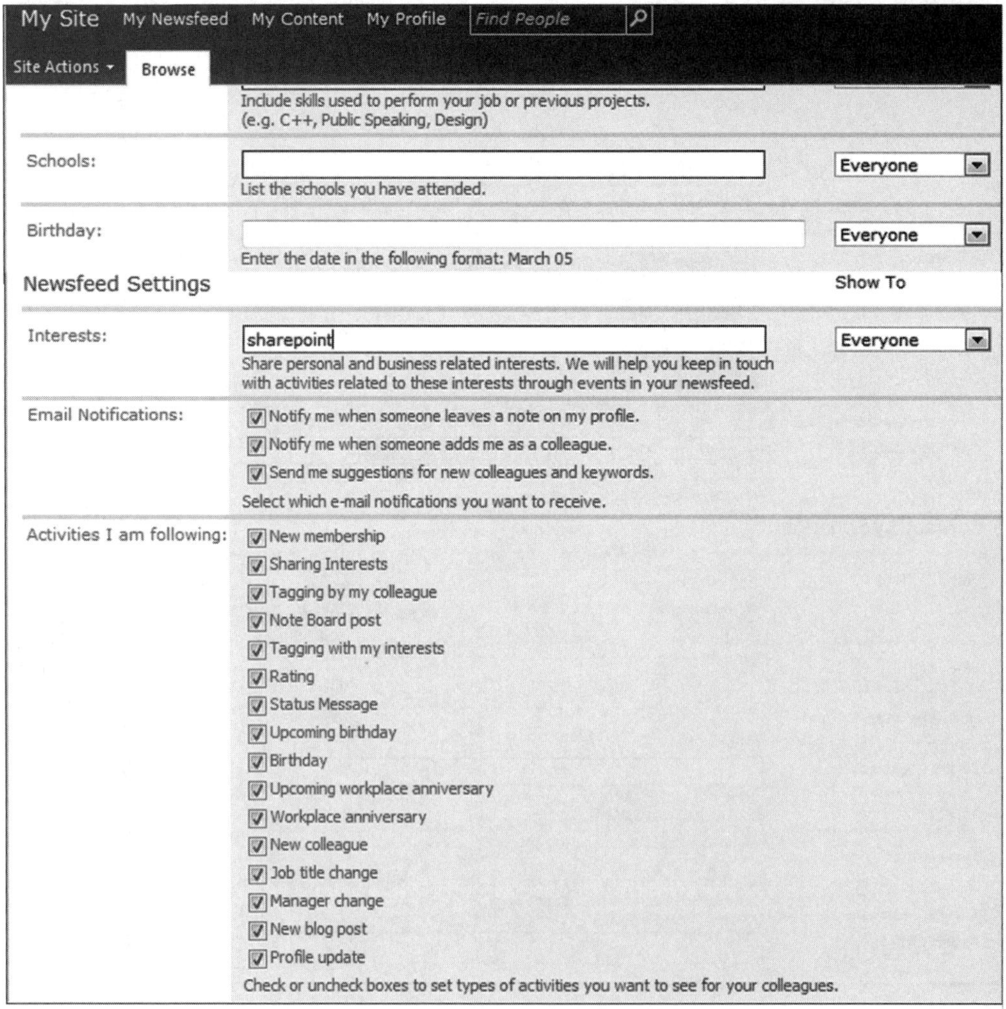

Figure 11.39 Configuring the activities you follow

You now know how you can get started using My Site from a social computing perspective, but what about using it to manage content?

11.4.5 Managing your content

My Site is a great way to store your content for your use only or to share with a subset of people. You can also create blog posts, manage link lists, upload pictures, and take part in many other collaboration activities that are specific to you and what you want to communicate. An example of a My Content area is shown in figure 11.40.

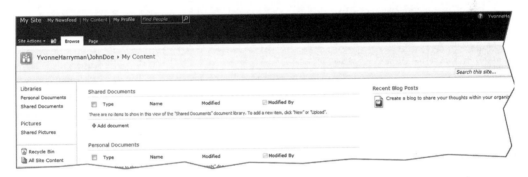

Figure 11.40 My Content area of a My Site

Lastly, you should understand your public profile page. All the areas that we discussed are tied to your internal My Site pages, to help you configure and work with your data, but some of this information is shared out to your public profile page.

11.4.6 Your public profile page

A public profile page is often visited by other users who are doing a people search and/or selecting your name next to some content that you worked on. This is primarily populated by your profile information and any information that it is syncing to, such as Active Directory, to gather further information about you. An example of my profile page is shown in figure 11.41.

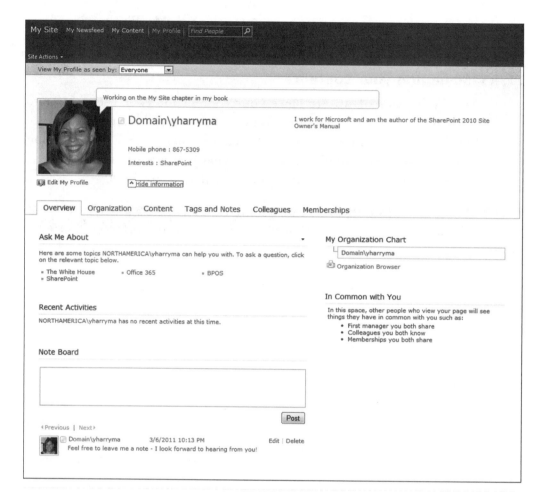

Figure 11.41 Public profile page

Although the interactive collaboration capabilities are minimal here, you do have some options with the note board and status updates to share information with your peers.

Good job! You've finished this chapter and hopefully the book. You should feel confident in your knowledge of SharePoint 2010 as a tech-savvy business user. Before I let you go, let's quickly summarize some core concepts that you should now understand from reading this chapter.

11.5 Summary

Following is a summary to help you understand the functionality that you should now be comfortable with implementing after reading this chapter:

- Leveraging search functionality by adding search web parts and configuring Search Centers
- Options for using My Sites
- Some key differences between site collections and subsites and how they tie into your information architecture
- How to use the Content Query web part
- RSS
- Using the Site Aggregator
- Managing and creating groups tied to permission levels
- Options for reporting on site usage

Let's test your knowledge. A couple of questions that you should be able to answer are as follows:

- What Search Center templates are available with SharePoint Server 2010 Standard?
  Basic Search Center and Enterprise Search Center
- What are some shared elements that span subsites in a site collection but not across site collections?
  Navigation, permissions, site templates, reports, and branding
- Can you have a user profile without a My Site?
  Yes

Appendix A

Setting up a test environment

This appendix covers

- How to determine what operating system you're using
- Upgrading your PC to 64-bit
- References for install steps to configure SharePoint on your PC
- Alternate option for configuring an Office 365 site

In this appendix we'll walk through the steps to set up a nonproduction environment of SharePoint on Windows 7 or Vista. You can then use this environment to experiment with the scenarios in the chapters.

In the book, we'll go through step-by-step scenarios allowing you to experiment and learn how to configure and customize your SharePoint sites. Having a SharePoint environment to do this in is critical. Historically, experimenting was difficult to do because SharePoint prior to the 2010 release wouldn't run on a PC operating system. Now the Share-Point team has made it much easier to set up a test environment, and you can install and configure SharePoint Foundation or SharePoint Server on Windows Vista or 7. I look forward to walking you through the steps so you can have your own personal playground on which to learn Share-Point! This will give you your own development environment, so you won't have to rely on someone else's installation. This is also a good exercise to begin learning the configuration and installation aspects of SharePoint.

There are other options for creating a development/test environment. You could install it directly on Windows Server 2008 R2 x64 or set up a virtual environment with Hyper-V. Because most power users won't have access to a server environment, we focus on an install in a PC environment. More information about setting up a server environment can be found on MSDN.

A.1 Ensuring your computer meets the requirements

I wish I could tell you that SharePoint will run on all computers, but I can't. Although SharePoint has made improvements on enabling end users to run it in a PC environment with the SharePoint 2010 release, it does now require that the operating system (OS) be 64-bit. If you're not certain what OS you're using, I'll explain how you can check in section A.1.1. If you find out it isn't 64-bit, I'll point you to the steps for upgrading to a 64-bit OS in section A.2.

A.1.1 Is your system 64-bit?

As stated in the introduction, with the release of SharePoint 2010, you now have the ability to run SharePoint directly on your PC operating system if you have Vista SP 1 (or higher) or Windows 7. Please note that this type of install is meant to be used only for test or development purposes. This type of install should never be used for production. But it still requires you to have a 64-bit operating system. If you're not certain, here's how you can check:

Step	Action	Result/Notes
1	Select the Windows menu (Start).	

Step	Action	Result/Notes
2	Right-click Computer and select Properties.	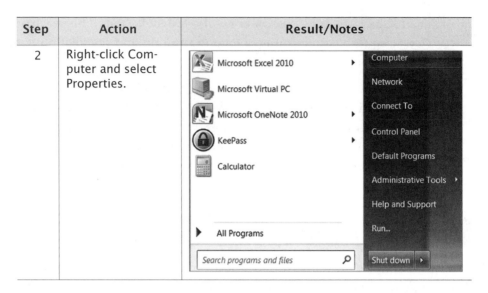

Your operating system will be shown next to System type in the System details, as shown in figure A.1.

Don't forget to also check your RAM while you're here. Although 4 GB of RAM is ideal for SharePoint Foundation, you can run it on 2 GB. For SharePoint Server, it's recommended that you have 6–8 GB of RAM.

System
Manufacturer:	Microsoft IT
Rating:	5.3 Windows Experience Index
Processor:	Intel(R) Core(TM)2 Duo CPU T7500 @ 2.20GHz 2.20 GHz
Installed memory (RAM):	4.00 GB
System type:	64-bit Operating System

Figure A.1 You can see the system details when you check your computer properties. You can check if you have a 64-bit operating system and also see your current RAM.

A.1.2 Upgrading to a 64-bit operating system

If you're not running a 64-bit operating system and your computer is 64-bit (you may need to check the manufacturer's website), you can easily upgrade by rerunning the installation and selecting the upgrade option if you're running Windows 7. This will preserve your current programs and files. It's common for your license to contain both 32-bit and 64-bit installs. So before you run out to buy the 64-bit version, check your current upgrade options to ensure you don't already own it.

If you're running Windows Vista, upgrading can be a bit tricky. Ideally, you've purchased the full version of Windows Vista. If you have, you can back up your data using Windows Easy Transfer. Afterward, you can go through the install process, starting the computer from the Windows Vista 64-bit DVD. Make sure you select Custom as your installation choice and restore the data once installation is complete. If you have an upgrade license, you'll need to uninstall Vista and reinstall Windows XP and then upgrade.

A.2 Prerequisites and installing SharePoint

To begin you'll need to prep your environment. The steps can be found on MSDN.Microsoft.com in an article titled "Setting Up the Development Environment for SharePoint 2010 on Windows Vista, Windows 7, and Windows Server 2008;" see http://msdn.microsoft.com/en-us/library/ee554869.aspx. Now that you've prepped your environment, let's get started with the actual install. These steps can be found in the same article under the section titled "Install SharePoint 2010."

Prior to doing this, you'll need to copy the SharePoint.exe install files to your computer. If you don't have a license and/or the install files for SharePoint, you can go to TechNet and download the trial version.

When you finish your SharePoint install, you'll be taken to the SharePoint web application that was created. Here you'll need to do some additional steps to configure your site. Once the site opens, you'll most likely be prompted for your credentials. To avoid this, you can add this site to the list of trusted sites in your IE options. This will allow

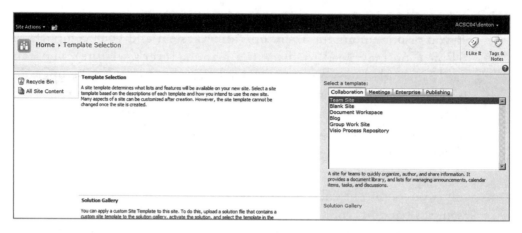

Figure A.2 Once you've run through the SharePoint Products Configuration Wizard, you'll need to run though some steps to set up your site. The step shown here is for selecting a template.

the credentials that you used for logging onto the computer to be passed to the site.

The first step will request you to do a template selection. For the purposes of our scenarios you'll always be starting from a Blank Site template, which is found under the Collaboration tab, or you'll be using a Publishing Site template, which is found under Publishing. The publishing site will be available only if you did the SharePoint Server install. An example of the templates you'll see if you did a SharePoint Server install is shown in figure A.2.

The next step will request you to set up groups for the site. Leave this at the defaults for the time being, as shown in figure A.3.

That was the last step in the setup for the site. You'll now see the site you configured. Figure A.4 shows what the publishing site will look like after creation.

Now you can begin to design your SharePoint site. This gives you the flexibility to access SharePoint from your personal PC without requiring internet access. You now have the ease and flexibility to follow along with the rest of this book without needing anyone else to provide a SharePoint environment for you.

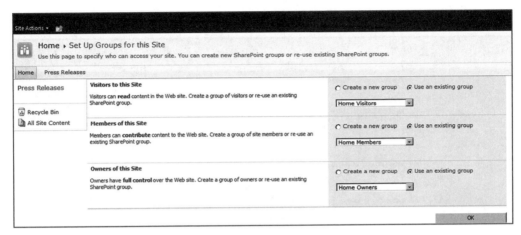

Figure A.3 Step to set up the site permissions. At this point, leave them at the defaults and click OK.

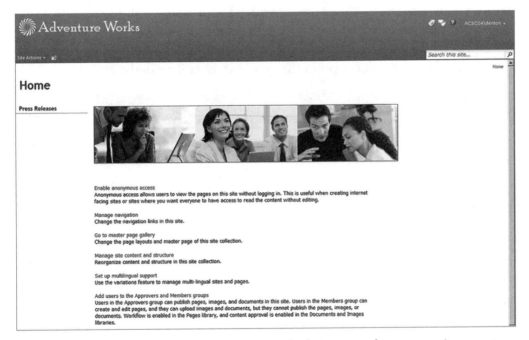

Figure A.4 Publishing site after creation. Good job! You now have an environment to use while you learn SharePoint.

> **Tip: IIS mapping**
>
> If you have other web-based applications, you may find that you need to reconfigure SharePoint to use another port besides the default port 80.
>
> When I first went through the install, I changed the IIS bindings for the SharePoint default site. I changed this to 88 using IIS. Right-click SharePoint 80, select Edit Bindings, and change Port to HTTP. That worked for the default site. But when I added a site collection, it still tried to point to my default site on port 80. To get around this, I changed it using Central Administration > Alternate Access Mappings > Edit Internal URL. This is shown in figure A.5.

Way to go! If you've completed this appendix successfully, you've probably worked through the hardest part of this book. You should be proud of yourself. You now understand some of the configuration and setup aspects of SharePoint, and you also have complete control of your own SharePoint environment. Not bad skills for an everyday end user! If you weren't able to complete the steps above, no problem; there's an alternate option that you can complete that's much easier.

A.3 Configuring a site with Office 365

An alternate option to configuring your PC to run a SharePoint 2010 environment is to use Microsoft's publicly available SharePoint environment. This is part of the Office 365 offering. Office 365 contains

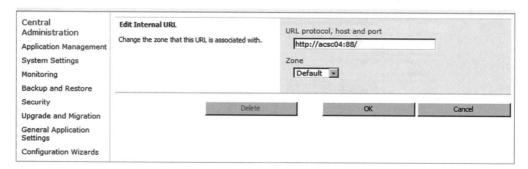

Figure A.5 How to reconfigure your web application to an alternate port

a suite of tools, so in addition to SharePoint you will get to play around with email, instant messaging, and Office Web Apps. Setting this up is a simple and easy process. First, go to the Microsoft.com site and search for *Office 365 trial*. Select the midsize business and enterprise free trial. From this point follow the steps to sign up, as shown in figure A.6. This account will last for 30 days and give you all the functionality that you will need to have a SharePoint environment to complete the scenarios in this book.

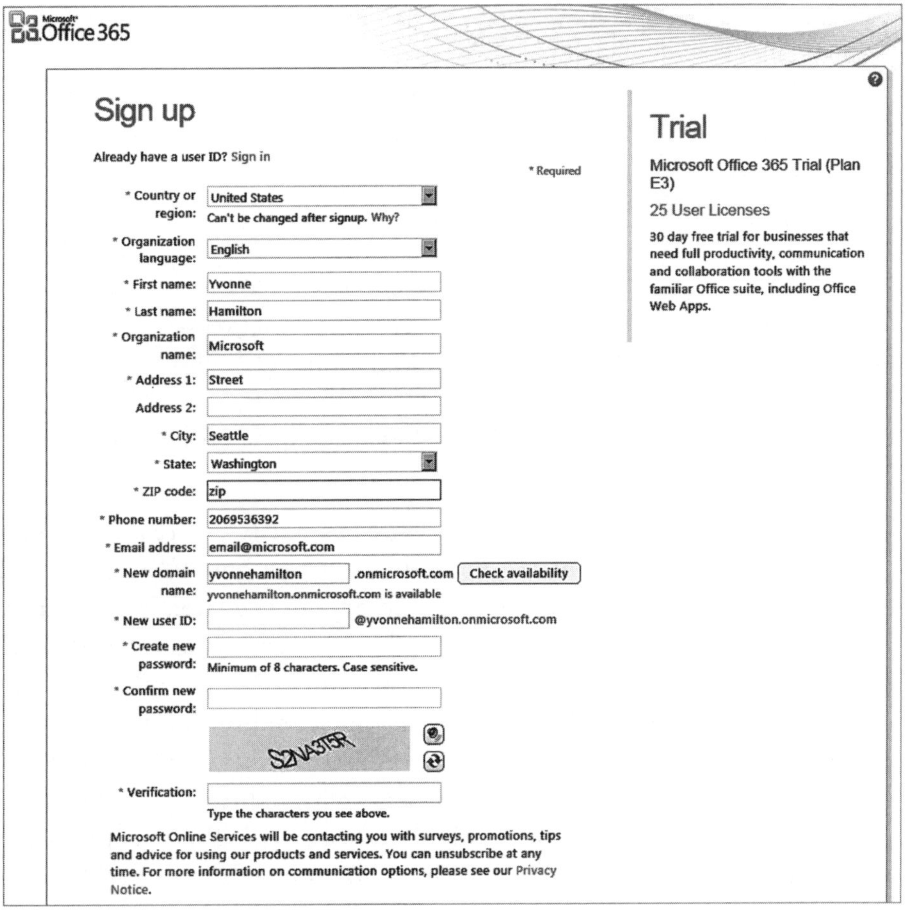

Figure A.6 Sign Up page for Office 365

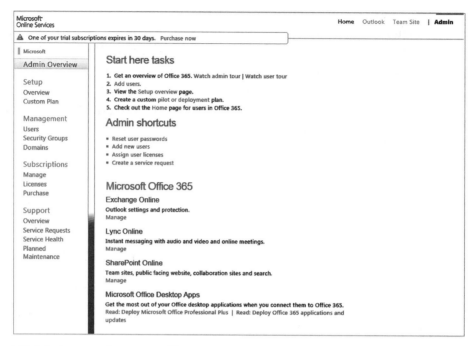

Figure A.7 Admin page for your Office 365 account

Once you've completed these steps, you'll be redirected to your admin homepage, as shown in Figure A.7.

For the purpose of this book we're primarily interested in SharePoint Online. To learn more about the features and functionality that are available to you, make sure you download the latest service description for SharePoint Online Standard. The service is continuously being updated to include new features, so you'll need to reference this document to understand the full set of functionality that is available to you. The service description at the point of release for this book has a release date of August 2010. Most functionality to complete the scenarios of the book will be available to you with the exception of anonymous access, which is discussed in chapter 6. You can still complete the steps in chapter 6, but your users will be required to log in to see any of the content.

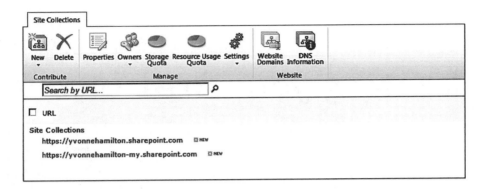

Figure A.8 Site collections created for your Office 365 account

To get to your site, select Manage under SharePoint Online in the Admin page. This will redirect you a page that displays the site collections that have been created for you, as shown in figure A.8.

Browse to the URL shown in the first link to get to your SharePoint site. You are now ready to get started. Remember this is free for only a trial period, so you better get started!

Appendix B

Creating your first site

In chapter 1, I introduced you to the steps for creating your first site. I covered it at a high level, but I wanted to provide you with the detailed steps in case you're interested in following along. To do this I assume you have a SharePoint environment readily available. If you don't, you should first work through appendix A, which covers the steps for creating a development/test environment.

B.1 Initial creation of your site

In this section, I'm going to discuss two options for creating a site. First, you'll create a site using the Blank Site template; the second option creates a site using the Publishing Site template. The latter is available only for users who have SharePoint Server.

B.1.1 Site creation properties

Select New Site under the Site Actions menu and this will take you to the New SharePoint Site creation page. If you're working with SharePoint Foundation, select Advanced Options, which will display the site creation page with the following options.

> NOTE If you're running SharePoint Server and it's a migrated SharePoint Server 2007 environment, you'll still see the site creation page with the options listed here if you haven't undertaken a visual upgrade.

Title and Description

In this section you need to enter the title that will be displayed on all your sites and a description. The description is important because it helps users understand the purpose of the site. Creating a site is just half the battle. Getting users to understand it and use it correctly is just as important in building a successful site; having a meaningful description can make all the difference. Don't worry if you're not sure what title and description you want. Go ahead and create your site, and you can always modify this information later.

Web Site Address

It's important here to follow naming conventions that are similar to your other sites. For example, if you abbreviate words on other sites, try to do the same here. I also recommend not putting spaces in the address because doing so will make *%20* appear in your URL. Keep the address short and descriptive. You can also change this later, but note that changing it will break any links from external applications. All links within SharePoint will automatically update to the new URL, and yes, this includes links lists, navigation links, and links entered into the Content Editor web part.

If you choose to modify the Title and Description or Web Site Address fields at a later time, you can do so by going to Site Actions > Site Settings, and under Look and Feel there will be an option called Title, Description and Appearance.

Template Selection

This section gives you different options based on the version of SharePoint you're running and what your administrator has installed. Later in this appendix we'll discuss how to create your own templates from the sites you created. In the meantime, refer to chapter 3's overview of the site templates and the descriptions displayed to the left as you navigate through your options.

Permissions

Here you have the option to use the same permissions as the parent site. This is a good option if you don't want to manage permissions and

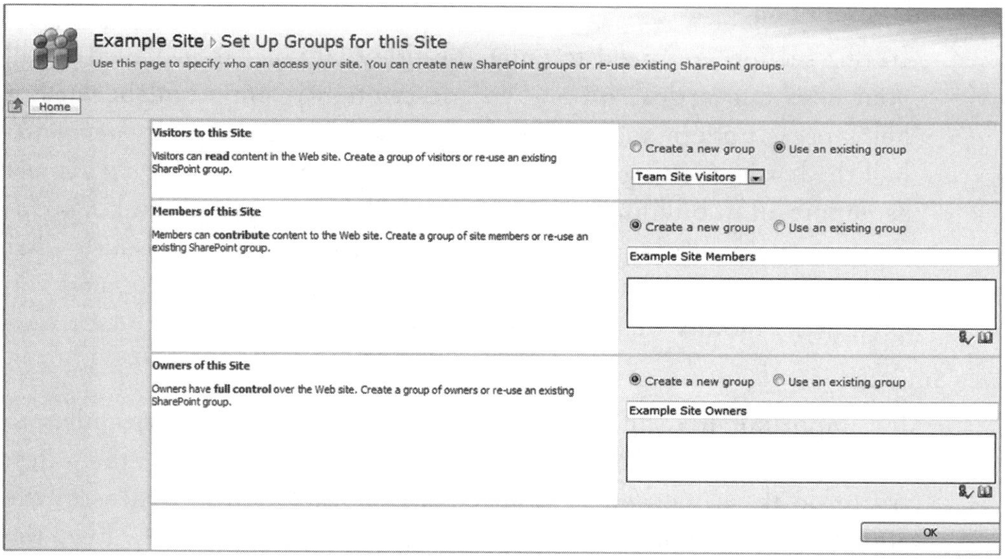

Figure B.1 If you choose to use unique permissions when creating a site, you'll need to create the visitors, members, and owners groups.

you want to have the permissions of the parent site automatically applied to your child site. This means that if a new user is added to the parent site at a later time, they'll automatically get access to your site as well. If your permissions need to be different, you can select the option Use Unique Permissions.

If you select Use Unique Permissions, you'll be asked to set up groups for the visitors, members, and owners of the new site, as shown in figure B.1.

Navigation

This option is broken up into two sections. The first covers Quick Launch navigation and the second covers the top link bar. Here you can choose how you want your site to display in either of these navigation bars, if at all, as shown in figure B.2.

> **NOTE** You can modify the Quick Launch and top link bars under the Look and Feel section in your site settings. Here you can add your own links, and for the Quick Launch bar you can add headings and modify the order of appearance.

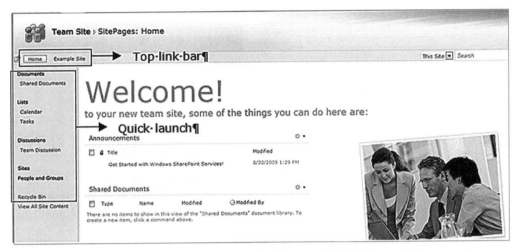

Figure B.2 Navigation options for the top link bar and Quick Launch bar are displayed on all sites by default.

Navigation Inheritance

> This option determines the starting point of your navigation items. You can include any parent sites, or you can set it to start from the site itself and not display the parent sites.

> If you're working with a SharePoint Server page, your interface will be different for creating sites. Here it will bring up a Silverlight interface, which will allow you to navigate through the various site templates. A refinement panel will allow you to easily filter down to the sites you're interested in. Once you choose your site template, you'll see an option to enter a title and URL. Next to the Create button you'll see a More Options button. This will take you to the additional site properties discussed previously.

> Now that you understand the basic options for configuring your site, we'll walk through the steps of creating a site. This is a simple exercise if you have a SharePoint environment available. If you don't have access to a SharePoint environment, come back and revisit this section after you work through appendix A.

B.1.2 Site creation

I'll demonstrate two options for creating your first site, which you can continue using in the scenarios in part 2 of this book. The first option is a blank site, and the second is a publishing site. Both sites have advantages and disadvantages that you should consider when making a decision about which to choose. If you don't have SharePoint Server, the decision is made for you; you have to use the Blank Site template because the publishing site is available only with SharePoint Server. Figure B.3 shows several of the options that you might see when creating a site if you're using SharePoint Server. Chapter 3 discusses the different templates, what they can do, and what version of SharePoint they're associated with.

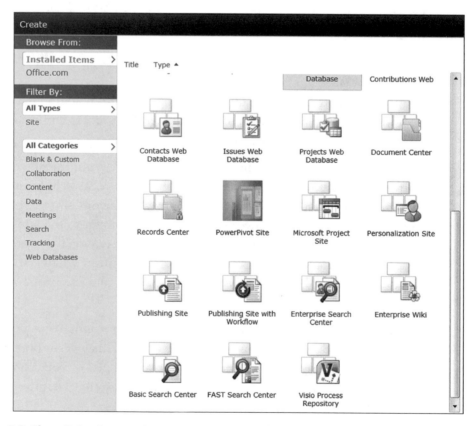

Figure B.3 SharePoint Server site creation options that you might have

Advantages and disadvantages specific to the Publishing Site template will be discussed in further detail in the section *Creating a publishing site*. Let's start with the directions for creating a blank site.

Creating a blank site

You'll need to complete the following steps to create a blank site or a publishing site. You'll need to complete these steps at the beginning of each scenario in part 2 in order to create your site. The scenarios will then walk you through a series of different customizations to leverage SharePoint's out-of-the-box capabilities:

Step	Action	Result/Notes
1	Select Site Action.	A list of administration options will appear. This enables site owners to access much of the administrative functionality for your site.
2	Select New Site.	This will direct you to a separate page to enter your site-creation information.
3	Enter a title, description, and website address.	If you don't see all of these options, click the More Options button.
4	For the template selection, select Blank Site under the Collaboration tab. Alternate steps: if you want to create a publishing site, select Publishing Site under the Content tab.	This will create a blank site that has no lists or web parts, enabling you to start from scratch to build out your site.
5	Leave the rest of the selections at their default value, and click Create.	[Create] [More Options]

An alternative to the blank site is a publishing site.

Creating a publishing site

A publishing site, which is available with SharePoint Server, offers advantages over the blank site because it allows the site administrators to make modifications to a checked-out version of the page and not disrupt the view of the current users. Your users won't see your modifications until the changes have been completed and published.

The disadvantage is that saving a publishing site as a site template isn't supported. If you plan to use your site as a site template for the creation of additional sites in the future, you may want to consider using a blank site instead.

Figure B.4 is an example of a publishing site with the page editing toolbar displayed. As you can see in the Status area, the site is currently checked out, and the edited version can't be viewed by the end users.

If you choose to use a publishing site as your foundation site, you'll need to complete the steps listed in the previous section but follow the alternate steps mentioned in step 4 for the template selection.

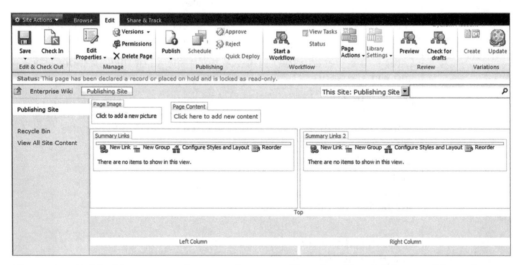

Figure B.4 Publishing site with page editing toolbar displayed. This enables administrators to modify the site without impacting the end users.

Index

355

RELATED MANNING TITLES

SharePoint 2010 WebParts in Action
by Wictor Wilén

ISBN: 978-1-935182-77-1
448 pages, $44.99
April 2011

SharePoint 2010 Workflows in Action
by Phil Wicklund

ISBN: 978-1-935182-71-9
360 pages, $44.99
February 2011

jQuery in Action, Second Edition
by Bear Bibeault and Yehuda Katz

ISBN: 978-1-935182-32-0
488 pages, $44.99
June 2010

Website Owner's Manual
by Paul A. Boag

ISBN: 978-1-933988-45-0
296 pages, $34.99
November 2009

For ordering information go to www.manning.com